INJURED ON THE JOB: EMPLOYEE RIGHTS, WORKERS' COMPENSATION & DISABILITY

by
Margaret C. Jasper

Oceana's Legal Almanac Series:
Law for the Layperson

Oceana®

Information contained in this work has been obtained by Oceana®
from sources believed to be reliable. However, neither the Publisher nor
its authors guarantee the accuracy or completeness of any information
published herein, and neither the Publisher nor its authors shall be responsible for any errors, omissions or damages arising from the use of
this information. This work is published with the understanding that
the Publisher and its authors are supplying information, but are not
attempting to render legal or other professional services. If such services are required, the assistance of an appropriate professional
should be sought.

You may order this or any Oxford University Press publication by visit-
ing the Oxford University Press and Oceana websites at www.oup.com
and www.oceanalaw.com, respectively.

Library of Congress Control Number: 2005934465

ISBN 978-0-379-11399-0

Oceana's Legal Almanac Series: Law for the Layperson
ISSN 1075-7376

©2005 Oxford University Press, Inc.

Oceana® is a registered trademark of Oxford University Press, Inc.

Manufactured in the United States of America on acid-free paper.

To My Husband Chris

Your love and support
are my motivation and inspiration

-and-

In memory of my son, Jimmy

Table of Contents

CHAPTER 3:
WORKERS' COMPENSATION

ABOUT THE AUTHOR

MARGARET C. JASPER is an attorney engaged in the general practice of law in South Salem, New York, concentrating in the areas of personal injury and entertainment law. Ms. Jasper holds a Juris Doctor degree from Pace University School of Law, White Plains, New York, is a member of the New York and Connecticut bars, and is certified to practice before the United States District Courts for the Southern and Eastern Districts of New York, the United States Court of Appeals for the Second Circuit, and the United States Supreme Court.

Ms. Jasper has been appointed to the panel of arbitrators of the American Arbitration Association and the law guardian panel for the Family Court of the State of New York, is a member of the Association of Trial Lawyers of America, and is a New York State licensed real estate broker and member of the Westchester County Board of Realtors, operating as Jasper Real Estate, in South Salem, New York. Margaret Jasper maintains a website at http://www.JasperLawOffice.com.

Ms. Jasper is the author and general editor of the following legal almanacs: AIDS Law; The Americans with Disabilities Act; Animal Rights Law; The Law of Attachment and Garnishment; Auto Leasing; Bankruptcy Law for the Individual Debtor; Individual Bankruptcy and Restructuring; Banks and their Customers; Becoming a Citizen; Buying and Selling Your Home; The Law of Buying and Selling; The Law of Capital Punishment; The Law of Child Custody; Your Rights in a Class Action Suit; Commercial Law; Consumer Rights Law; The Law of Contracts; Co-ops and Condominiums: Your Rights and Obligations As Owner; Copyright Law; Credit Cards and the Law; The Law of Debt Collection; Dictionary of Selected Legal Terms; The Law of Dispute Resolution; Drunk Driving Law; DWI, DUI and the Law; Education Law; Elder Law; Employee Rights in the Workplace; Employment Discrimination Under Title VII; Environmental Law; Estate Planning; Everyday Legal Forms; Executors and Personal Representatives: Rights and Responsibilities; Harassment in the Workplace; Health Care and Your Rights; Hiring Household Help and Contractors: Your Rights and Obligations Under the Law; Home Mortgage Law Primer; Hospital Liability Law; How To Change Your Name; How To Protect Your Challenged Child; Identity Theft and How To Protect Yourself; Injured on the Job: Employee rights, Worker's Compensation and Disability; Insurance Law; The Law of Immigration; International Adoption; Juvenile Justice and Children's Law; Labor Law; Landlord-Tenant Law; Lemon Laws; The Law of Libel and Slander; Living Together: Practical Legal Issues; Marriage and Divorce; The Law of Medical Malpractice; Motor Vehicle Law; The Law of No-Fault Insurance; Nursing Home Negligence; The Law of Obscenity and Pornography; Patent Law; The Law of Personal Injury; The Law of Premises Liability; Prescription Drugs; Privacy and the Internet: Your Rights and Expectations Under the Law; Probate Law; The Law of Product Liability; Real Estate Law for the Homeowner and Broker; Religion and the Law; Retirement Planning; The Right to Die; Rights of Single Parents; Law for the Small Business Owner; Small Claims Court; Social Security Law; Special Education Law; The Law of Speech and the First Amendment; Teenagers and Substance Abuse; Trademark Law; Victim's Rights Law; The Law of Violence Against Women; Welfare: Your Rights and the Law; Your Rights Under the Family and Medical Leave Act; You've Been Fired: Your Rights and Remedies; What if it Happened to You: Violent Crimes and Victims' Rights; What if the Product Doesn't Work: Warranties & Guarantees; Workers' Compensation Law; and Your Child's Legal Rights: An Overview.

INTRODUCTION

This almanac discusses the rights and remedies of workers who become injured or disabled on the job. The inability to work can mean financial disaster for many, who depend on a steady income to pay their bills and provide food and shelter for their family. A number of federal and state laws have been enacted to protect workers who unfortunately find themselves in such a situation.

State workers' compensation programs cover most workers who are not federal employees. Although these laws may vary, this almanac sets forth a general discussion of the common characteristics of a workers' compensation program. However, the reader is advised to check his or her own jurisdiction concerning issues that are state-specific, such as procedural rules or benefit amounts.

In addition to state workers' compensation programs, many employers provide their employees with disability insurance coverage, which is also discussed in this almanac. Currently, five states require employers to provide state disability insurance coverage for their employees. A disabled worker's eligibility for social security disability benefits is also discussed.

This almanac also presents an overview of workers' compensation programs established under various federal laws, including The Federal Employment Compensation Act ("FECA")—the primary federal statute governing compensation for disabled non-military federal employees; The Longshore and Harbor Workers' Compensation Program, which provides compensation benefits to maritime employees and other related groups; and The Black Lung Benefits Act, which provides compensation benefits to coal miners suffering from an occupational respiratory illness known as "black lung" disease. The benefits available to soldiers who are injured during military service, including disability compensation, vocational rehabilitation, and medical benefits are also explored.

This almanac also discusses the workplace health and safety laws that have been enacted to ensure that employers follow basic safety standards in order to reduce the number of workplace deaths, injuries and illnesses. This almanac examines the employee's right to a safe and healthy working environment, and the manner in which an employee can enforce this right. Further, an injured employee's right to recover damages from responsible third parties is also discussed.

The Appendix provides applicable statutes, sample forms, and other pertinent information and data. The Glossary contains definitions of many of the terms used throughout the almanac.

CHAPTER 1:
INJURIES IN THE WORKPLACE

PROMOTING SAFETY IN THE WORKPLACE

Over the past 35 years, there has been a concerted effort by America's workers to have effective legislation passed which would protect their health and safety in the workplace. Through this effort, they have been successful in getting some major legislation enacted which addresses health and safety concerns on the job. Thus, all businesses are now required by law to provide a safe and healthy workplace for their employees.

Statistics demonstrate that these efforts to reduce workplace injuries have had positive results. Since 1970, there has been a 50% reduction in workplace fatalities, and occupational injury and illness rates have been steadily declining. Nevertheless, nearly 50 American workers are still injured every minute of the 40-hour workweek, and almost 17 workers die each day.

Information on making sure your workplace is safe and healthy, as well as your rights and remedies under the law, are discussed in Chapter 2 of this almanac.

Despite these statistics, there is still a low risk of serious or fatal workplace injuries for most workers. According to the Bureau of Labor Statistics (BLS), the fatality rate for all occupations is 4.1 per 100,000 workers. However, BLS statistics also demonstrate that the fatality rate for workers in certain occupations is significantly higher. Surprisingly, the occupations that present the greatest danger are not ones that would immediately come to mind, such as a fire fighter or police officer.

For example, agriculture ranks among the most hazardous industries, particularly for children. In an average year, 110 American farm workers are crushed to death by tractor rollovers, and every day, about 228 agricultural workers suffer injuries which result in lost time at work.

Approximately 5% of those injuries result in permanent impairment. In addition, an average of 103 children are killed annually on farms, and approximately 40 percent of these deaths are work-related.

The ten most dangerous occupations in the United States according to the Bureau of Labor Statistics are set forth at Appendix 1.

OVERVIEW OF DISABILITY COMPENSATION PROGRAMS

As further discussed in this almanac, there are a number of disability compensation programs that have been established under federal and state laws in order to provide financial assistance to workers who are injured on the job. These laws have helped disabled workers avoid the financial disaster associated with loss of income and mounting medical bills, and have virtually eliminated the need for litigation over workplace injury claims.

Workers' Compensation Programs

Each state has a workers' compensation law designed to ensure that employees who are injured or disabled on the job are provided with fixed monetary awards, eliminating the need for litigation. These laws also provide benefits for dependents of those workers who are killed because of work-related accidents or illnesses. Some laws also protect employers and fellow workers by limiting the amount an injured employee can recover from an employer and by eliminating the liability of co-workers in most accidents.

Workers' Compensation is discussed more fully in Chapter 3 of this almanac.

Federal Disability Compensation Programs

As set forth below, there are three federal disability compensation programs, all of which are administered by The Office of Workers' Compensation Programs ("OWCP") under the jurisdiction of the U.S. Department of Labor:

1. The Federal Employees' Compensation Program;

2. The Longshore and Harbor Workers' Compensation Program; and

3. The Black Lung Benefits Program.

In administering these programs, OWCP's goal is to protect the interests of workers, employers and the Federal Government by ensuring timely and accurate claims adjudication and provision of benefits, by responsibly administering the funds authorized for this purpose, and by helping injured workers return to the workforce when their injury or illness permits. There are 12 OWCP district offices located throughout the United States.

A directory of the OWCP District Offices is set forth at Appendix 2.

The Federal Employment Compensation Act [5 U.S.C. §§ 8101 – 8193]

The Federal Employment Compensation Act (FECA) established a workers' compensation program that provides compensation for non-military, federal employees who are injured on the job. Many of FECA's provisions are typical of most state workers' compensation laws.

Selected provisions of the Federal Employee Compensation Act are set forth at Appendix 3.

Under the FECA, a disabled employee receives two-thirds of his or her normal monthly salary during their period of disability, and may receive more for permanent physical injuries, or if he or she has dependents. FECA also covers medical expenses due to the disability, and provides compensation for survivors of employees who are killed on the job. However, awards are limited to "disability or death" sustained while in the performance of the employee's duties, which are not caused wilfully by the employee, or by the employee's intoxication.

The Federal Employment Compensation Act is discussed more fully in Chapter 4 of this almanac.

The Longshore and Harbor Workers' Compensation Act [33 U.S.C. §§ 901 – 950]

The Longshore and Harbor Workers' Compensation Act (LHWCA) provides workers' compensation to approximately one-half million maritime workers injured or killed upon the navigable waters of the United States, as well as employees working on piers, docks and terminals.

Selected provisions of the Longshore and Harbor Workers' Compensation Act are set forth at Appendix 4.

The LHWCA also covers overseas employees of defense contractors; employees at military post exchanges, workers engaged in the extraction of natural resources on the outer continental shelf, and certain other classes of private industry workers. The LHWCA provides lost wages compensation, medical benefits, and rehabilitation services, to employees who suffer work-related injuries or illness.

The Longshore and Harbor Workers' Compensation Act is discussed more fully in Chapter 5 of this almanac.

The Black Lung Benefits Act [30 U.S.C. §§ 901 – 945]

Under the Black Lung Benefits Act, monthly compensation payments and medical treatment are provided to coal miners who are totally disabled as a result of work-related black lung disease.

Selected provisions of the Black Lung Benefits Act are set forth at Appendix 5.

In addition to disability compensation benefits, if the worker dies, his or her surviving dependents are eligible to receive benefits. The Black Lung Benefits Act also established a fund administered by the Secretary of Labor providing disability payments to miners where the mine operator is unknown or unable to pay.

The Black Lung Benefits Act is discussed more fully in Chapter 6 of this almanac.

The Federal Employment Liability Act [45 U.S.C. §§ 51 – 60]

The Federal Employment Liability Act (FELA), while not a workers' compensation statute, provides that railroad workers injured in a railroad-related accident have the right to recover compensation. However, in order to recover, the worker must demonstrate that his or her injuries are the result of the railroad's negligence

The text of the Federal Employee Liability Act is set forth at Appendix 6.

Under the FELA, the injured worker may recover lost wages, medical expenses and treatments, pain and suffering, and compensation for partial or permanent disability. If a worker is killed on the job, his or her survivors are entitled to recover damages that they have suffered as a result of the worker's death.

The Federal Employment Liability Act is discussed more fully in Chapter 7 of this almanac.

The Merchant Marine Act [46 U.S.C. § 688]

The Merchant Marine Act—also known as "The Jones Act"—provides seamen with the same protection from employer negligence as FELA provides railroad workers.

The text of the Merchant Marine Act is set forth at Appendix 7.

Under the Act, injured seaman are entitled to transportation, lost wages, and medical expenses and treatments. If the seaman can prove that his or her injuries were the result of negligence, a seaman may also recover damages for pain and suffering from the employer and ship owner.

The Merchant Marine Act is discussed more fully in Chapter 7 of this almanac.

Disability Insurance

Disability insurance is designed to provide financial benefits to an injured or disabled worker. However, unlike the other workers' compensation programs discussed in this almanac, disability insurance applies to injuries that are sustained outside of the workplace.

Disability insurance may be privately purchased by an individual worker, or it may be provided by an employer under a group disability insurance policy. In five states, employers are required for provide disability insurance to their employees.

Disability insurance is discussed more fully in Chapter 8 of this almanac.

Social Security Disability Insurance

Under the Social Amendments of 1954, a disability insurance program was implemented which provides workers with additional benefits if they have to stop working at any time before age 65 due to health reasons.

Social Security Disability Insurance is discussed more fully in Chapter 8 of this almanac.

Veterans' Disability Compensation

Veterans' Disability Compensation is a monetary benefit paid to a military veteran who suffered an injury or disease while on active duty. The Veterans' Administration also provides vocational rehabilitation and medical care for disabled veterans.

Veterans' Disability Compensation is discussed more fully in Chapter 9 of this almanac.

THIRD PARTY CLAIMS

If you are injured on the job, and your injury was due to the responsibility of a third party—not your employer—you may be able to recover damages from the third party. This may occur, for example, if you are injured using a defective piece of machinery, in which case the manufacturer of the defective device may be liable for you injuries. However, in order to recover damages, unless you are able to settle your claim, you will usually be required to go to court and prove your case.

Third party liability is discussed more fully in Chapter 10 of this almanac.

CHAPTER 2:
MAINTAINING A SAFE AND
HEALTHY WORKPLACE

IN GENERAL

A number of laws now establish basic safety standards which have as their goal a reduction in the number of workplace deaths, injuries and illnesses. These workplace safety and health laws consist primarily of federal and state statutes. Federal laws and regulations preempt state laws where they overlap or contradict one another.

Statutory requirements may vary from state to state. Therefore, it is essential that the reader investigate the particular requirements of his or her jurisdiction.

THE OCCUPATIONAL SAFETY AND HEALTH ADMINISTRATION

The Occupational Safety and Health Administration (OSHA) is a division of the U.S. Department of Labor. Along with its state government counterparts, OSHA employs a combined staff that includes inspectors, complaint discrimination investigators, engineers, physicians, educators, standards writers, and other technical and support personnel. The OSHA staff establishes and enforces protective standards to be used in the workplace, and sponsors workplace safety and health programs for employers and employees.

Because Federal and state OSHA programs have only about 2,500 inspectors to cover 111 million workers at seven million worksites, workers are encouraged to play an active role in spotting workplace hazards and asking their employers to correct them.

OSHA administers the Occupational Safety and Health Act of 1970 (The OSH Act), The OSH Act is designed to provide job safety and health protection for workers by promoting safe and healthy working conditions throughout the nation.

THE OCCUPATIONAL AND SAFETY ACT OF 1970 [29 U.S.C. §§ 651 – 678]

The Occupational and Safety Act (The OSH Act) is the main statute protecting the health and safety of workers in the workplace. Congress enacted the OSH Act under its constitutional authority to regulate interstate commerce. Every private employer who engages in interstate commerce is subject to the regulations promulgated under the OSH Act by the Secretary of Labor.

Under the OSH Act, states are not allowed, without permission of the Secretary of Labor, to promulgate any laws that regulate an area directly covered by the OSHA regulations. States may, however, regulate in areas not governed by OSHA regulations. If a state wishes to regulate an area covered by OSHA regulations, the state must submit a plan for federal approval.

Under the OSH Act, employers are required to maintain their facilities free from any recognized hazards that are causing, or are likely to cause, death or serious harm to an employee. The OSH Act protects just about every working individual with the exception of miners, transportation workers, certain public employees and self-employed persons. Under the OSH Act, employees are also required to comply with all applicable sections of the occupational safety and health standards issued by OSHA.

UNDER THE OSHA ACT, YOU HAVE THE FOLLOWING RIGHTS:

The Right to Training

Under the OSH Act, you have the right to obtain training from your employer about the health effects of chemicals you are exposed to at work, including information on how to protect yourself from harm. Your employer must label chemical containers, and make material safety data sheets with detailed hazard information available to employees. You also have the right to get trained on a variety of other health and safety hazards, and the standards your employer is required to follow, including blood borne pathogens, construction hazards, confined spaces, etc.

The Right to Information

Under the OSH Act, you have the right to request information from your employer about OSHA standards, worker injuries and illnesses, job hazards and workers' rights. You are entitled to information concerning chemicals used in your workplace, tests your employer has done to measure chemical, noise and radiation levels, precautions you should take and procedures to be followed if you or other employees are exposed to hazardous chemicals or other toxic substances.

You may also observe any monitoring or measuring of toxic materials or chemicals, as well as harmful physical agents, such as noise, and view the resulting records. In addition, you may request copies of the OSHA standards, rules, regulations, and requirements that your employer is required to make available to employees.

Under the OSH Act, you are permitted access to relevant exposure and medical records. Employers must inform you of the existence, location and availability of your medical and exposure records when you first begin employment and at least annually thereafter.

The Right to Request Action

Under the OSH Act, you may ask your employer to correct hazards even if they are not violations of specific OSHA standards. You should make your requests in writing and keep copies of all requests you make to your employer to correct hazards in the workplace.

The Right to File a Complaint

Under the OSH Act, you are entitled to file a confidential complaint with OSHA if you believe there are either violations of OSHA standards or serious workplace hazards.

The Right to be Involved

Under the OSH Act, you are entitled to have an authorized employee representative accompany the OSHA compliance officer during his or her inspection of your workplace. The employer is not permitted to choose the workers' representative. If there is no employee representative, the OSHA inspector must talk confidentially with a reasonable number of workers during the course of the investigation. Whether or not there is a workers' representative, you are still entitled to speak privately and confidentially with the compliance officer. You may point out hazards, and describe injuries or illnesses in the workplace.

The Right to Obtain Results

Under the OSH Act, you are entitled to know the results of the OSHA Inspection, and request a review if OSHA doesn't take action, e.g. issue a citation. You may also attend any meetings or hearings held to discuss you employer's objections to OSHA's actions.

You can also check to see whether your employer has ever been inspected by OSHA by researching your employer's inspection history through OSHA's Establishment Search online [www.osha.gov/]. You simply type in the name of your company and select the dates you want to investigate.

The Right to Appeal

Under the OSH Act, you are entitled to file an appeal with OSHA concerning the deadlines given to your employer to correct any violations if you believe that the employer has been given too long to improve the conditions.

The Right to File a Discrimination Complaint

Under the OSH Act, if you believe you have been punished or discriminated against because you filed a complaint, or refused to work under conditions that pose an immediate health and/or safety threat, you may file a discrimination complaint with OSHA.

The Right to Request an Evaluation

Under the OSH Act, you have the right to request the National Institute for Occupational Safety and Health (NIOSH) to conduct a health hazard evaluation if you are concerned about toxic effects of a substance in the workplace.

The Right to Testify

Under the OSH Act, you are entitled to provide comments and testify before OSHA concerning rulemaking on any new standards.

Additional Rights Under State Law

If you live in a state that has an OSHA-approved state plan, you are entitled to at least the same rights and protections afforded under the OSH Act and, in some cases, you may have additional rights under your state's law.

FILING A COMPLAINT WITH OSHA

As set forth above, if you believe your working conditions are unsafe or unhealthy, you have the right to file a complaint with OSHA. However, before you file a complaint, you should first try and bring the condition to your employer's attention. If your employer wants to improve the working conditions, they can contact OSHA for information and guidance on rectifying any unsafe or unhealthy conditions that may exist. OSHA offers free assistance to employers in identifying and correcting workplace safety and health hazards without risking a citation or penalty.

If the workplace conditions or so bad that they present a risk of death or serious physical injury, and your employer has not responded to your request to improve conditions, you may have a legal right to refuse to work under hazardous conditions. If the situation does not present an immediate threat to your health, but you believe there may be a violation of an OSHA standard or a serious safety or health hazard at work that your employer has not remedied, you should file your complaint with OSHA and request the agency to conduct an inspection of your workplace. Your complaint can be filed by telephone, mail, fax, or electronically on the internet. OSHA's 24-hour hotline for reporting workplace safety and health emergencies is 1-800-321-OSHA.

A Directory of regional OSHA offices is set forth at Appendix 8.

In order to prevail on your OSHA complaint, you must generally prove that:

1. The employer failed to keep the workplace free of a hazard; and

2. The particular hazard was recognized as being likely to cause death or serious physical injury.

CITATIONS

If OSHA determines, after an inspection, that an employer is in violation of the law, a citation is issued against that employer. The citation specifies each and every violation alleged to have been committed by the employer and the date by which the violation must be corrected. The employer is required to display the citation at or near the location of the violation for a period of three days or until the violation is corrected, whichever date is later. The purpose of this provision is to warn the employees about the dangerous condition.

PENALTIES FOR NONCOMPLIANCE

The penalties for failure to adhere to the OSH Act are serious. For example, there are mandatory civil penalties of up to $7,000 per violation against employers for serious violations of the law, and optional penalties of up to $7,000 for nonserious violations. If an employer fails to correct a violation within the allotted time period, additional penalties of up to $7,000 per day can be assessed until the violation is finally corrected.

Willful violations of the OSH Act can result in penalties ranging from a minimum of $5,000 to a maximum of $70,000. Repeated violations can also result in a fine of up to $70,000. An employer can also be assessed a penalty of up to $7,000 for failure to display the citation as required.

In addition to the civil penalties, criminal penalties may be assessed if a willful violation of the OSH Act results in the death of an employee. Upon conviction, such a violation is punishable by a fine of up to $250,000 or by imprisonment of up to six months, or both. If the employer is a corporation, the maximum fine is $500,000. There are additional penalties that may be imposed for subsequent convictions.

WHISTLE BLOWER PROTECTION

As set forth above, if you believe your workplace is unsafe or unhealthy, you can file a confidential complaint with OSHA and request an inspection. In fact, most workplace safety laws, to be effective, rely on employees to report employment hazards. These employees are generally known as "whistle blowers." You can request OSHA to keep your name confidential if you don't want your employer to know you filed the complaint.

A Notice to OSHA of Alleged Safety or Health Hazards is set forth at Appendix 9.

To prevent retaliation and encourage compliance, it is illegal for employers to fire or otherwise discriminate against employees who report unsafe conditions to the proper authorities. If an employee who "blew the whistle" believes that they have suffered discrimination as a result, the employee can file a discrimination complaint with OSHA within 30 days of the alleged incident.

SAFETY INITIATIVES

Some safety initiatives your employer can take to make sure the workplace is safe for the employees include:

1. Performing regular in-house safety inspections;

2. Establishing a comprehensive safety plan for all employees;

3. Maintaining an adequately stocked first-aid kit readily available;

4. Keeping telephone numbers for emergency medical assistance on display for quick reference if the need arises.

5. Maintaining adequate protective clothing and equipment where the nature of business operations requires such precautions.

If an employer wants to make sure they are in compliance with the law, they may engage the services of a workplace safety consultant, who specializes in bringing companies into compliance with the law.

SMOKING IN THE WORKPLACE

It has been clearly established that tobacco smoke is detrimental to one's health. This health hazard also applies to secondhand smoke one inhales when in the company of smokers. A recent Environmental Protection Agency report estimated that secondhand tobacco smoke causes approximately 3,000 lung cancer deaths and 37,000 heart disease deaths in nonsmokers each year. To protect nonsmokers from smokers, many employers either restrict smoking to designated areas, or prohibit it altogether.

Presently, there are no federal laws which prohibit smoking in the workplace. However, a majority of states have enacted legislation restricting smoking on the job. For example, California, Connecticut, New Jersey, Rhode Island and Vermont have enacted laws that specifically limit smoking in the workplace. Some states require the company to have designated smoking areas in the workplace, and other states require nonsmokers to be segregated from smokers. In fact, due to the high costs of health care insurance and related factors, some companies reportedly will not hire applicants who smoke.

On the other hand, many states also have laws that prohibit discrimination against smokers who smoke during nonworking hours. In addition, anti-smoking legislation commonly contains exceptions, e.g., for smoking during private social functions, and smoking in a private office occupied solely by smokers. Thus, the reader is advised to check the law of his or her jurisdiction.

CHAPTER 3:
WORKERS' COMPENSATION

IN GENERAL

If you suffer a work-related injury or illness, and as a result become disabled and unable to work, you may be entitled to receive certain benefits under a system known as workers' compensation. Presently, the Federal Government, all 50 states, Puerto Rico, the U.S. Virgin Islands, American Samoa and Guam have workers' compensation laws.

Because statutory provisions vary depending on the particular jurisdiction, the reader is advised to check the law of his or her own jurisdiction concerning specific questions. This chapter sets forth a general discussion of workers' compensation law applicable to most jurisdictions. The Federal Employees' Compensation program is discussed in Chapter 4 of this almanac.

Making a false or fraudulent workers' compensation claim is a felony which, depending on the state, may subject the offender to imprisonment and/or a fine. It is also a felony for an employee to make a false statement for the purposes of obtaining compensation benefits, or for an employer to make a false statement for the purposes of denying compensation benefits.

A more detailed discussion of state and federal Workers' Compensation programs can be found in this author's book entitled *Workers' Compensation Law*, published by Oceana Publishing Company.

PURPOSE OF WORKERS' COMPENSATION LAWS

Before workers' compensation laws were enacted, injured employees were forced to sue their employer and prove liability in order to recover damages. Workers' compensation laws dispensed with these lawsuits and replaced them with a type of no-fault system. Under the workers' compensation system, disabled workers no longer have to prove that their employer was negligent.

Thus, an employer who maintains workers' compensation insurance coverage for his or her employees is generally immune from employee lawsuits for work-related injuries or illnesses. There are some exceptions to this general immunity. For example, an employer who intentionally causes injury to an employee is not immune from a lawsuit.

STATE VERSUS FEDERAL COVERAGE

Most workers are covered by their own state's workers' compensation program unless they fall under those categories entitled to Federal coverage. Federal statutes have been enacted to provide coverage for certain classes of employees. The Federal Employees Compensation Program protects U.S. Government civilian employees; The Longshore and Harborworkers' Compensation Act protects maritime workers and certain other classes of workers; and the Black Lung Act protects coal miners.

A discussion of the Federal workers' compensation programs administered by the Office of Workers' Compensation Programs under the auspices of the U.S. Department of Labor is set forth in Chapters 4 of this almanac. Because many of the provisions of the Federal Employees' Compensation Act are typical of state workers' compensation laws, the full text of the Act is set forth at Appendix 3 as a model workers' compensation statute.

COMPULSORY VS. ELECTIVE WORKERS' COMPENSATION LAWS

Depending on the jurisdiction, workers' compensation laws may be either compulsory or elective. The majority of states have enacted compulsory workers' compensation laws. This means that employers are required to maintain workers' compensation coverage for their employees. Employers who fail to maintain the required insurance may be sued by the employee, and are liable for damages. Depending on the jurisdiction, non-complying employers may be further penalized.

Nevertheless, state laws may exempt certain employers, such as small companies, and certain workers, such as agricultural workers, domestic workers, and independent contractors.

A table setting forth coverage requirements for agricultural and domestic workers is set forth at Appendix 10.

A minority of jurisdictions, including New Jersey, South Carolina and Texas, have elective workers' compensation laws. Under an elective law, the employer may choose to reject the workers' compensation system. However, if a suit for damages is brought by an injured employee, an uninsured employer is not permitted to assert the three common law defenses to negligence: (1) contributory negligence; (2) assumption of risk; and (3) fellow servant negligence doctrines.

INSURANCE COVERAGE

Workers' Compensation insurance is usually purchased from an authorized private insurance carrier. Employers are free to choose from any number of private insurance companies that offer this coverage. In addition, an employer may elect to be self-insured. A self-insured employer assumes liability for workers' compensation, and generally sets up a reserve fund to pay benefits to disabled employees. Self-insurance usually requires authorization by the appropriate State Workers' Compensation Board officials. The employer seeking to be self-insured must demonstrate that it has the financial ability to carry the associated risks.

A Directory of State Workers' Compensation Boards is set forth at Appendix 11.

In a minority of jurisdictions, employers are required to obtain insurance through the state insurance fund and privately obtained workers' compensation insurance is not permitted, although some of these jurisdictions still permit employer self-insurance. Although state insurance funds are generally adequately funded, they are criticized for their inefficiency, such as the timeliness in making compensation payments.

The cost of workers' compensation coverage is the responsibility of the employer, and cannot be charged, in whole or in part, to the employee.

A table setting forth the type of insurance required under state workers' compensation programs is set forth at Appendix 12.

TYPES OF WORKERS' COMPENSATION CLAIMS

Workers' compensation claims generally fall into three categories: (1) Injury Claims; (2) Occupational Disease Claims; and (3) Death Claims. In order to prevail on a workers' compensation claim, the employee is generally required to prove that the injury or illness is causally related to their employment, i.e., the injury or illness must be one that "arises out of and in the course of the employment."

Injury Claims

The injury or accident claim is the most common type of workers' compensation claim. It is generally called a "traumatic" injury claim in that it is a sudden and unexpected occurrence caused by a particular event. For example, a back injury caused by lifting a heavy object, or a laceration caused by a meat-slicing machine, would be considered traumatic injuries.

Some state statutes specifically define an injury or accident claim so as to differentiate it from an occupational disease claim. In other jurisdictions, the two types of claims overlap with a focus on whether the employee's disability is work-related, regardless of whether the disability is caused by injury or illness.

Under certain circumstances, an employee may not be covered under workers' compensation. For example, an injury or illness that is caused by the employee's intoxication—e.g., by drugs or alcohol—is not eligible for compensation. Coverage may also be denied in situations involving:

1. Self-inflicted injuries, or injuries sustained while attempting to injure another;

2. Injuries sustained while committing a crime;

3. Injuries sustained when the employee was not on the job; and

4. Injuries sustained when the employee's conduct violated company policy.

Work-Related Requirement

In order to demonstrate that an injury is work-related, it must be shown that the time and place of the injury was so closely connected to the employment that it justifies coverage under the workers' compensation system. In most cases, when an injury occurs at the place of employment, the work-relatedness of the injury is rarely in dispute.

Injuries which occur away from the employee's place of employment may or may not be compensable. For example, compensability is less clearly defined in circumstances when the employee is away from his or her place of business, although there may be some indirect connection, such as a business luncheon. If the luncheon were clearly for the benefit of the employer, most courts would allow the compensation claim.

An employee who is injured while attending an off-site function held by the employer, such as a convention or party, is generally entitled to compensation since it can be assumed that the employee's attendance at the function was expected. In addition, an employee whose business is primarily conducted away from the office, such as a salesperson, would be entitled to compensation provided the injury occurred while the employee was performing his or her work-related duties.

Questions of work-relatedness also arise in situations where an employee is injured while attending to personal matters on company time.

An important factor to consider would be whether the employer permitted employees to engage in personal activities while on the job. For example, an employee on his or her lunch or coffee break on company premises is generally held to be covered. However, jurisdictions differ on whether an employee is covered for injuries sustained while on lunch or coffee break off-premises.

An employee en route to and from his or her place of employment is generally not covered, however, exceptions have been made in certain cases, e.g., where the employee is paid for their travel time; the employee engages in a work-related task during the trip to or from work; or the employer provides for the employee's transportation, etc.

Occupational Disease Claims

The occupational disease claim applies when the employee suffers a work-related illness. Occupational disease is primarily distinguishable from an injury because it is not characterized by the suddenness or unexpectedness that usually accompanies a work-related injury or accident.

Work-Related Requirement

The specific disease must be one which is characteristic of the employee's occupation. An illness that is characteristic of an employee's occupation is generally held to be one that "arises out of and in the course of the employment." For example, employees who are engaged in employment that requires heavy lifting may develop back problems. Employees whose duties involve repetitive movements may develop arthritis. These conditions would likely be considered work-related for the purpose of claiming compensation.

In addition, an occupational disease may also be attributed to "continuous trauma." Continuous trauma refers to a gradual deterioration of the employee's physical condition as a result of repetitive work. For example, carpal tunnel syndrome—a condition known to be caused by repetitive hand or wrist movements such as those made in the operation of a computer—would likely fall under the category of occupational disease. Of course, the focus would again be on whether the specific illness is work-related, rather than a disease that is ordinarily encountered in one's life, or which is not characteristic of the employee's occupation.

Many jurisdictions maintain a schedule of diseases that are known to occur in specific occupations or trades. If an employee contracts such a disease during the course of his or her employment in that specific occupation or trade, a presumption may be drawn that it was causally related to the employment. If a statutory presumption exists, it is the employer's duty to rebut the presumption. If the disease is not scheduled, and thus there is no statutory presumption, the employee has the burden of proving that he or she contracted the illness as a result of the employment.

The employee usually submits medical documentation to prove the causal relationship. Therefore, it is important that the employee fully detail all of his or her symptoms and complaints to the treating physician. The medical report is crucial in substantiating the disability claim.

A sample Worker's and Physician's Report for Workers' Compensation Claim is set forth at Appendix 13.

The employee cannot depend on the insurance carrier's physician to make his or her disability case. The insurance carrier's physicians are more likely to minimize the seriousness of the disability, or determine that a pre-existing condition is, in fact, the cause of the disability. If an employee's compensation claim is denied based upon a doctor's report that no injury exists, the employee is generally entitled to get a second opinion from a doctor of his or her choice, at the expense of the insurance carrier.

Aggravation of a Pre-Existing Condition

If the employee's disability is caused by aggravation of an employee's pre-existing condition, he or she is entitled to compensation provided the "aggravation" is causally related to the employment. However, if the disability were caused by a natural progression of the pre-existing condition that is unrelated to the employment, it would not be compensable. If the claim were deemed compensable, the employee would be fully covered for the entire disability. There is no apportionment between the pre-existing condition and the aggravation of the condition.

Jurisdictions are split on whether aggravation of a pre-existing condition is compensable as an occupational disease. This is because an occupational disease is one that is caused by the employment. By definition, a pre-existing illness could not have been caused by the employment.

Because of concerns that employers would not hire persons with disabilities due to the financial risk, a "second injury" fund was instituted. A second injury fund distributes the costs of claims that are caused by pre-existing conditions, among the entire workers' compensation system. In order to qualify for participation in the second injury fund, an employer must demonstrate that it had knowledge of the employee's pre-existing condition. There may be other statutory requirements; therefore, the reader is advised to check the law of his or her own jurisdiction.

Death Claims

A death claim is one which is made by the survivors of an employee who died as a result of a work-related injury or illness. Death benefits generally include compensation to the employee's dependents, and payment of funeral expenses. Even if the employee settled a compensation claim, or never even brought such a claim in their lifetime, the survivors are still permitted to make the claim following his or her death. Of course, the survivors must prove that the death was caused by an injury or disease that was causally related to their decedent's employment.

Survivors who are entitled to compensation on a death claim generally include certain classes of dependents. Depending on the jurisdiction, eligible dependents may include:

1. The surviving spouse;

2. Surviving minor children, including adopted children;

3. Children who, while not minors, are full-time students and were dependent on the decedent;

4. Other family members who were living with the decedent at the time of his or her death and can prove their dependency on the decedent, such as parents, grandparents, grandchildren, and siblings of the decedent.

In general, if an individual is not within the classes of persons set forth in the statute, he or she cannot claim survivor benefits even if they can establish their dependency upon the decedent.

FILING A WORKERS' COMPENSATION CLAIM

A claim for workers' compensation benefits is not a lawsuit. It is an application for benefits under an insurance policy for which the employer has paid a premium. In some jurisdictions, the employer is entitled to deduct a small contribution from the employee's salary to help defray the cost of the insurance.

Most workers' compensation statutes set forth specific procedural requirements designed to move claims expeditiously through the various administrative stages. Thus, it is important that the disabled employee follow the procedural steps set forth under their state workers' compensation law in a timely manner in order to preserve their claim. Initiating a workers' compensation claim generally includes the following steps.

Notice to the Employer

It is extremely important to report all injuries at work to the employer as soon as possible. An untimely or post-termination reporting of the injury will result in a loss of entitlement to benefits. In general, a work-related accidental injury is required to be reported within a certain number of days of its occurrence. Nevertheless, if it is determined that the injured employee could not give timely notice of the claim, e.g., due to the nature and extent of the injuries suffered, etc., the untimely claim will generally not be barred.

Filing the Claim with the Insurance Carrier

A claim for workers' compensation benefits must be filed with the insurance carrier. The employer is required to provide the employee with the necessary forms to be filed. However, if the disability occurs over a prolonged period of time, such as a gradually developing occupational illness, it must be reported as soon as the employee discovers that he or she is suffering from the illness.

The employer will submit the claim to the insurance carrier. The employer is given an opportunity to respond to the claim. If the employer does not contest the claim, the insurance carrier will make payment of medical bills and wages. However, if the employer contests the claim to determine whether, or how much, compensation is owed to the employee, a hearing with the workers' compensation board will be scheduled.

A sample California State Workers' Compensation Claim Form is set forth at Appendix 14.

The Workers' Compensation Hearing

Although it is not necessary to be represented by an attorney in a workers' compensation proceeding, it may be advisable in certain circumstances, e.g., if the claim is particularly complex, or if the claim has already been denied. Attorney fees for workers' compensation claims are fixed by statute and/or subject to approval by the judge. Thus, many workers' compensation attorneys work on a volume basis. They are usually quite familiar with the workers' compensation system, and can assist a claimant with the procedural steps.

A table setting forth attorney fees in workers' compensation claims is set forth at Appendix 15.

Workers' compensation matters are generally held before some type of administrative agency, such as a workers' compensation board. The first appearance is usually a conference at which time the parties attempt to settle the claim. Many states have initiated alternative dispute resolution measures to assist in resolving claims. If a settlement cannot be reached, a trial date is set. Trial dates are frequently adjourned in an attempt to settle cases, in large part due to the limited resources of the workers' compensation boards. If the case goes to trial, it is held before a workers' compensation judge, also known as a "referee" in some jurisdictions. Generally, there are no jury trials held in the workers' compensation system.

A workers' compensation hearing is designed to be informal. Although the employee has the burden of proving that he or she is entitled to compensation, formal rules of evidence are not usually followed. The degree of proof necessary to prevail on a workers' compensation case is generally "a preponderance of the evidence."

Findings and Award

Following the trial, the judge will issue a decision setting forth the judge's conclusions about the case. This is known as a "finding." The judge will also issue an "award." The award sets forth: (1) the total percentage of disability; (2) the number of weeks payable for the disability; and (3) the amount to be paid per week. There will also usually be a finding as to whether future medical treatment is needed.

Filing an Appeal

If the employee loses their claim at the hearing, most states allow the employee to appeal the decision to an appeals board. If the employee is unsuccessful at this level, most states also permit judicial review of a final administrative decision. However, most appellate courts are only permitted to review questions of law. Some states do permit limited review of factual issues. All parties, including the administrative agency, are bound by the court's decision.

BENEFITS

Workers' compensation is designed to cover a disabled worker's economic losses, thus most state workers' compensation programs provide the following benefits: (1) wage loss compensation; (2) medical benefits; and (3) rehabilitation benefits.

Wage Loss Compensation

Wage loss compensation is generally paid according to whether the disability is deemed temporary, permanent, partial or total. Workers' compensation statutes generally require a waiting period before lost wages compensation are payable. However, if an employee's disability continues for a specific number of days or weeks, lost wages compensation begins, and is usually retroactive back to the date of injury.

A table setting forth the waiting periods for workers' compensation benefits, by state, is set forth at Appendix 16.

Temporary Total Disability

An employee who suffers a temporary total disability is one who is totally disabled during the period when compensation is paid, but is expected to return to employment once recovered. An employee in this category is generally entitled to a weekly benefit that is paid during the period of time the employee cannot work because of the employment-related injury. The weekly benefit is set forth as a percentage of the employee's gross salary, and continues until the employee is able to return to work.

A table of the percentage of wages payable for temporary total disability under state workers' compensation laws is set forth at Appendix 17.

Permanent Total Disability

An employee who suffers a permanent total disability is one who is deemed totally disabled and is unable to return to employment. An employee who suffers a permanent total disability is generally entitled to a weekly benefit based on his or her diminished ability to compete in the job market. The weekly benefit is set forth as a percentage of the employee's gross salary, payable for a stated number of weeks, calculated according to the extent of the permanent disability.

Employees who have suffered a severe injury such that he or she is presumed to be permanently and totally disabled, generally receives compensation checks throughout his or her entire life. This compensation continues until either the employee returns to gainful employment or the employee dies. In some jurisdictions, compensation ends when the employee reaches the maximum allowable benefit.

A table of the percentage of wages payable for permanent total disability under state workers' compensation laws is set forth at Appendix 18.

Temporary Partial Disability

An employee who suffers a temporary partial disability is usually entitled to wage loss replacement. This is because a partial disability generally affects the employee's current earnings or wage earning ability. The compensation amount is expressed as a percentage of the employee's wages, and is calculated as the difference between earnings before the injury and earnings after the injury. Because the disability is temporary, the compensation ends when the employee returns to his or her pre-injury status.

Permanent Partial Disability

An employee who suffers a permanent partial disability is also entitled to wage loss replacement because the partial disability affects the employee's current earnings or wage earning ability. Again, the compensation amount is expressed as a percentage of the employee's wages, and is calculated as the difference between earnings before the injury and earnings after the injury.

A table of the percentage of wages payable for permanent total disability under state workers' compensation laws is set forth at Appendix 19.

Scheduled Disabilities

Depending on the jurisdiction, certain disabilities are statutorily listed as "scheduled" injuries. A scheduled injury is one that involves the loss—or loss of use of—a specific body part. Wage loss is presumed based on the type of injury suffered. Depending on the particular statute, compensation for a scheduled disability is calculated by attributing a specific number of weeks of benefits to the particular body part involved, e.g., loss of an eye = 300 weeks. This number of weeks is then multiplied by a weekly benefit amount, which is based on the employee's earnings at the time of the injury, in order to arrive at a compensation sum.

Medical Benefits

An extremely important benefit of the workers' compensation program is the right to receive good medical care. An employee is generally entitled to receive these medical benefits without limitation on duration or cost. In addition, the waiting period for the lost wages benefit does not apply to medical benefits. Medical care benefits, including hospitalization, are effective immediately.

Under the workers' compensation system, the employee is usually permitted to choose his or her treating physician provided the employer is notified of the choice before the injury occurs. This is known as "pre-designating" a physician for workers' compensation purposes. Employers are generally required to advise the employees of their right to pre-designate a physician. If you pre-designate your physician, you must do so in writing. In the notice to your employer, include the following information:

1. The name, address and phone number of the physician and/or medical facility you choose to pre-designate.

2. Your desire that your pre-designated physician provides your medical care in case you are injured or become ill on the job.

3. Sign and date the notice.

You can pre-designate a physician who has treated you in the past and has your medical records, or you can pre-designate the medical facility where the physician treated you.

It is advisable to pre-designate your doctor in case you need to file a workers' compensation claim. Your choice of physician is very important to your claim, and it is best to treat with a physician who you are comfortable with, and with whom you have a personal relationship, rather than one selected by the insurance carrier. Your treating doctor is responsible for the type of medical care you receive, and will provide medical reports that will impact the benefits you receive. Your treating doctor also helps decide the kind of work you can do during your recovery period, and determines when you can safely return to work.

Depending on the jurisdiction, if you have not pre-designated your treating physician, you may be forced into treatment with a physician who is selected by the employer for a certain time period, e.g. 30 days. However, once the specified time period ends, the employee is then usually permitted to choose his or her own treating physician.

Rehabilitation Benefits

A disabled employee is generally entitled to both medical and vocational rehabilitation. It is to the mutual benefit of both employer and employee that such rehabilitation begins as soon as possible. The purpose of vocational rehabilitation is to assist a disabled employee in finding a new job when the employee is no longer able to function in his or her former position due to the work-related disability.

RETALIATION

It is illegal for your employer to retaliate against you for filing a workers' compensation claim if you are injured or become ill at work. If you believe you are the victim of retaliation, you should file a petition for discrimination with your state Workers' Compensation Board.

In addition, there are federal and state laws that prohibit discrimination against an employee because he or she has a disability, such as the Americans with Disabilities Act (ADA), and state laws offering similar protection to disabled workers.

A more detailed discussion of this topic may be found in this author's book entitled The Americans with Disabilities Act, published by Oceana Publishing Company.

Further, under the Family and Medical Leave Act (FMLA), if your employer has 50 or more employees, you are entitled to take up to 12 weeks of unpaid leave to take care of a serious medical condition.

A more detailed discussion of this topic may be found in this author's book entitled Your Rights Under the Family and Medical Leave Act, published by Oceana Publishing Company.

LIMITS ON COMBINED BENEFITS

You are entitled to obtain both state workers' compensation benefits and federal social security disability benefits at the same time, however, there are limits on the amount of money you can recover. Generally, the limit is a percentage of your average current earnings as computed by the Social Security Administration.

In this situation, some states have a statutory reverse offset that allows the employer's workers' compensation insurance carrier to take a credit. In most jurisdictions, however, the offset is taken by the social security system. In general, there is no offset after an employee reaches age 62.

Social Security Disability Insurance is discussed more fully in Chapter 8 of this almanac.

INDEPENDENT MEDICAL EXAMINATIONS

Your employer's insurance carrier may require you to undergo periodic medical examinations. These examinations are referred to as "independent" medical examinations, although the insurance carrier selects the doctors. You must attend these examinations in order for your workers' compensation benefits to continue. The insurance carrier pays all of the costs for the medical examination, including your transportation expenses to and from the examination.

If your benefits are discontinued based on the results of the IME, and your doctor disagrees with the IME findings, you may be able to request another medical examination by a physician selected by the Workers' Compensation Board. Generally, you must first appeal the denial of benefits based on the IME report, and request an examination. Your request should include a copy of the denial letter and medical documentation from your physician showing that he or she did not concur with the IME findings.

INDEPENDENT CONTRACTORS

Workers' compensation programs, as well as the other disability compensation programs discussed in this almanac, generally apply only to employees. Individuals who work for themselves—called independent contractors—are not entitled to any disability benefits in connection with the work they perform, unless they have purchased a private disability compensation policy.

An independent contractor is generally defined as a person who contracts with another to perform services for that person, but who is not controlled by the other nor subject to the other's right to control with respect to the performance. Thus, if an employer has the right to control when the work is done, where it is done, and how it is done, the worker would likely be considered an employee. If the worker controls these conditions, he or she would more likely be considered an independent contractor, particularly if the worker provides his or her own equipment.

A court may be called upon to make the determination as to whether a worker is an employee or independent contractor if a dispute—e.g., over workers' compensation benefits—should arise. In making this determination, the court will usually look at the nature of the employer-employee relationship, including the degree of control the employer had over the worker.

To determine whether an individual is as an employee or an independent contractor, courts have established 20 common law factors which must be taken into account. The factors that may indicate employee status are the following:

1. Whether the worker is required to comply with the employer's instructions as to when, where, and how he or she is to work.

2. Whether the employer trains the worker to perform in a particular manner.

3. Whether the employer requires the worker to render personal service.

4. Whether the employer hires, supervises, and pays the worker's staff.

5. Whether the employer and the worker have a continuing relationship.

6. Whether the worker is required to work during hours set by the employer.

7. Whether the worker is required to work full-time for the employer.

8. Whether the worker performs the work on the employer's premises, particularly if the work could be performed elsewhere.

9. Whether the employer requires the worker to perform services in a particular order or sequence.

10. Whether the worker is required to submit oral or written reports to the employer.

11. Whether payment is made by the hour, week, or month as opposed to a per job basis.

12. Whether the employer pays the worker's business or travelling expenses.

13. Whether the employer furnishes the tools and materials to the worker.

14. Whether there is a lack of investment by the worker in the facilities required to perform services and dependence on the employer for such facilities.

15. Whether the worker realizes a profit or loss as a result of the services rendered.

16. Whether the worker works exclusively for the employer.

17. Whether the worker makes his or her services available to the general public.

18. Whether the employer maintains the right to discharge the worker, which would not be possible if the individual were an independent contractor working under a contract.

19. Whether the worker has the right to end the relationship with the employer without continuing to render services. An independent contractor would be bound by the contract to finish the job.

20. Whether the worker's services are integral to the business operations.

CHAPTER 4:
THE FEDERAL EMPLOYEES'
COMPENSATION ACT

IN GENERAL

The Federal Employees' Compensation Program was established pursuant to the Federal Employees' Compensation Act (FECA), a law which provides benefits for civilian employees of the United States who have suffered work-related injuries or occupational diseases. These benefits include payment of medical expenses and compensation for wage loss. The FECA also provides for payment of benefits to dependents of employees who die from work-related injuries or diseases.

Selected provisions of the Federal Employees' Compensation Act are set forth at Appendix 3.

The program provides compensation benefits to more than three million civilian employees of the United States who suffer disability due to work-related personal injury or illness. This includes the executive, legislative and judicial branch employees, civilian defense workers, medical workers in veterans' hospitals, and the 800,000 workers of the Postal Service, the country's largest civilian employer.

Coverage under the program is extended to Federal employees regardless of the length of time on the job or the type of position held. Probationary, temporary, and term employees are covered on the same basis as permanent employees. Also, part-time, seasonal, and intermittent employees are covered.

The program is administered by the Office of Workers Compensation Programs pursuant to the authority contained in the Federal Employees' Compensation Act (FECA). The costs are paid from the Employees' Compensation Fund, which OWCP administers. Federal civilian employees are covered by virtue of their employment status. Each year, every employer reimburses the Fund for the amounts paid to its employees in workers' compensation benefits during the previous year. Thus, a Federal employee is not required to contribute to the cost of compensation coverage

A Directory of National OWCP District Offices is set forth at Appendix 2.

TYPES OF FEDERAL WORKERS' COMPENSATION CLAIMS

Federal workers' compensation claims generally fall into the same three categories as claims under state workers' compensation statutes: (1) Traumatic Injury Claims; (2) Occupational Disease or Illness Claims; and (3) Death Claims.

Traumatic Injury Claims

A traumatic injury is a wound or other condition of the body caused by external force, including stress or strain. The injury must occur at a specific time and place, and it must affect a specific member or function of the body. The injury must be caused by a specific event or incident, or a series of events or incidents, within a single day or work shift.

Traumatic injuries include damage solely to or destruction of prostheses, such as dentures or artificial limbs. Traumatic injuries also include damage to or destruction of personal appliances, such as eyeglasses or hearing aids, when a personal injury requiring medical services occurred.

Occupational Disease or Illness Claims

An occupational disease or illness is a condition produced by the work environment over a period longer than one workday or shift. The condition may result from infection, repeated stress or strain, or repeated exposure to toxins, poisons, fumes or other continuing conditions of the work environment.

ESTABLISHING THE FACT OF THE INJURY OR ILLNESS

In order to establish an injury or illness, it must be shown that the employee actually sustained the injury or illness. Two factors are involved:

1. It must be shown that an incident occurred at the time and place and in the manner claimed. This is determined on the basis of factual evidence, including statements from the employee, the supervisor, and any witnesses. Nevertheless, an injury need not be witnessed to be compensable.

2. It must be shown that the employee has a medical condition that may be related to the incident. This is determined on the basis of the attending physician's statement.

Aggravation of a Pre-Existing Condition

Diseases and illnesses aggravated, accelerated or precipitated by the job are also covered. The employee must submit medical and factual evidence showing that the employment aggravated, accelerated, or precipitated the medical condition to receive compensation.

Death Claims

A death claim is one which is made by the survivors of an employee who died as a result of a work-related injury or illness. Death benefits generally include compensation to the employee's dependents, and payment of burial expenses. Of course, the survivors must prove that the death was caused by an injury or disease that was causally related to their decedent's employment.

PERFORMANCE OF DUTY REQUIREMENT

In order to prevail on a federal workers' compensation claim, the employee is required to prove that the injury or illness occurred while the employee was performing his or her duties. Generally, this means that the injury or illness must occur on the employer's premises during working hours while the employee is performing assigned duties or engaging in an activity that is reasonably associated with the employment. Workers who perform assigned duties away from the employer's premises are also covered.

Lunch and Breaks

In addition, an employee is considered to be in performance of duty during a break or at lunch on the employer's premises. Unless the employee is in travel status or is performing regular duties off the premises, an injury that occurs during lunch hour off the premises is not usually covered.

Recreation Activities

Further, injuries that occur during recreation which the employee is required to perform as a part of training or assigned duties, or which occur while the employee is in pay status, are considered to be in performance of duty for compensation purposes. Injuries that occur during informal recreation on the employer's premises may also be covered, including injuries that may occur while an employee is engaged in activities approved as part of an individual plan developed under a formal physical fitness program managed by the employer.

Injuries that occur during informal recreation off the employer's premises, such as playing on an employer-sponsored baseball team, may also be covered. In that connection, the employer must explain what benefit it derived from the employee's participation, the extent to which the employer sponsored or directed the activity, and whether the employee's participation was required or not.

Travel Time

Employees are not generally covered for injuries that occur before they reach the employer's premises or after they have left it. However, coverage may be extended when the employer provides transportation to and from work, when the employee is required to travel during a curfew or an emergency, or when the employee is required to use his or her automobile during the workday.

Nevertheless, an employee considered to be in travel status is covered 24 hours a day for all activities incidental to the work assignment. Such activities include obtaining meals, using the hotel room, and travelling between the hotel and the work site. However, this does not include recreational or sightseeing trips.

BENEFITS

Benefits available to disabled federal employees are similar to those provided under state workers' compensation systems. As discussed below, benefits include wage loss compensation, medical care, vocational rehabilitation, and death benefits resulting from a work-related injury or illness.

Employees are not entitled to any benefits if:

1. The injury or death is caused by the wilful misconduct of the employee;

2. The injury or death is caused by the employee's intention to bring about his or her injury or death or that of another; or

3. If intoxication by alcohol or drugs is the proximate cause of the employee's injury or death.

Wage Loss Compensation

Temporary Disability

The FECA provides non-taxable compensation benefits to federal employees for temporary disability due to work-related injury or disease. An injured employee is entitled to continuation of pay (COP) from the employing agency for up to 45 days of disability after a three-day waiting period in a non-paid status. However, if the disability causing wage loss lasts longer than 14 days from the time compensation begins, compensation is retroactive to the first day of disability.

Continuation of pay benefits do not apply to occupational disease cases. However, the employee may use sick or annual leave, or enter a leave without pay status and claim compensation.

Compensation is generally payable at the rate of two-thirds of the employee's pre-disability gross earnings if the employee has no dependents. Employees with dependents are generally entitled to compensation payable at the rate of three-fourths of pre-disability gross earnings. The term "dependent" as defined in the FECA includes a husband, wife, unmarried child under 18 years of age, and a wholly dependent parent.

An unmarried child may qualify as a dependent after reaching the age of 18 if incapable of self-support by reason of mental or physical disability, or as long as the child continues to be a full-time student at an accredited institution, until he or she reaches the age of 23 or has completed four years of education beyond the high school level.

Permanent Disability

The FECA also provides compensation benefits for work-related loss, or loss of use of, specified members, organs, and functions of the body. Benefits are calculated based on scheduled awards and loss of earning capacity. For example, an award of 160 weeks of compensation is payable to an employee who loses total vision in one eye due to a work-related occurrence.

In addition, compensation for loss of earning capacity may be paid if the employee is unable to resume his or her usual work because of the work-related disability. This compensation is paid on the basis of the difference between (1) the employee's capacity to earn wages after an injury; and (2) the wages of the job he or she held when injured.

Medical Benefits

Under the FECA, a disabled employee is entitled to:

1. Medical services;

2. Surgical services;

3. Hospital services;

4. Necessary medical supplies; and

5. Transportation necessary to obtain medical care.

Initially, the injured employee is entitled to choose a physician or hospital to provide necessary treatment. If the physician selected has been excluded from participating in the compensation program, the OWCP District Office will advise the employee of the exclusion and the need to select another physician. The employee may also use agency medical facilities if available.

After the employee's initial choice of physician has been made, he or she may not change physicians without obtaining OWCP authorization. If the employee changes physicians without OWCP authorization, OWCP will not pay for the unauthorized treatment. However, this provision does not apply when the attending physician has referred the employee to another medical provider. In addition, an employee is entitled to a referral to a medical specialist for a second opinion examination where required by the worker's medical condition or the office's need for additional medical information.

The term "physician" as used in the FECA includes surgeons, osteopathic practitioners, podiatrists, dentists, clinical psychologists, optometrists and chiropractors within the scope of their practice as defined by State law. Payment for chiropractic services is limited to treatment consisting of manual manipulation of the spine to correct a subluxation as demonstrated by x-ray to exist.

An injured employee who is unable to return to his or her employment within a specified period of time is also entitled to the services of a registered nurse. The nurse ensures that appropriate medical care is rendered and assists the worker in returning to employment. If the employee's condition requires a constant attendant, an additional amount not to exceed $1500 per month may be allowed.

Vocational Rehabilitation

An disabled employee is entitled to vocational rehabilitation services if he or she is unable to return to work at the employing agency, or in his or her previous job category. OWCP may provide a maintenance allowance not to exceed $200 per month. A disabled employee participating in an OWCP-approved training or vocational rehabilitation program is paid at the compensation rate for total disability.

Death Benefits

If an employee dies due to a work-related injury or illness, his or her family members are entitled to compensation, as follows:

1. If the employee had no eligible children, the surviving spouse's compensation is 50 percent of the employee's pay at the time of death.

2. If the employee had a child or children eligible for benefits, the surviving spouse is entitled to 45 percent of the employee's pay at the time of death, and each child is entitled to 15 percent.

3. If the employee's children are his or her sole survivors, 40 percent of the employee's pay at the time of death is paid to the first child and 15 percent for each additional child, to be shared equally.

4. Other related persons such as dependent parents, brothers, sisters, grandparents, and grandchildren may also be entitled to benefits.

In any event, the total compensation paid to the employee's survivors may not exceed 75 percent of the employee's pay, or the pay of the highest step for the federal employee grade of GS-15 as per the General Schedule, except when such excess is created by authorized cost-of-living increases.

Compensation paid to an employee's surviving spouse terminates upon the spouse's death or remarriage, unless the remarriage takes place after the age of 55. Awards to children, brothers, sisters and grandchildren terminate at the age of 18 unless: (1) the dependent is incapable of self-support; or (2) continues to be a full-time student at an accredited institution until he or she has completed four years of education beyond the high school level, or has reached the age of 23, whichever occurs first.

Burial expenses in an amount not to exceed $800 are also payable. If the death occurs away from the employee's former residence in the United States, transportation of the body is provided. In addition to any burial expenses or transportation costs, a $200 allowance is paid for the administrative costs of terminating an employee's status with the Federal Government.

Cost-of-Living Increases

Compensation payments on account of a disability or death which occurred more than one year before March 1 of each year, are increased on that date by any percentage change in the Consumer Price Index published for December of the preceding year.

FILING A WORKERS' COMPENSATION CLAIM UNDER THE FECA

Legal Representation

An employee does not need an attorney or other representative to file or pursue a claim for compensation. However, the employee may obtain the services of an attorney or other representative if desired. A Federal employee may not serve as a representative unless he or she is an immediate family member of the injured worker, or is acting in his or her official capacity as a union representative. An OWCP employee may not act as a representative under any circumstances. The employee must advise OWCP in writing of the name of the representative.

If the employee hires an attorney, the employee is responsible for paying the fee. The OWCP will not direct the payment of a fee or help collect a fee. The employee and representative must resolve these matters. The employee should not pay any legal fee until the OWCP has approved the amount. The OWCP will approve a fee based on an itemized statement submitted by the representative showing the work performed, along with a statement from the employee indicating his or her agreement, or lack of agreement, with the requested fee.

Written Notice of a Traumatic Injury

Every injury should be immediately reported to the employee's supervisor. Written notice of a traumatic injury is required to be reported on Form CA-1. This form may be obtained from the federal employer or the OWCP office, and should be filed within 30 days. Any claim that is not submitted within 3 years will be barred by statutory time limitations unless the immediate superior had actual knowledge of the injury or death within 30 days of occurrence.

Further, Form CA-1 must be filed within the 30-day period to qualify for continuation of pay (COP) for a disabling traumatic injury. COP may be terminated if medical evidence of the injury-related disability is not submitted to your employer within 10 workdays. It is the employee's responsibility to make sure that the proper medical evidence is submitted to his or her employer.

A Sample Federal Employee's Notice of Traumatic Injury and Claim for Continuation of Pay/Compensation (Form CA-1) is set forth at Appendix 20.

Written Notice of Occupational Disease

Written notice of an occupational disease or illness must be reported on Form CA-2. This form may also be obtained from the federal employer or the OWCP office, and should be filed within 30 days. Form CA-2 may be obtained from the federal employer or the OWCP office.

A Sample Federal Employee's Notice of Occupational Disease and Claim for Compensation (Form CA-2) is set forth at Appendix 21.

Authorization for Medical Treatment

In case of injury, an employee should seek medical attention even if the injury is minor. While many minor injuries heal without treatment, a few result in serious prolonged disability that could have been prevented had the employee received treatment when the injury occurred. For traumatic injuries, the employer must authorize medical treatment prior to the employee's visit to the doctor. An employer may authorize medical treatment for occupational illness only with the prior approval of OWCP.

The employee should submit medical bills promptly. Bills for medical treatment may not be paid if submitted to OWCP more than one year after the calendar year in which treatment was rendered, or in which the condition was accepted as compensable.

Establishing the Necessary Elements of the Claim

The employee must be able to establish the elements of his or her claim to prevail. For example:

1. The employee must prove that he or she is a covered employee under the FECA;

2. The employee must prove that benefits were applied for in a timely manner;

3. The employee must prove that the injury occurred as reported, and while in performance of duty; and

4. The employee must prove that his or her condition is causally related to the employment. The medical connection must be based entirely on medical evidence provided by physicians who have examined and treated the employee.

The OWCP assists employees in gathering evidence and meeting their burden of proof on these elements.

Continuation of Pay

If the employee continues to lose pay after the dates initially claimed, he or she must submit to his or her employer a Claim for Continuing Compensation (Form CA-12), to claim additional compensation until he or she is able to return to work.

A sample Claim for Continuation of Compensation under the Federal Employees' Compensation Act (Form CA-12) is set forth at Appendix 22.

If the employee chooses to use leave time, he or she may, with the employer's approval, request to "buy back" their leave time. Any compensation payment is to be used to partially reimburse the employer for the leave pay.

The employee must also arrange to pay the employer the difference between the leave pay based on the full salary, and the compensation payment that was paid at 2/3 or 3/4 of the employee's salary. The employer will then recredit the leave to the employee's leave record.

Penalties for Filing a False Claim for Compensation

It is illegal to file a false claim for federal workers' compensation benefits:

> Whoever knowingly and wilfully falsifies, conceals, or covers up a material fact, or makes a false, fictitious, or fraudulent statement or representation, or makes or uses a false statement or report knowing the same to contain any false, fictitious, or fraudulent statement or entry in connection with the application for or receipt of compensation or other benefit or payment under subchapter I or III of chapter 81 of title 5, shall be guilty of perjury, and on conviction thereof shall be punished by a fine under this title, or by imprisonment for not more than 5 years, or both; but if the amount of the benefits falsely obtained does not exceed $1,000, such person shall be punished by a fine under this title, or by imprisonment for not more than 1 year, or both. [18 U.S.C. 1920].

RETURN TO WORK PROVISIONS

Under the FECA, injured workers have the right to reclaim their Federal jobs within one year of the onset of wage loss. Thus, the employee should return to work as soon as he or she is able to do so.

Employees who fully or partially recover from their injuries are expected to return to work. The FECA provides vocational rehabilitation services to partially disabled employees for this purpose. If the employer gives the employee a written description of an available light duty job, he or she must provide a copy to the doctor and ask if and when the duties described could be performed, and if there are any work restrictions.

In any event, the employer is entitled to written verification of the doctor's return to work instructions for the employee. Compensation may be terminated if the employee refuses work that is within these medical restrictions without good cause, or if the employee fails to respond within specified time limits to a job offer from the employer.

In appropriate cases, the OWCP provides assistance in arranging for reassignment to lighter duties in cooperation with the employer. In addition, injured employees have certain other specified rights under the jurisdiction of the Office of Personnel Management, such as reemployment rights if the disability has been overcome within one year.

TIME LIMITS IN ADJUDICATING A FEDERAL COMPENSATION CLAIM

Injured Employees

Employees who suffer traumatic injuries generally receive a decision within 45 days of receipt of the claim, unless the case is particularly complex. If the case is accepted, and the medical evidence supports the disability, compensation payments are usually made within 14 days of submission to the OWCP district office by the employing agency.

Approved medical bills, whether submitted directly by the providers or as reimbursement requests by injured workers, are usually paid within 28 days of receipt.

Occupational Disease

A simple occupational disease claim is usually decided within 90 days of receipt of the claim. Decisions in cases that require more extensive evidentiary development may take up to six months. However, if the claim is particularly complex, it may take up to 10 months of receipt of the claim for a decision.

APPEAL RIGHTS

An employee or survivor who disagrees with a final OWCP determination may appeal the decision. Appeal rights include the following:

1. The employee has the right to an oral hearing before an OWCP representative. The employee claiming benefits can testify and present written evidence. The hearing is held at a location near the employee's home. The employee may have legal representation at the hearing, but it is not necessary.

2. The employee has the right to a review of the written record by an OWCP representative. The employee claiming benefits will not be asked to attend or testify, but he or she may submit written evidence.

3. The employee has the right to reconsideration of a decision by district office staff that were not involved in making the decision. The request must clearly state the grounds for requesting reconsideration, and it must include evidence not submitted before or a legal argument not made before.

4. The employee has the right to a review by the Employees' Compensation Appeals Board (ECAB). The ECAB is part of the U.S. Department of Labor, but separate from the OWCP. Review by the ECAB is limited to the evidence of record, and no new evidence may be submitted. The individual claiming benefits may be represented by an

attorney or by any other person authorized by that individual. The ECAB must approve any fee for such representation.

Unlike state workers' compensation systems, if the federal employee is dissatisfied with the decision reached on appeal, he or she cannot obtain review through a state or Federal court system.

RECOVERY FROM LIABLE THIRD PARTIES

If a third party, other than the United States, is liable to the employee for his or her work-related injury or death, the OWCP is entitled to a portion of the cost of compensation and other benefits paid by OWCP if there is any recovery from such third party. OWCP will assist in obtaining a settlement with the third party.

The FECA guarantees that the employee may retain a certain portion of the settlement after any attorney fees and costs are deducted, even if the cost of compensation and other benefits exceeds the amount of the settlement.

CHAPTER 5:
THE LONGSHORE AND HARBOR WORKERS' COMPENSATION ACT

IN GENERAL

In addition to the Federal Employees' Compensation Program, The Office of Workers' Compensation Programs ("OWCP") is responsible for administering The Longshore and Harbor Workers' Compensation Program pursuant to the Longshore and Harbor Workers' Compensation Act of 1927 (33 U.S.C. §§901-950) (LHWCA). The LHWCA offers compensation and medical care to approximately one-half million maritime workers injured or killed upon the navigable waters of the U.S., as well as employees working on adjoining piers, docks and terminals, plus a number of other groups.

The Act also covers a variety of other workers through the following extensions to the Act: (1) the Defense Base Act of 1941; (2) the Nonappropriated Fund Instrumentalities Act of 1952; and (3) the Outer Continental Shelf Lands Act of 1953. Under these extensions to the Act, the following workers are covered: (1) overseas employees of defense contractors; (2) employees at military post exchanges; (3) workers engaged in the extraction of natural resources on the outer continental shelf; and (4) other classes of private industry workers that are entitled to compensation benefits.

The Act does not cover the following individuals if they are covered by a state workers' compensation law: (1) Individuals employed exclusively to perform office clerical, secretarial, security, or data processing work; (2) Individuals employed by a club, camp, recreational operation, restaurant, museum, or retail outlet; (3) Individuals employed by a marina and who are not engaged in construction, replacement, or expansion of such marina; (4) Individuals who: (a) are employed by suppliers, transporters, or vendors; (b) are temporarily doing business on the premises of a maritime employer; and (c) are not engaged in work normally performed by employees of that employer covered under this Act; (5) Aquaculture workers; (6) Individuals employed to build, repair, or dismantle any recreational vessel under sixty-five feet in length; (7) A master or member of a crew of any vessel; (8) Any person engaged by a master to load or unload or repair any small vessel under eighteen tons net; and (9) Employees of the United States government or of any state or foreign government.

BENEFITS

The LHWCA provides lost wages compensation, medical benefits, and rehabilitation services, to employees who suffer work-related injuries or illness. The Act also offers benefits to dependents if the injury causes the employee's death. These benefits are paid by an insurance company or by an employer who is authorized by the OWCP to be self-insured. In some cases, benefits are paid from a special fund consisting of employer contributions.

The Division of Longshore and Harbor Workers' Compensation (DLHWC) is responsible for administering this special fund, and ensuring that disabled workers or their survivors receive the benefits they are entitled to in an expedient manner. The DLHWC is also responsible for providing authorization to qualified insurance carriers and self-insured employers.

The program pays out over $747 million in monetary, medical and vocational rehabilitation benefits in more than 66,000 cases annually. In addition the program maintains over $2.8 billion in securities to ensure the continuing provision of benefits for these injured workers in cases of employer insolvency.

Medical Benefits

Medical benefits include all medical, surgical, and hospital treatment and other medical supplies and services required by the employment related injury, as well as the cost of travel and mileage incidental to such treatment.

The employee may obtain medical treatment from a physician of his or her choice. The term "physician" includes doctors of medicine (MD), surgeons, podiatrists, dentists, clinical psychologists, optometrists, and osteopathic practitioners within the scope of their practice as defined by state law. Chiropractors are also included only to the extent that their treatment consists of manual manipulation of the spine to correct subluxation.

An employee may not choose a physician who is currently not authorized by the Department of Labor to render medical care under the Act.

The list of physicians not authorized is available from the local OWCP district office.

Disability Compensation

Disability is defined as the employee's inability to earn the same wages he or she was earning at the time of injury. Compensation is payable for disabilities that are permanent total, temporary total, permanent partial, or temporary partial.

Disability compensation is paid every two weeks during an employee's total disability because of a work-related injury. Compensation is paid at a lesser rate if the employee is only partially disabled for his regular work.

Permanent Total and Temporary Total Disability

Compensation under this category is two-thirds of the employee's average weekly wage, subject to a maximum amount. The maximum rate payable for temporary total disability changes each October 1, based on the current National Average Weekly Wage for the affected period. Compensation for permanent total disability is adjusted each October 1, based on the percentage change in the national average weekly wage from the previous year, subject to a maximum adjustment of 5%.

Permanent Partial Disability

Compensation under this category is payable for the permanent loss or loss of use of certain parts or functions of the body, such as the loss of the arm, hand, fingers, leg, foot, toes, hearing or vision. Compensation is payable for a certain number of weeks for each type of disability as specified in the Act. For example, total loss of use of a foot entitles the employee to 205 weeks of compensation.

Temporary Partial and Non-Scheduled Permanent Partial Disability

Compensation under this category is two-thirds of the employee's weekly wage loss or loss of wage-earning capacity.

Permanent Partial Disability for Retirees

If a worker suffers the onset of a latent occupational disease after retirement, compensation is two-thirds of the National Average Weekly Wage (NAWW) multiplied by the percentage of impairment resulting from the disease.

Vocational Rehabilitation

A disabled worker is entitled to vocation rehabilitation. Vocational rehabilitation may include evaluation, testing, counseling, selective placement, and retraining, if the employee is injured and cannot return to the former job. Rehabilitation services may include the cost of tuition, books and supplies. A maintenance allowance not to exceed $25.00 per week is also provided during retraining. The cost of vocational rehabilitation services is paid by the U. S. Department of Labor.

Death Benefits

Death benefits are paid to a widow or widower or other eligible survivors if the injury causes the employee's death. Other eligible survivors include children, parents, brothers, sisters, grandparents and grandchildren who were dependent on the employee. Reasonable funeral expenses are paid, up to a maximum of $3,000.

Compensation payable under the Act may not exceed 200% of the national average weekly wage, applicable at the time of injury, or the employee's full average weekly wage, whichever is less.

Widow/Widower

The employee's widow or widower receives 50% of the average weekly wage of the deceased employee for life or until remarriage. Upon remarriage, a widow or widower receives a lump sum payment of compensation covering two years.

Children

Additional compensation is payable at a rate of 16-2/3% of the employee's average weekly wage for one or more children. If children are the sole survivors of the employee, 50% of the employee's average weekly wage is paid on behalf of the first child. Where more than one child is entitled to benefits, a maximum of 66-2/3% applies, shared equally.

Benefit payments to children, brothers, sisters, and grandchildren terminate when they reach 18, but may be extended to age 23 if the child or beneficiary is a student. Payments may continue indefinitely if a child remains incapable of self-support due to mental or physical disabilities.

WAITING PERIOD

No compensation is allowed for the first three days of disability unless the disability lasts longer than fourteen days. In such cases, compensation is paid retroactively from the first day of wage loss. The first installment of compensation is due 14 days after the employee begins to lose time from work due to the injury, or as directed by the OWCP.

FILING A CLAIM

If you are injured on the job, you must notify your employer immediately. If you need medical treatment, ask your employer to give you the necessary forms that authorize treatment by a doctor of your choice. You should obtain medical treatment as soon as possible.

In any event, you must give written notice of your injury to your employer within 30 days of the date of injury. Notice of death must also be given within 30 days. Additional time is provided for certain hearing loss and occupational disease claims.

A written claim for compensation must be filed within one year after the date of injury or last payment of compensation, whichever is later. A claim for survivor benefits must be filed within one year after the date of death. The time for filing claims in certain occupational disease cases has been extended to two years.

A sample Longshore and Harbor Worker's Compensation Claim Form (Form LS-203) is set forth at Appendix 23.

ALTERNATIVE DISPUTE RESOLUTION

A primary function of the Longshore and Harbor Workers' Compensation Program is to resolve claims through alternative dispute resolution methods. Claims that are resolved voluntarily in mediation are beneficial to all parties. Mediation avoids the delays encountered during the more formal procedures. Thus, the worker and his or her family do not have to suffer the financial difficulties associated with loss of income and benefits while their claims are pending.

In addition, mediation provides the employer a way to minimize litigation expenses. The government also saves money because mediation conferences are far less expensive than formal hearings. For example, an informal conference can be conducted for an estimated average of $300, while each formal hearing costs over $2,000. During fiscal year 2005, over 2,900 informal conferences were conducted in disputed claims.

If the parties cannot resolve their controversy through this informal method, they must request a formal hearing before an Administrative Law Judge.

CHAPTER 6:
THE BLACK LUNG BENEFITS ACT

IN GENERAL

In addition to the Federal Employees' Compensation Program, The Office of Workers' Compensation Programs ("OWCP") is also responsible for administering The Black Lung Benefits Program.

The Federal Coal Mine Health and Safety Act of 1969 established a system for providing monthly cash payments and medical benefits to coal miners who suffer from pneumoconiosis—commonly referred to as "black lung disease"—a crippling respiratory condition, arising from their employment in or around the nation's coal mines. Surviving dependents of the miner are also entitled to benefits if he or she dies as a result of coal mine dust exposure.

The Black Lung Benefits Program was initially administered by the Social Security Administration (SSA) under Part B of the Act. However, in 1973, jurisdiction over new claims was transferred to the Department of Labor's Office of Workers' Compensation Programs ("OWCP"), under Part C of the Act, pursuant to the 1972 amendments to the Act. Claims filed prior to implementation of the 1972 amendments remain under the jurisdiction of the Social Security Administration.

Part B of the Act was set up as a temporary system to compensate past victims of coal mine dust exposure from government funds. Part C of the Act made the program permanent, and diverted the responsibility for payment of benefits from the U.S. Government to the coal mining industry.

THE DIVISION OF COAL MINE WORKERS' COMPENSATION

The Division of Coal Mine Workers' Compensation ("DCMWC") has been set up to administer the Black Lung Benefits Program under the jurisdiction of the OWCP. The DCMWC adjudicates and processes disability compensation claims filed by the nation's coal miners and their survivors. There are 17 DCMWC offices nationwide, including a national office, nine district offices, and seven field stations.

The DCMWC accepts, reviews and makes eligibility determinations on benefit applications. Ninety-eight percent (98%) of the claims the DCMWC receives are decided within 180 days. The Division began fiscal year 2004 with 5,049 claims for benefits pending, and received an additional 4,489 claims during the year. Decisions were issued in 6,495 claims, leaving 3,149 determinations to be made. The Division also initiated payments to 1,549 survivors who were automatically entitled to benefits following the death of the miner. In 2004, a total of over 102,000 beneficiaries and 18,000 dependents received benefits.

INSURANCE REQUIREMENT

The Black Lung Benefits Act requires each coal mine operator to secure the payment of its benefits liability by either qualifying as a self-insurer or by purchasing and maintaining in force a commercial insurance contract, including a policy or contract procured from a State agency.

Any coal mine operator who is required to secure the payment of benefits and who fails to do so is subject to a civil penalty of up to $1,000 for each day of noncompliance. In addition, the president, treasurer and secretary of an uninsured coal mine operator that is a corporation may be liable for the payment of benefits owed to former employees.

Coal transportation and coal mine construction employers who are not also coal mine operators do not have to secure benefit payments in advance; however, once an employee is awarded benefits, the employer may be required to secure a bond or otherwise guarantee payment.

THE BLACK LUNG DISABILITY TRUST FUND

Generally, the last coal mine operator for whom the miner worked for a cumulative period of at least one year is usually responsible for the payment of benefits; however, the Black Lung Disability Trust Fund pays benefits when:

1. The miner's last coal mine employment was before January 1, 1970;

2. There is no liable coal mine operator; or

3. The miner's most recent employment of at least one year with an operator ended while the operator was authorized to self-insure, and such operator is no longer financially capable of securing benefit payments.

BENEFITS

Monthly Benefits Rate for 2005

On January 1, 2005, new monthly rates went into effect for Black Lung benefits that included a 2.5% increase over the 2004 benefit amounts. The new rates are as follows:

Part-B Black Lung Monthly Benefit Rates

Primary beneficiary - $562.00

Primary beneficiary and one dependent - $844.00

Primary beneficiary and two dependents - $984.00

Primary beneficiary and three or more dependents - $1,125.00

Part-C Black Lung Monthly Benefit Rates

Primary beneficiary - $562.80

Primary beneficiary and one dependent - $844.10

Primary beneficiary and two dependents - $984.80

Primary beneficiary and three or more dependents - $1,125.50

Medical Benefits

The program provides medical treatment for respiratory conditions related to treatment for black lung disease. Two types of medical services related to black lung disease are provided: (1) diagnostic testing for all miner-claimants to determine the presence or absence of black lung disease and the degree of associated disability; and, (2) for miners entitled to monthly benefits, medical coverage for treatment of black lung disease and disability.

Diagnostic testing includes a chest x-ray, pulmonary function study (breathing test), arterial blood gas study, and a physical examination. Medical coverage includes, but is not limited to, costs for prescription drugs, office visits, and hospitalizations. Also provided, with specific approval, are items of durable medical equipment, such as hospital beds, home oxygen, and nebulizers; outpatient pulmonary rehabilitation therapy; and home nursing visits.

In fiscal year 2004, approximately 336,000 medical treatment bills were processed. Medical treatment bills are monitored and subject to audit to ensure that the requested treatments are necessary and that payments are correct.

Death Benefits

Surviving dependents of the miner are also entitled to benefits if he or she dies as a result of coal mine dust exposure. A survivor whose claim is filed on or after January 1, 1982, in which there has been no previous compensation award, must generally prove that the miner's death was causally related to pneumoconiosis.

FILING A CLAIM UNDER THE BLACK LUNG ACT

To file a claim under the Black Lung Act, the worker must contact the DCMWC to fill out the appropriate claim forms. The DCMWC staff is available to assist disabled workers in completing the required forms. Claims may be filed by present and former coal miners and their surviving dependents, including surviving spouses, orphaned children, and totally dependent parents, brothers and sisters of the worker. Once the claim has been opened, a medical examination of the worker will be held to determine whether he or she suffers from black lung disease.

A sample Miner's Claim For Benefits Under The Black Lung Benefits Act (Form CM-911) is set forth at Appendix 24.

Under The Black Lung Amendments of 1981, certain presumptions of disease and disability were eliminated in claims filed on or after January 1,1982. The 1981 Amendments also eliminated presumptions of death due to pneumoconiosis in survivor claims.

For all claims filed after January 19, 2001, following is the claims processing procedure.

Development of Evidence

When a claim for benefits is received, the district office obtains a complete history of the miner's employment from the claimant. They then gather other evidence regarding the nature and duration of the miner's employment, and any other information necessary to resolve the claim.

If the claim is filed by or on behalf of a miner, a complete pulmonary evaluation is authorized and paid for by the Black Lung Disability Trust Fund. The miner must select a physician or medical facility to conduct the evaluation from a list provided by the district office. The list includes physicians and facilities located in the miner's state of residence and contiguous states who have been authorized to conduct complete pulmonary evaluations.

If the claim is filed by or on behalf of a survivor, the district office obtains whatever medical evidence is necessary and available to evaluate the claim.

THE BLACK LUNG BENEFITS ACT

In the event the district office determines that the evidence supports an award and that there is no coal mine operator responsible for the payment of benefits, they will issue a proposed decision and order an award of benefits payable by the Trust Fund.

If the district office determines the evidence does not support an award and that there is no operator responsible for the payment of benefits, they will issue a Schedule for the Submission of Additional Evidence. In that instance, the district office will be entitled to exercise the same rights as a responsible operator, subject to certain limitations. In all cases where an operator may be liable for the payment of benefits, however, the district director will issue a Notice of Claim.

Notice of Claim

If, after developing evidence related to the miner's employment history, the district office identifies one or more operators who may be liable for the payment of benefits should they be awarded, they send a Notice of Claim to those operators and their insurers of record. These operators are called "potentially liable operators."

The Notice advises the operators and insurers of the existence of the claim and that they have been made parties to the claim. The district office sends a copy of the claimant's application and all of the evidence that has developed pertaining to the miner's employment history along with the Notice.

An operator who receives a Notice of Claim must respond within 30 days of receipt of the Notice and indicate its intent to accept or contest its identification as a potentially liable operator. The operator must send a copy of its response to the claimant.

An operator who contests its potential liability must state the precise nature of its disagreement with its designation by accepting or denying that:

1. It was an operator for any period after June 30, 1973;

2. It employed the miner as a miner for a cumulative period of not less than one year;

3. The miner was exposed to coal mine dust while working for the operator;

4. It employed the miner at least one day after December 31, 1969;

5. It is capable of assuming liability for the payment of benefits.

If a notified operator fails to respond within 30 days, it will not be allowed to contest its liability for the payment of benefits in later proceedings on any of these five grounds, although it will retain the right

Injured on the Job: Employee Rights, Workers' Compensation & Disability 53

to assert that another operator is liable for the particular claim involved.

Within 90 days of the date on which it receives the Notice of Claim, an operator may submit documentary evidence in support of its position. Documentary evidence relevant to the five grounds listed above must be submitted to the district office. If the operator does not submit the documentary evidence, it will not be admitted in any further proceedings absent a showing of exceptional circumstances.

The 30 and 90-day response periods may be extended for good cause shown if an extension request is filed with the district office before the response period expires.

Submission of Additional Evidence

Once the district office completes the development of medical evidence and receives responses and evidence regarding liability from potentially liable operators, they will issue a "Schedule for the Submission of Additional Evidence." The district office will send a copy of the Schedule, together with a copy of the evidence developed, to the claimant and all designated potentially liable operators.

The Schedule will include:

1. A summary of the results of the initial complete pulmonary evaluation or, for survivors' claims, a summary of the medical evidence developed;

2. The preliminary analysis of the medical evidence;

3. The designation of the "responsible operator" liable for the payment of benefits; and

4. A notice to the claimant and the designated responsible operator that they have a right to submit evidence on the claimant's entitlement to benefits and the responsible operator's liability for them.

The responsible operator named in the Schedule must respond to the schedule within 30 days of issuance indicating whether it agrees or disagrees with its designation as the responsible operator liable for the payment of benefits. If it does not timely respond, the responsible operator will be deemed to have accepted liability should benefits be awarded, and to have waived its right to challenge its liability in any further proceedings. On the merits of the claim, the responsible operator may file a statement accepting the claimant's entitlement to benefits; otherwise, the responsible operator will be deemed to have contested the claim.

The Schedule will give the claimant and the responsible operator no less than 60 days to submit additional evidence on both the liability and entitlement issues, and will allow an additional 30 days within which to respond to evidence the other party submits. These time periods may be extended for good cause if an extension request is filed with the district office before the time period expires.

Development of Evidence by the Claimant and the Responsible Operator

Documentary Evidence Regarding Liability

During the time periods set out in the Schedule for the submission of affirmative and rebuttal evidence, the responsible operator may submit evidence to the district office demonstrating it is not the potentially liable operator that most recently employed the miner. Other parties as well may submit evidence regarding the designated responsible operator's liability.

There is no limitation on the amount of evidence regarding liability a party may submit. A copy of any documentary evidence submitted must be mailed to all other parties. Absent extraordinary circumstances, no documentary evidence pertaining to this aspect of the liability determination shall be admitted in any further proceeding conducted with respect to the claim unless it is submitted to the district office in compliance with the schedule for the submission of additional evidence.

Documentary Medical Evidence

Documentary medical evidence is treated differently. A party may submit medical evidence either to the district office in compliance with the Schedule, or to the Administrative Law Judge (ALJ) up to 20 days before the hearing.

The amount of documentary medical evidence a party may submit is limited. Each side may submit two chest x-ray interpretations, the results of two pulmonary function tests, two arterial blood gas studies and two medical reports as its affirmative case. Each side may also submit one autopsy report and one report of each biopsy.

In addition, each party may submit one piece of evidence in rebuttal of each piece of evidence submitted by the opposing party. In a case in which rebuttal evidence has been submitted, the party that originally submitted the evidence subjected to rebuttal may submit one additional statement to rehabilitate its evidence.

Documentary medical evidence exceeding these limits will not be admitted absent a showing of good cause. Notwithstanding these limitations, any record of a miner's hospitalization or medical treatment for a respiratory or pulmonary or related disease may be submitted. Each party must serve a copy of any documentary medical evidence it submits on all other parties. If the claimant is unrepresented, the district office will mail copies of the claimant's evidence to the other parties.

At the end of the period for submission of additional evidence, the district office will review the claim on the basis of all evidence submitted. They may notify additional operators of their potential liability, issue a new schedule for the submission of additional evidence identifying another potentially liable operator as the responsible operator, schedule an informal conference, issue a proposed Decision and Order, or take any other action that considered appropriate. If the district office chooses to designate a different operator as the responsible operator, they will suspend development of medical evidence until the operator issue is resolved.

Informal Conference

The district office may determine that an informal conference is not warranted in a particular case. In that instance, they will generally issue a proposed Decision and Order at the conclusion of the period allowed for submission of evidence. The district office may, however, conduct an informal conference in any claim where it appears that a conference will assist in the voluntary resolution of any issue raised with respect to the claim.

The district office must hold the conference no later than 90 days after the conclusion of the period for submission of additional evidence unless a party, based on good cause shown, obtains an extension. A conference may be held only if all parties have representation. A coal mine operator that is either self-insured or covered by a commercial insurance policy for the claim in question, is considered represented.

The unexcused failure of any party to appear at an informal conference will be grounds for the imposition of sanctions: if the claimant does not appear, the claim may be denied as abandoned; if the operator does not appear, it will be deemed to have waived its right to contest its liability and, within the district office's discretion, to have waived its right to contest the claimant's eligibility.

At the end of the conference, the district office will prepare, and all parties will sign, a stipulation of contested and uncontested issues. Within 20 days after the termination of all conference proceedings, the district office will prepare and send to the parties a proposed Decision and Order.

Proposed Decision and Order

A proposed Decision and Order is a document, generally issued by the district office after the evidentiary development of the claim is completed, which attempts to resolve the claim on the basis of all of the evidence. The proposed Decision and Order will set forth the district office's determination of the merits of the claim, i.e., an award or a denial of benefits.

The proposed Decision and Order will also contain the district office's final designation of the responsible operator liable for the payment of benefits, and will dismiss all other potentially liable operators. The proposed Decision and Order will advise the parties of their right to request a formal hearing before the Department of Labor's Office of Administrative Law Judges.

If a party requests a hearing before the district office concludes it's adjudication of the claim, and the later determination is adverse to that party, the district office will forward the claim to the Office of Administrative Law Judges unless the party affirmatively states that it no longer desires a hearing.

Otherwise, within 30 days after the date the proposed Decision and Order is issued, any party may request a revision of the proposed Decision and Order or a hearing. Such requests must be made in writing to the district office and served on all other parties. If any party requests a hearing within the 30-day period, the district office will refer the claim to the Office of Administrative Law Judges. If no party responds to a proposed Decision and Order, it will become final and effective upon the expiration of the applicable 30-day period.

Administrative Law Judge Hearing and Review

Once a case is forwarded to the Office of Administrative Law Judges for hearing, it is assigned to an Administrative Law Judge (ALJ). In most cases, the ALJ will hold an oral hearing, receive testimony and other evidence in accordance with all applicable rules, and render a written decision on the claim. The decision will address the relevant issues in dispute between the parties and adjudicate the claim. If the ALJ awards benefits, the responsible coal mine operator must begin paying monthly benefits to the claimant, and pay any retroactive benefits to which the claimant is entitled.

Any party dissatisfied with the ALJ's decision has 30 days from the date the decision is filed with OWCP either to ask the ALJ to reconsider it or to appeal to the Department of Labor's Benefits Review Board. The Board reviews the ALJ's decision to determine whether it is supported by substantial evidence and in accordance with law, and issues a written decision disposing of the appeal.

Any party adversely affected or aggrieved by the Board's decision may, within 60 days of its issuance, petition the court of appeals where the miner was exposed to coal mine dust for review of the Board's decision. Finally, a party may seek review of the court's decision in the Supreme Court. If the award becomes final, the responsible coal mine operator must reimburse the Trust Fund for any benefits paid to the claimant on an interim basis.

Final Decision

Once a decision becomes final, there are no rights to further proceedings with respect to the claim except for filing a request for modification. At any time before one year after the decision becomes final, or within one year of the last payment of benefits, a party may request modification of the Decision and Order based upon a change in conditions or because of a mistake in a determination of fact.

A claimant whose previous claim was finally denied more than one year earlier may file a subsequent claim for benefits. The subsequent claim will be processed and adjudicated in the same manner as an initial claim, except that the claim will be denied unless the claimant demonstrates that one of the applicable conditions of entitlement has changed since the date on which the order denying the prior claim became final.

A directory of Black Lung district offices and the jurisdictions they serve is set forth at Appendix 25.

CHAPTER 7:
THE FEDERAL EMPLOYMENT
LIABILITY ACT (FELA)

IN GENERAL

In 1908, Congress passed the Federal Employers' Liability Act (FELA). The goal of FELA is to provide railroad employees with a safe place to work, and provide benefits to employees and the families if a railroad employee is injured on the job. Unlike the worker's compensation programs discussed in this almanac, FELA is not a "no-fault" statute, and benefits are not awarded automatically. As set forth below, FELA requires the injured employee to prove that the railroad was liable for causing his or her injury. Once the employee proves that the employer is liable, he or she is entitled to full compensation.

Under the law, a railroad employee is entitled to damages when: (1) The road on which the employee works is engaged in interstate commerce, e.g., it runs across state lines or handles interstate freight; and (2) injury to the worker is the result of the negligence of any officer, agent or employee of the railroad, or the injury is caused by any defect in the cars, engines, appliances, machinery, track, road bed, or any other equipment of the road.

The Federal Employment Liability Act is set forth at Appendix 6.

Under FELA, injured employees can seek compensation for wage loss, future wage loss, medical expenses and treatments, pain and suffering, and for partial or permanent disability. If an employee is killed on the job, survivors are entitled to recover death benefits.

DAMAGES

The amount of money an injured railroad employee may recover depends on (1) the seriousness of his or her injuries, and (2) whether the injured employee can demonstrate that the injury was caused by the negligence of the railroad or its employees in failing to provide a safe workplace, or by a defect in the equipment.

The contributory negligence of the railroad employee is not a bar to recovery, although compensation may be reduced in proportion to the employee's degree of negligence unless the employee's injuries were caused by the employer's violation of a safety statute designed to protect employees. In addition, the injured employee cannot be held to have assumed the risks of employment if their injury or death was caused by negligence or the violation of a safety statute.

FILING A CLAIM

You should immediately report the accident and your injury to your union. You should also notify your employer. You are required to complete an accident report, however, you should not sign any statements concerning the accident until you have first consulted with a legal representative familiar with FELA, who can advise you of your rights. Most union agreements with railroads provide that an employee is entitled to representation. In addition, under FELA, an injured employee has the right to representation during all stages of their claim.

Although you are required to complete the accident report as soon as possible, if you are in extreme pain, you may be able to delay filling out the form. You do not want to unwittingly defeat your case by signing a statement that contains inaccuracies that may undermine your claim of negligence against the employer. Request copies of every document you sign, at the time you sign them, including the accident report and any written statements concerning the accident. You will need copies of these documents to pursue your claim.

Insofar as you will be required to demonstrate negligence or unsafe working conditions, it is important to keep a journal which details the facts surrounding the accident. This includes the exact time and place of the accident, and the manner in which the accident happened. You should obtain the names and addresses of any witnesses to the accident. If permitted, you should photograph the scene of the accident. It is also important to document your physical condition after the accident; therefore, you should have your injuries photographed.

You do not have to fear retaliation if you report your accident and injury. Under the law, employers are prohibited from retaliating against an employee who files a claim for benefits:

§ 60. Penalty for suppression of voluntary information incident to accidents.

"Any contract, rule, regulation, or device whatsoever, the purpose, intent, or effect of which shall be to prevent employees of any common carrier from furnishing voluntarily information to a person in interest as to the facts incident to the injury or death of any employee, shall be void, and whoever, by threat, intimidation, order, rule, contract, regulation, or device whatsoever, shall attempt to prevent any person from furnishing voluntarily such information to a person in interest, or whoever discharges or otherwise disciplines or attempts to discipline any employee for furnishing voluntarily such information to a person in interest, shall, upon conviction thereof, be punished by a fine of not more than $1,000 or imprisoned for not more than one year, or by both such fine and imprisonment, for each offense..."

SETTLEMENT

If you are able to establish your injury claim by showing that the your employer's negligence or an unsafe workplace caused your accident, the following factors must be taken into account when considering a settlement offer:

1. The seriousness of your injury, e.g. permanent, temporary, total or partial disability.

2. The amount of your past lost wages and the amount of wages you will likely lose in the future due to your injury.

3. The amount of money you have spent on medical treatment, including medical bills, medication, hospitalization, surgery, etc.

4. The amount of money you expect to spend on future medical treatment.

5. Vocational evaluation and retraining, if necessary.

6. A sum of money that represents your past, present and future pain and suffering.

If you are unable to settle your injury claim, you can bring a lawsuit in either a state court or Federal court. You are entitled to a trial by jury.

THE MERCHANT MARINE ACT

The Merchant Marine Act—also called "The Jones Act"—is a federal law enacted in 1920, that provides seaman with workers' compensation coverage. Under the Act, maritime workers are provided the same protection from employer negligence as the Federal Employment Liability Act affords railroad workers discussed above.

The Merchant Marine Act is set forth at Appendix 7 of this almanac.

Covered Employees

In 1995, the U.S. Supreme Court ruled that any worker who spends more than thirty percent of his time in the service of a vessel on navigable waters qualifies as a seaman under the Merchant Marine Act. [Chandris, Inc., v. Latsis, 515 U.S. 347, 115 S.Ct. 2172 (1995)]

Requirements for U.S.-Flagged Vessels

The Merchant Marine Act requires U.S.-flagged vessels to be built in the United States, owned by United States citizens, and documented under the laws of the United States. To be documented in the United States means that the vessel is registered, enrolled, or licensed under the laws of the United States. In addition, 75% of the crew and all of the officers of the vessel must be United States citizens. Vessels that meet the above requirements are designated the "Jones Act fleet."

Workers' Compensation Provisions

Under the Merchant Marine Act, injured seaman may recover damages for pain and suffering from their ship owner or employer if the ship owner, captain, or fellow crew members are determined to be negligent. An action under the Act may be brought either in a U.S. federal court or in a state court.

The Merchant Marine Act expands coverage of the Federal Employment Liability Act that pertains to recovery by railroad workers, by making it applicable to sailors. The applicable provision reads as follows:

> Any seaman who shall suffer personal injury in the course of his employment may, at his election, maintain an action for damages at law, with the right of trial by jury, and in such action all statutes of the United States modifying or extending the common-law right or remedy in cases of personal injury to railway employees shall apply; and in case of the death of any seaman as a result of any such personal injury the personal representative of such seaman may maintain an action for damages at law with the right of trial by jury, and in such action all statutes of the United States conferring or regulating the right of action for death in the case of railway employees shall be applicable. [46 U.S.C. 688(a)].

The Merchant Marine Act entitles injured sailors to "transportation, wages, maintenance, and cure." This means that the ship owner or employer must transport the injured sailor home; pay the sailor his or her wages while unable to work; and provide medical care for the sailor's injuries until the sailor has recovered to the degree possible.

CHAPTER 8:
DISABILITY INSURANCE

IN GENERAL

If you are employed, you should have a disability insurance policy in place in case you are injured or become ill and unable to work. This is particularly important if you are the breadwinner of your family, and your income is crucial to keep up with your financial obligations. Any savings you have could quickly disappear if you are disabled for a lengthy period of time without any income.

Disability insurance is similar to a state workers' compensation programs in that it provides "wage-replacement" during the period of time you are unable to work due to an injury or illness. The benefits payable are generally a percentage of your regular income while you are disabled. However, unlike a state workers' compensation program that covers employees who suffer a work-related injury or illness, private disability insurance covers you for injuries and illnesses that are not job-related.

You should check with your employer to find out whether you are covered under a group disability insurance policy. If your employer does not provide group disability insurance, you should consider purchasing an individual policy in order to protect yourself from a financial catastrophe.

TYPES OF DISABILITY POLICIES

Disability insurance policies fall into two general categories: (1) private insurance and (2) government insurance.

Private Insurance

A private disability insurance policy is one that is purchased from a private insurance carrier. A private policy may be an individual policy or a group policy. An employer may purchase a group policy as an employee benefit. Private disability policies generally offer more comprehensive benefits than government insurance.

Government Insurance

Government disability insurance is provided through state or federal government. Workers' Compensation is an example of state government disability insurance. Worker's Compensation is discussed more fully in Chapter 3 of this almanac. Social Security Disability Insurance (SSDI) is an example of federal government disability insurance. SSDI is discussed more fully below.

COVERAGE

Disability policies may offer either (1) short-term coverage; or (2) long-term coverage, as discussed below.

Short-Term Disability Insurance

Short-term disability insurance covers employees who will be out of work due to a non-work-related disability, e.g., a short-term illness or injury, pregnancy, or childbirth. Short-term coverage usually begins after you have been out of work for a certain number of days, e.g. eight days. Employees do not receive 100% of their regular earnings during this time period. This serves as an incentive for workers to return to work as soon as they are able.

Long-Term Disability Insurance

Long-term disability generally begins after the short-term disability coverage period ends. Statistics show that one out of seven workers will suffer a long-term disability—e.g., one that lasts five years or longer—before the age of 65. Therefore, long-term disability provides important financial protection if you are out of work for an extended period of time.

EMPLOYER-PROVIDED GROUP DISABILITY INSURANCE

In the majority of states, employers are not required to provide disability insurance for employees, however, many choose to do so. Employers may purchase a group disability insurance policy from a commercial insurance carrier, or may self-insure a private disability plan. The cost of coverage is usually funded by contributions deducted from the employee's regular salary. Your employer may also contribute to the cost of coverage. The actual insurance policy or plan agreement determines the extent of coverage under the plan.

MANDATORY STATE DISABILITY PROGRAMS

Five states—California, Hawaii, New Jersey, New York, and Rhode Island—have mandatory laws that require employers to provide short-term disability coverage to disabled workers through state-run programs, or by private or self-insurance coverage that mirror the state-run program. Rhode Island, however, requires employers to obtain coverage solely through the state-run program. The state-run programs do not provide long-term coverage, and generally provide only minimal benefits.

New Jersey State Disability Insurance Program

New Jersey's disability program is typical of an employer-provided state-run disability program. Under the New Jersey program, an employee who works for a New Jersey covered employer is entitled to receive temporary disability benefits regardless of where they reside.

Disabled employees have 30 days to file a claim for disability. If the claim is submitted more than 30 days from the date the disability began, the claimant must show good cause as to why the claim was not filed timely. If good cause cannot be shown, the claimant's benefits may be reduced or the claim denied. Nevertheless, the claim form should not be filed until the disability period begins, even if the claimant knows the date when disability will begin, e.g., the date of the claimant's surgery.

Benefits are payable on the eighth consecutive day of disability. The first seven days of disability are known as the "waiting week." If the claimant's disability continues for three consecutive weeks, benefits for the waiting week will be paid retroactively.

To continue receiving benefits, the claimant must be under continuous care of their physician. The insurance carrier will request periodic medical reports from the physician to verify continued eligibility. In addition, the claimant may be required to submit to independent medical examinations. Failure to attend these medical examinations may result in a discontinuation of benefits.

Work-related injuries or illnesses are not compensable under the state disability program, but may be covered under the state workers' compensation program. However, if the workers' compensation claim is contested, a disabled worker may be eligible for temporary disability benefits until the workers' compensation claim is decided. If the workers' compensation issues are resolved in the claimant's favor, the disability insurer has the right to file a lien against any subsequent workers' compensation award to recover any benefits paid through the disability program. This is known as subrogation.

If an employee is covered under his or her employer's private disability insurance, and exhausts all of the benefits under that program, the employee is not eligible to start receiving benefits under the state-run program. However, coverage may be sought under the Social Security Disability Insurance program (SSDI) as further discussed below.

A copy of the New Jersey Temporary Disability Claim Form is set forth at Appendix 26.

SOCIAL SECURITY DISABILITY INSURANCE

The Social Security Amendments of 1954 initiated a disability insurance program that provides workers with additional coverage against economic insecurity if they have to stop working at any time before age 65 due to health reasons. Under the social security disability insurance program, you may be eligible for benefits if:

1. You meet the Social Security Administration (SSA) standard for disability; and

2. You are deemed "insured" because you have worked the required number of quarters for a person your age, and you contributed to the Social Security system.

If you are deemed disabled, benefits may start as early as five months after you become disabled. In addition, you may be entitled to retroactive benefits for up to one year, depending on how much time elapsed between the onset of your disability and the date you filed your application for benefits.

Applying for Social Security Disability Benefits

You should apply for social security disability benefits as soon as you become disabled. The waiting period begins with the first full month after the date the SSA determines your disability began. In addition, the claims process for disability benefits is generally longer than for other types of Social Security benefits—i.e., from 60 to 90 days. This is because the agency must obtain medical information to assess the nature of your disability, and make a determination as to whether you are able to work.

You can expedite this process by providing the original or certified copy of certain documents and having necessary information readily available when you apply for benefits, including:

1. Your social security number;

2. Your birth certificate or other evidence of your date of birth;

3. Your military discharge papers, if you served in the military;

4. Your spouse's birth certificate and social security number if your spouse is applying for benefits;

5. Your children's birth certificates and social security numbers if your children are applying for benefits;

6. Your checking or savings account information so your benefits can be directly deposited;

7. The names, addresses, and phone numbers of doctors, hospitals, clinics, and institutions that treated you, and the dates of your treatment;

8. The names of all medications you are taking;

9. Copies of your medical records from your doctors, therapists, hospitals, clinics, and caseworkers;

10. Your laboratory and test results;

11. A summary of where you worked in the past 15 years and the kind of work you performed;

12. A copy of your W-2 Form (Wage and Tax Statement) or, if you are self-employed, your federal tax return for the past year; and

13. The dates of any prior marriages if your spouse is applying for benefits.

Determining Disability

Qualifying disabilities are usually determined by the state agency that handles health issues—generally known as a disability determination service. To be eligible for benefits, the agency must find that you are suffering from a physical or mental impairment that meets SSA criteria. This would include a determination as to whether the disability prevents you from participating in "any substantial gainful activity." In addition, the disability must have lasted a full year, be expected to last a full year, or be expected to result in death within a year.

Some of the factors that determine whether you suffer from a qualifying disability include:

1. Present Employment - If you are working, and your earnings average more than the SSA-designated monthly limit, you generally cannot be considered disabled.

2. Severity of Condition—Your impairment must interfere with basic work-related activities for your claim to be considered.

3. Disabling Impairment - The SSA will check to see if your condition is on their list of disabling impairments. This list contains impairments for each of the major body systems that are so severe they au-

tomatically mean an applicant is disabled. If your condition is not on the list, the SSA must decide if your condition is of equal severity to an impairment on the list. If so, your claim will be approved. If not, a further determination must be made.

4. Ability to Perform Prior Work - If your condition is severe, but not of the same or equal severity as an impairment on the SSA list, then they must determine if your impairment interferes with your ability to do the work you performed in the last 15 years. If it does not interfere, your claim will be denied. If it does interfere, your claim will be given further consideration.

5. Ability to Work - If you cannot do the work you performed in the last 15 years, the SSA must then determine whether you can do any other type of work. The SSA will take into consideration your age, education, past work experience, and transferable skills, and the job demands of various occupations, in making this determination. If it is determined that you cannot do any other kind of work, your claim will be approved. However, if the SSA determines that you can perform other types of work, your claim will be denied.

In order to assist in their determination, the SSA will require you to complete a disability report. The report includes the following information:

1. The type and extent of the your disability;

2. The affect the disability has had on your ability to work;

3. Information about the your employment;

4. Information about your medical records; and

5. Information about your education and training.

Offset of Other Disability Benefits

Social security disability benefits may be reduced if you receive disability payments through a state workers' compensation program or other government disability program. The sum of all disability payments to you and your family may not exceed 80% of your average earnings before you became disabled.

Appeal Rights

The SSA will provide you with a written decision regarding your eligibility for social security disability benefits. If your claim is denied, you have a right to appeal the decision to the Administrative Law Judge in charge of handling social security disability appeals. If you do not prevail at the administrative level, you can further appeal the decision to a United States District Court.

CHAPTER 9:
VETERANS' DISABILITY PROGRAMS

IN GENERAL

If you were injured while serving in the United States military, you may be entitled to a number of disability benefits. The United States Department of Veterans Affairs (VA) administers disability programs for service members who are disabled as a result of their military service.

DISABILITY COMPENSATION

Disability compensation is a benefit paid to a veteran because of injuries or diseases that happened while he or she was on active duty in the military. Disability compensation is also paid to a veteran if an injury or illness was made worse by active military service. There is no deadline to apply for disability benefits.

Eligibility

You may be eligible for disability compensation benefits if:

1. You were discharged under other than dishonorable conditions; and

2. You have a service-related disability.

Amount of Benefits

The disability compensation program pays monthly benefits to military veterans who are to determined to be at least 10% degree disabled as a result of their military service. The degree of disability determination attempts to represent the average loss in wages resulting from service-connected injuries and diseases, and their complications in civil occupations. Generally, the degrees of disability specified are also designed to compensate for considerable loss of working time from exacerbations or illnesses.

The amount of the basic disability compensation benefit ranges from $108 to $2,299 per month, depending on your degree of disability. Disability compensation benefits are tax-free. You may be entitled to an additional amount in certain cases, e.g., (1) if you have a severe disability or loss of limb(s); (2) you have a spouse, children or dependent parents; or (3) you have a seriously disabled spouse.

Applying for Disability Compensation Benefits

You can apply for disability compensation benefits by filing an Application for Compensation or Pension (VA Form 21-526). The following items must accompany your application, if applicable:

1. Dependency records, such as your marriage certificate or your child's birth certificate.

2. Medical evidence of your disability, such as doctor and hospital reports.

Related Benefits

Related benefits to which you may be entitled include:

1. Priority Medical Care

2. Vocational Rehabilitation

3. Clothing Allowance

4. Service-Disabled Veterans Insurance

5. Grants for Specially Adapted Housing

6. Automobile Grant & Adaptive Equipment

7. Federal Employment Preference

8. State/Local Veterans Benefits

9. Military Exchange & Commissary Privileges

DISABILITY COMPENSATION FOR SEXUAL OR PERSONAL TRAUMA

The VA has established a disability compensation program to assist male and female veterans who have suffered sexual or other personal trauma while serving on active military duty. Sexual or personal trauma is defined as events of human design that threaten or inflict harm, including rape; physical assault; domestic battering; and stalking.

Veterans who have experienced sexual or personal trauma may struggle with fear, anxiety, embarrassment, or profound anger as a result of their experiences. They are often diagnosed with post traumatic stress disorder (PTSD) secondary to sexual or personal trauma. Post traumatic stress disorder is defined as a recurrent emotional reaction to a terrifying, uncontrollable or life-threatening event. The symptoms may develop immediately after the event, or may be delayed for years. The symptoms include:

1. Sleep disturbances and nightmares;

2. Emotional instability;

3. Feelings of fear and anxiety;

4. Impaired concentration;

5. Flashbacks; and

6. Problems in intimate and other interpersonal relations.

Eligibility

You may be eligible for disability compensation benefits if:

1. You were discharged under other than dishonorable conditions; and

2. You are currently suffering from disabling symptoms related to sexual or personal trauma.

Amount of Benefits

The disability compensation program pays monthly benefits to military veterans who are suffering from disabilities due to sexual or personal trauma.

Applying for Disability Compensation Benefits

You can apply for disability compensation benefits relating to sexual or personal trauma by filing an Application for Compensation or Pension (VA Form 21-526). In addition, VA counsellors are available for assistance.

DISABILITY PENSION

The VA also pays a monthly disability pension to wartime veterans who have limited income and are no longer able to work. There is no deadline to apply for a disability pension.

Eligibility

You may be eligible for disability compensation benefits if:

1. You were discharged under other than dishonorable conditions; and

2. You served 90 days or more of active duty with at least 1 day during a period of war time. However, anyone who enlists after Septem-

ber 7, 1980 generally has to serve at least 24 months or the full period for which a person was called or ordered to active duty in order to receive any benefits based on that period of service;

3. You are permanently and totally disabled, or are age 65 or older; and

4. Your countable family income is below a yearly limit set by law.

Amount of Benefits

The VA pays the difference between your countable family income and the yearly income limit established by the VA for your family size. This amount is generally paid in 12 equal monthly payments.

Applying for Disability Pension Benefits

You can apply for disability pension benefits by filing an Application for Compensation or Pension (VA Form 21-526). The following items must accompany your application, if applicable:

1. Dependency records, such as your marriage certificate or your child's birth certificate.

2. Medical evidence of your disability, such as doctor and hospital reports.

Related Benefits

Related benefits to which you may be entitled include:

1. Vocational Rehabilitation Program

2. Medical Care

VOCATIONAL REHABILITATION PROGRAM

The VA operates a vocational rehabilitation program to assist eligible disabled veterans find and maintain suitable employment. The VA also helps seriously disabled veterans achieve independence in daily living. Some of the services the VA provides include:

1. Job Search - The VA operates a job search program that prepares veterans with service-connected disabilities for their return to work. Veterans are also given assistance in finding and maintaining suitable employment.

2. Vocational Evaluation - The VA conducts an evaluation of the disabled veteran's abilities, skills, interests and needs.

3. Career Exploration—The VA offers the disabled veteran vocational counseling and planning.

4. Vocational Training—The VA provides disabled veterans with training, such as on-the-job training and non-paid work experience, if needed.

5. Education Training—The VA provides disabled veterans with educational training so that they can accomplish their rehabilitation goal.

6. Rehabilitation Service—The VA offers supportive rehabilitation and counseling services and, for veterans who have more serious disabilities.

Services generally last up to 48 months, but they can be extended in certain instances.

Eligibility

To be eligible for vocational rehabilitation services, you must meet the following criteria:

1. You must first be awarded a monthly VA disability compensation payment, with limited exceptions.

2. You must have served in the military on or after September 16, 1940; and

3. Your service-connected disabilities must be rated at least 20% disabled by the VA or 10% disabled if you have a serious employment handicap; and

4. It has been less than 12 years since the VA notified you of your eligibility status, unless certain conditions prevented you from vocational rehabilitation training, in which case your eligibility for this benefit may be extended.

Amount of Benefits

If you need vocational rehabilitation training, the VA will pay for the training costs, including tuition and fees, books, supplies, equipment, and special services, if needed. The VA also pays a monthly benefit—called a subsistence allowance—to help you with your living expenses while you are in training.

Applying for Vocational Rehabilitation Benefits

You can apply for vocational rehabilitation benefits by filing a Disabled Veterans Application for Vocational Rehabilitation (VA Form 28-1900).

Related Benefits

Related benefits to which you may be entitled include:

1. Work Study Allowance

2. Tutorial Assistance

3. Revolving Fund Loan

HOUSING ASSISTANCE

In addition to the guaranteed loans available to eligible veterans and military personnel, the VA offers special grants to certain disabled veterans and military personnel, in order to acquire housing suitable, or adapt current housing, according to their needs. There is no time limit for a veteran to apply for a VA home loan.

BURIAL BENEFITS

The VA offers certain benefits and services for deceased veterans. All eligible veterans are entitled to: (1) a headstone to mark the veteran's grave; (2) a presidential memorial certificate; (3) an American flag to drape the veteran's casket; (4) a $300 allowance for burial and funeral expenses; (5) a $300 allowance for a plot or burial in a VA national cemetery.

In addition, the burial allowance for veterans who die due to a service-related cause is increased to $2,000.

There is no time limitation for making a claim for reimbursement of burial expenses for a service-related death. In all other cases, a reimbursement claim must be filed within 2 years of the date of the veteran's burial.

DEPENDENTS' AND SURVIVORS' BENEFITS

The VA pays dependency and indemnity compensation to certain survivors of: (1) service members who died while on active duty; (2) veterans who died from service-related disabilities; and (3) certain veterans who were being paid a 100% disability compensation at their time of death.

In addition, a death pension is payable to some surviving spouses and children of deceased wartime veterans. This benefit is based on the financial need of the family.

There is no time limit to apply for the dependents' and survivors' benefits.

HEALTH CARE SERVICES

The VA provides a variety of health care services, including:

1. Hospital, outpatient medical, dental, pharmacy, and prosthetic services.

2. Domiciliary, nursing home, and community-based residential care.

3. Sexual trauma counseling.

4. Specialized health care for women veterans.

5. Health and rehabilitation programs for homeless veterans.

6. Readjustment counseling.

7. Alcohol and drug dependency treatment.

8. Medical evaluation for military service exposure, including Gulf War, Agent Orange, radiation, or other environmental hazards.

In addition to the above, the VA will provide combat veterans with free medical care for any illness that is possibly associated with service against a hostile force in a war after the Gulf War or during a period of hostility after November 11, 1998. This benefit may be provided for two years from the veteran's release from active duty.

SERVICE-DISABLED VETERANS INSURANCE

Service-Disabled Veterans Insurance—also called "RH Insurance—is life insurance for service-disabled veterans. The basic coverage is $10,000. However, if the premium payments for the basic policy are waived due to the veteran's total disability, he or she may be eligible for a supplemental policy of up to $20,000. Veterans have two years after being notified of their service-connected disability to apply for basic insurance coverage.

BENEFITS FOR SELECTED RESERVE AND NATIONAL GUARD MEMBERS

Active Duty Service

Selected Reserve and National Guard members who served on regular active duty are eligible for the same VA benefits as other veterans, as discussed above. The member must also meet the same length of service requirement for any benefit.

Non-Active Duty Service

Selected Reserve and National Guard members may be eligible for the following VA benefits based on non-active duty service:

Compensation

Selected Reserve and National Guard members are eligible for a monthly benefit paid for disabilities that resulted from a disease or injury incurred while on active duty for training, or an injury, heart attack or stroke incurred during inactive duty for training. These disabilities are considered "service-connected" disabilities.

Medical Care

Selected Reserve and National Guard members are entitled to medical care for service-connected disabilities.

Vocational Rehabilitation

Selected Reserve and National Guard members who have service-connected disabilities are entitled to services and assistance in finding and maintaining suitable employment. The VA also helps members with serious service-connected disabilities achieve independence in daily living.

CONTACT INFORMATION

Additional information regarding specific benefit programs may be obtained from the Veterans Administration, by telephone and via the internet, as follows:

Main Toll Free Number:	1-800-827-1000
Main Website:	http://www.va.gov
Online Benefits	http://vabenefits.vba.va.gov

CHAPTER 10:
THIRD PARTY LIABILITY

EMPLOYER IMMUNITY

If you are receiving workers' compensation benefits due to a work-related injury or illness, you cannot file a lawsuit against your employer or a co-worker for negligence. Workers' compensation is the exclusive remedy for an employee to obtain wage replacement for work-related injuries or illnesses, and your employer is generally immune from liability.

Nevertheless, you retain your right to sue any negligent third parties who may be responsible for causing or contributing to your injury. For example, an employee who is injured while using a defective piece of machinery is still permitted to bring a product liability lawsuit against the manufacturer of the defective product, in addition to receiving benefits under their state's workers' compensation program.

EXCEPTIONS TO EMPLOYER IMMUNITY

If your employer does not have workers' compensation insurance, you are generally entitled to sue your employer and recover damages if you can prove that your employer's negligence caused your injuries.

In addition, your employer would not be entitled to immunity if they intentionally caused your injuries. An intentional tort differs from an act of negligence in that it requires the element of intent. Common intentional tort claims include assault and battery and defamation.

THE STATUTE OF LIMITATIONS

If it appears that a third party is responsible for your injuries, you must start your lawsuit before the statute of limitations expires. A statute of limitations is a law that sets forth a time period within which you must initiate a lawsuit. If you do not start the lawsuit before the statute of limitations runs out, you will be forever barred from bringing the lawsuit. The time period varies according to the state and the type of claim being made.

The reader is advised to check the law of his or her jurisdiction to determine the applicable statute of limitations.

PROVING NEGLIGENCE

Negligence encompasses unintentionally caused harms. The basis of liability is the creation of an unreasonable risk of harm to another. A third party cannot be held liable for your injuries unless those injuries were negligently caused. You bear the burden of proving that a third party was responsible for negligently causing your injuries in order to recover damages in a lawsuit.

The elements of a negligence claim which must be proved include: (1) a duty; (2) a breach of that duty; (3) foreseeability; (4) proximate cause, i.e., the breach caused the harm; and (5) a resulting injury.

Duty

Duty is defined as that degree of ordinary care owed to another under the circumstances. Ordinary care is the care a prudent and cautious person would take in the same situation. It is your responsibility to prove that a third party acted without ordinary care. The third party has the burden of proving contributory negligence on your part in order to reduce your damage award.

For example, if an independent contractor is hired to wax the floors where you work, he or she has a duty to make sure that the employees who work in the area are not injured. Thus, a prudent person would place signs indicating where the floors are wet and potentially dangerous. You may be able to prove that the contractor acted without ordinary care if he or she did not put up any signs, and you slip and fall on the wet and slippery surface. On the other hand, if you observe the danger sign, and decide to walk across the wet surface, you may be deemed to have contributed to your own injuries because you negligently ignored the warning sign.

Breach of Duty

Once it has been established that there is a relationship between the parties in which a duty has arisen, it must be shown that the third party breached that duty in some manner. Using the above example, the contractor's failure to place appropriate warnings signs would indicate a breach of duty.

Foreseeability

In order for the third party to be deemed negligent, there is a common law requirement that it is foreseeable that his or her conduct created the danger. If a reasonably prudent person could not have foreseen the probability that injury would occur as a result of his or her conduct, there is no negligence and no liability.

Using the above example, it is arguably foreseeable that the contractor's failure to warn employees about the wet and slippery floor created a potentially dangerous situation that could result in serious injuries.

Proximate Cause

In order to prevail in your negligence claim, you must further prove that the injury sustained as a result of the breach of duty were proximately caused by the negligent act or omission of the third party. The act is a proximate cause of the injury if it was a substantial factor in bringing about the injury, and without which the result would not have occurred.

Again, using the above example, the contractor's failure to place warning signs around the wet and slippery floor was a substantial factor in bringing about your injuries, and was thus the proximate cause of your injuries.

DAMAGES

Once you have established that a third party was liable for your injuries, you are entitled to recover damages. Damages are usually measured in terms of monetary compensation. The damage award represents an attempt to compensate you for the injuries you suffered by awarding you an amount of money that will restore you to your pre-injury condition. If complete restoration is not possible, damages may include the monetary value of the difference between your pre-injury and post-injury conditions. Typical items include: (1) medical expenses; (2) lost earnings and impairment of earning capacity; and (3) a monetary award for your pain and suffering.

DOCUMENT THE INCIDENT

As soon as practicable following your accident, you should document the facts and gather evidence in case you decide in the future that you are entitled to pursue a third party claim. You should file a written incident report with your employer. Make sure the facts are accurate and request a copy of the incident report at the time it is made. You should also obtain the names, addresses and telephone numbers of any witnesses to the accident, as well as any individuals who saw you imme-diately after the accident occurred. Even if these witnesses did not see the actual accident, they can still testify to your physical condition fol-lowing the accident, and the circumstances surrounding the accident.

If there is any physical evidence that contributed to your accident, or which demonstrates your injuries—e.g., a defective machine—you should try to preserve that evidence. If the evidence is not within your control, you should take photographs of the area, e.g. a dangerous floor condition. Make sure that you clearly label the photographs with the date and time they were taken

In addition, you should write down all of the circumstances surround-ing the accident while the facts are still fresh in your mind, including the manner in which you were injured. Small but important facts can fade in your memory over time, such as comments made by a witness or the responsible party.

Keep a journal of the progression of your pain, your symptoms and in-juries. Keep track of how much time you lost at work, and any other physical limitations caused by the accident, e.g., the amount of time spent in the hospital, and confined to your home and/or bed.

RETAIN AN ATTORNEY

If your injuries are serious and/or have caused you any significant damages, you should contact an attorney who will investigate the facts surrounding the incident, and will evaluate whether you have a viable third party claim.

At your first meeting with your prospective attorney, bring the docu-mentation and evidence you previously gathered. This will assist the attorney in investigating your case, and make it more likely that the at-torney will take the case and be able to obtain a favorable settlement or verdict on your behalf.

Prior to taking any action on a case, an attorney will typically require you to sign a retainer agreement. A retainer agreement is a contract be-tween you and the lawyer, which sets forth the responsibilities the law-yer is agreeing to undertake, and the compensation the lawyer expects to receive if there is a recovery, by verdict or settlement.

Most personal injury retainer agreements are contingency fee agree-ments. This means that you do not have to pay any money towards le-gal fees up front to the lawyer in order for the lawyer to take your case. In return, the lawyer receives a percentage—typically one-third—of the recovery, if there is one. If there is no recovery, the lawyer basically forgoes the legal fee. A personal injury lawyer may also advance some or all of the costs of the case, which are then deducted from the verdict or settlement amount.

Your attorney will contact the appropriate insurance carrier for the responsible third party, and place them on notice that your claim exists. The date, place and manner in which the claim arose will be provided to the insurance carrier, as well as a copy of any police, ambulance, hospital, and/or medical reports, to the extent available at that time.

A claims representative from the owner's insurance company may call to take a statement over the phone concerning the facts surrounding your accident. You should not provide a statement without first speaking with their attorney. The claims representative represents the responsible party, and does not represent your interests. The claims representative may attempt to get you to admit full or partial responsibility for the incident, or try to obtain a quick settlement at an amount well below the value of your claim.

In the months following your accident, your attorney will exchange correspondence and engage in settlement negotiations with the claims representative. During that time, all of your medical records will be provided to the insurance carrier, as well as documentation of lost wages, medical expenses and any other economic damages you may have suffered as a result of the accident. If a mutually agreeable settlement cannot be reached within a reasonable time period, formal legal action will likely be initiated.

A more detailed discussion of personal injury lawsuits can be found in this author's book entitled The Law of Personal Injury, published by Oceana Publishing Company.

APPENDIX 1:
TEN MOST DANGEROUS OCCUPATIONS

OCCUPATION	FATALITY STATISTIC	RISKS/COMMENTS
Logging Workers	92.4 per 100,000 workers	heavy, falling objects.
Aircraft Pilots/Flight Engineers	92.4 per 100,000 workers	statistic includes commercial pilots of small aircraft, crop dusters and air taxis
Fishers/Related Workers	86.4 per 100,000 workers	drowning
Structural Iron and Steel Workers	47 per 100,000 workers	falls
Refuse/Recyclable Material Collectors	43.2 per 100,000 workers	hazardous materials, traffic accidents
Farmers/Ranchers	37.5 per 100,000 workers	tractor accidents
Roofers	34.9 per 100,000 workers	falls, burns from flammable, toxic materials
Electrical Power Line Installers/Repairers	30 per 100,000 workers	falls, electrocution
Driver/Sales Workers/Truck Drivers	27.6 per 100,000 workers	traffic accidents due to amount of driving

Source: Bureau of Labor Statistics

APPENDIX 2:
DIRECTORY OF NATIONAL OWCP DISTRICT OFFICES

DISTRICT	AREA COVERED	ADDRESS	TELEPHONE
DISTRICT OFFICE 1—BOSTON	Connecticut, Maine, Massachusetts, New Hampshire, Rhode Island, and Vermont	U. S. Department of Labor, OWCP JFK Federal Building, Room E-260 Boston, MA 02203	617-565-2137
DISTRICT OFFICE 2—NEW YORK	New Jersey, New York, Puerto Rico, and the Virgin Islands	U. S. Department of Labor, OWCP 201 Varick Street, Room 740 New York, NY 10014	212-337-2075
DISTRICT OFFICE 3—PHILADELPHIA	Delaware, Pennsylvania, and West Virginia	U. S. Department of Labor, OWCP Gateway Bldg., Room 15200 3535 Market Street Philadelphia, PA 19104	215-596-1457

DISTRICT	AREA COVERED	ADDRESS	TELEPHONE
DISTRICT OFFICE 6—JACKSONVILLE	Alabama, Florida, Georgia, Kentucky, Mississippi, North Carolina, South Carolina, and Tennessee	U. S. Department of Labor, OWCP 214 North Hogan St., Suite 1006 Jacksonville, FL 32202	904-357-4777
DISTRICT OFFICE 9—CLEVELAND	Indiana, Michigan, and Ohio	U. S. Department of Labor, OWCP 1240 East Ninth Street, Room 851 Cleveland, OH 44199	216-522-3800
DISTRICT OFFICE 10—CHICAGO	Illinois, Minnesota, and Wisconsin	U. S. Department of Labor, OWCP 230 South Dearborn Street, Eighth Floor Chicago, IL 60604	312-353-5656
DISTRICT 11—KANSAS CITY	Iowa, Kansas, Missouri, and Nebraska; all employees of the Department of Labor, except Job Corps enrollees, and their relatives	U. S. Department of Labor, OWCP City Center Square 1100 Main Street, Suite 750 Kansas City, MO 64105	816-426-2195
DISTRICT 12—DENVER	Colorado, Montana, No. Dakota, So. Dakota, Utah, and Wyoming	U. S. Department of Labor, OWCP 1801 California Street, Suite 915 Denver, CO 80202-2614	303-844-1310
DISTRICT 13—SAN FRANCISCO	Arizona, California, Hawaii, and Nevada	U. S. Department of Labor, OWCP 71 Stevenson Street San Francisco, CA 94105	415-975-4090
DISTRICT OFFICE 14—SEATTLE	Alaska, Idaho, Oregon, and Washington	U. S. Department of Labor, OWCP 1111 Third Avenue, Suite 615 Seattle, WA 98101-3212	206-553-5508

DISTRICT	AREA COVERED	ADDRESS	TELEPHONE
DISTRICT OFFICE 16—DALLAS	Arkansas, Louisiana, New Mexico, Oklahoma, and Texas	U. S. Department of Labor, OWCP 525 Griffin Street, Room 100 Dallas, TX 75202	214-767-4707
DISTRICT OFFICE 25—WASHINGTON, D.C.	District of Columbia, Maryland, and Virginia; all areas outside the U.S., its possessions, territories, and trust territories; and all special claims	U. S. Department of Labor, OWCP 800 N. Capitol Street N.W., Room 800 Washington, D.C. 20211	202-565-9770

APPENDIX 3:
SELECTED PROVISIONS OF THE FEDERAL EMPLOYMENT COMPENSATION ACT
[5 U.S.C. §§ 8101 – 8193]

SUBCHAPTER I - GENERALLY

§8101. Definitions [Omitted]

§8102. Compensation for disability or death of employee

(a) The United States shall pay compensation as specified by this subchapter for the disability or death of an employee resulting from personal injury sustained while in the performance of his duty, unless the injury or death is—

(1) caused by willful misconduct of the employee;

(2) caused by the employee's intention to bring about the injury or death of himself or of another; or

(3) proximately caused by the intoxication of the injured employee.

(b) Disability or death from a war-risk hazard or during or as a result of capture, detention, or other restraint by a hostile force or individual, suffered by an employee who is employed outside the continental United States or in Alaska or in the areas and installations in the Republic of Panama made available to the United States pursuant to the Panama Canal Treaty of 1977 and related agreements (as described in section 3(a) of the Panama Canal Act of 1979), is deemed to have resulted from personal injury sustained while in the performance of his duty, whether or not the employee was engaged in the course of employment when the disability or disability resulting in death occurred or when he was taken by the hostile force or individual. This subsection does not apply to an individual—

(1) whose residence is at or in the vicinity of the place of his employment and who was not living there solely because of the exigencies of his employment, unless he was injured or taken while engaged in the course of his employment; or

(2) who is a prisoner of war or a protected individual under the Geneva Conventions of 1949 and is detained or utilized by the United States.

This subsection does not affect the payment of compensation under this subchapter derived otherwise than under this subsection, but compensation for disability or death does not accrue for a period for which pay, other benefit, or gratuity from the United States accrues to the disabled individual or his dependents on account of detention by the enemy or because of the same disability or death, unless that pay, benefit, or gratuity is refunded or renounced.

§8103. Medical services and initial medical and other benefits

(a) The United States shall furnish to an employee who is injured while in the performance of duty, the services, appliances, and supplies prescribed or recommended by a qualified physician, which the Secretary of Labor considers likely to cure, give relief, reduce the degree or the period of disability, or aid in lessening the amount of the monthly compensation. These services, appliances, and supplies shall be furnished—

(1) whether or not disability has arisen;

(2) notwithstanding that the employee has accepted or is entitled to receive benefits under subchapter III of chapter 83 of this title or another retirement system for employees of the Government; and

(3) by or on the order of United States medical officers and hospitals, or, at the employee's option, by or on the order of physicians and hospitals designated or approved by the Secretary. The employee may initially select a physician to provide medical services, appliances, supplies, in accordance with such regulations and instructions as the Secretary considers necessary, and may be furnished necessary and reasonable transportation and expenses incident to the securing of such services, appliances, and supplies. These expenses, when authorized or approved by the Secretary, shall be paid from the Employees' Compensation Fund.

(b) The Secretary, under such limitations or conditions as he considers necessary, may authorize the employing agencies to provide for the initial furnishing of medical and other benefits under this section. The Secretary may certify vouchers for these expenses out of the Employees' Compensation Fund when the immediate superior of the employee certifies that the expense was incurred in respect to an injury which was accepted by the employing agency as probably compensable under this subchapter.

The Secretary shall prescribe the form and content of the certificate.

§8104. Vocational rehabilitation

(a) The Secretary of Labor may direct a permanently disabled individual whose disability is compensable under this subchapter to undergo vocational rehabilitation. The Secretary shall provide for furnishing the vocational rehabilitation services. In providing for these services, the Secretary, insofar as practicable, shall use the services or facilities of State agencies and corresponding agencies which cooperate with the Secretary of Health, Education, and Welfare in carrying out the purposes of chapter 4 of title 29, except to the extent that the Secretary of Labor provides for furnishing these services under section 8103 of this title. The cost of providing these services to individuals undergoing vocational rehabilitation under this section shall be paid from the Employees' Compensation Fund. However, in reimbursing a State or corresponding agency under an arrangement pursuant to this section the cost to the agency reimbursable in full under section 32(b)(1) of title 29 is excluded.

(b) Notwithstanding section 8106, individuals directed to undergo vocational rehabilitation by the Secretary shall, while undergoing such rehabilitation, receive compensation at the rate provided in sections 8105 and 8110 of this title, less the amount of any earnings received from remunerative employment, other than employment undertaken pursuant to such rehabilitation.

§8105. Total disability

(a) If the disability is total, the United States shall pay the employee during the disability monthly monetary compensation equal to 66 2/3 percent of his monthly pay, which is known as his basic compensation for total disability.

(b) The loss of use of both hands, both arms, both feet, or both legs, or the loss of sight of both eyes, is prima facie permanent total disability.

§8106. Partial disability

(a) If the disability is partial, the United States shall pay the employee during the disability monthly monetary compensation equal to 66 2/3 percent of the difference between his monthly pay and his monthly wage-earning capacity after the beginning of the partial disability, which is known as his basic compensation for partial disability.

(b) The Secretary of Labor may require a partially disabled employee to report his earnings from employment or self-employment, by affidavit or otherwise, in the manner and at the times the Secretary specifies. The employee shall include in the affidavit or report the value of housing, board, lodging, and other advantages which are part of his earnings in employment or self-employment and which can be estimated in money. An employee who—

(1) fails to make an affidavit or report when required; or

(2) knowingly omits or understates any part of his earnings; forfeits his right to compensation with respect to any period for which the affidavit or report was required. Compensation forfeited under this subsection, if already paid, shall be recovered by a deduction from the compensation payable to the employee or otherwise recovered under section 8129 of this title, unless recovery is waived under that section.

(c) A partially disabled employee who—

(1) refuses to seek suitable work; or

(2) refuses or neglects to work after suitable work is offered to, procured by, or secured for him; is not entitled to compensation.

§8107. Compensation schedule

(a) If there is permanent disability involving the loss, or loss of use, of a member or function of the body or involving disfigurement, the employee is entitled to basic compensation for the disability, as provided by the schedule in subsection (c) of this section, at the rate of 66 2/3 percent of his monthly pay. The basic compensation is—

(1) payable regardless of whether the cause of the disability originates in a part of the body other than that member;

(2) payable regardless of whether the disability also involves another impairment of the body; and

(3) in addition to compensation for temporary total or temporary partial disability.

(b) With respect to any period after payments under subsection (a) of this section have ended, an employee is entitled to compensation as provided by—

(1) section 8105 of this title if the disability is total; or

(2) section 8106 of this title if the disability is partial.

(c) The compensation schedule is as follows:

(1) Arm lost, 312 weeks' compensation.

(2) Leg lost, 288 weeks' compensation.

(3) Hand lost, 244 weeks' compensation.

(4) Foot lost, 205 weeks' compensation.

(5) Eye lost, 160 weeks' compensation.

(6) Thumb lost, 75 weeks' compensation.

(7) First finger lost, 46 weeks' compensation.

(8) Great toe lost, 38 weeks' compensation.

(9) Second finger lost, 30 weeks' compensation.

(10) Third finger lost, 25 weeks' compensation.

(11) Toe other than great toe lost, 16 weeks' compensation.

(12) Fourth finger lost, 15 weeks' compensation.

(13) Loss of hearing—

(A) complete loss of hearing of one ear, 52 weeks' compensation; or

(B) complete loss of hearing of both ears, 200 weeks' compensation.

(14) Compensation for loss of binocular vision or for loss of 80 percent or more of the vision of an eye is the same as for loss of the eye.

(15) Compensation for loss of more than one phalanx of a digit is the same as for loss of the entire digit. Compensation for loss of the first phalanx is one-half of the compensation for loss of the entire digit.

(16) If, in the case of an arm or a leg, the member is amputated above the wrist or ankle, compensation is the same as for loss of the arm or leg, respectively.

(17) Compensation for loss of use of two or more digits, or one or more phalanges of each of two or more digits, of a hand or foot, is proportioned to the loss of use of the hand or foot occasioned thereby.

(18) Compensation for permanent total loss of use of a member is the same as for loss of the member.

(19) Compensation for permanent partial loss of use of a member may be for proportionate loss of use of the member. The degree of loss

of vision or hearing under this schedule is determined without regard to correction.

(20) In case of loss of use of more than one member or parts of more than one member as enumerated by this schedule, the compensation is for loss of use of each member or part thereof, and the awards run consecutively. However, when the injury affects only two or more digits of the same hand or foot, paragraph (17) of this subsection applies, and when partial bilateral loss of hearing is involved, compensation is computed on the loss as affecting both ears.

(21) For serious disfigurement of the face, head, or neck of a character likely to handicap an individual in securing or maintaining employment, proper and equitable compensation not to exceed $3,500 shall be awarded in addition to any other compensation payable under this schedule.

(22) For permanent loss or loss of use of any other important external or internal organ of the body as determined by the Secretary, proper and equitable compensation not to exceed 312 weeks' compensation for each organ so determined shall be paid in addition to any other compensation payable under this schedule.

§8109. Beneficiaries of awards unpaid at death; order of precedence

(a) If an individual—

(1) has sustained disability compensable under section 8107(a) of this title;

(2) has filed a valid claim in his lifetime; and

(3) dies from a cause other than the injury before the end of the period specified by the schedule; the compensation specified by the schedule that is unpaid at his death, whether or not accrued or due at his death, shall be paid—

(A) under an award made before or after the death;

(B) for the period specified by the schedule;

(C) to and for the benefit of the persons then in being within the classes and proportions and on the conditions specified by this section; and

(D) in the following order of precedence:

(i) If there is no child, to the widow or widower.

(ii) If there are both a widow or widower and a child or children, one-half to the widow or widower and one-half to the child or children.

(iii) If there is no widow or widower, to the child or children.

(iv) If there is no survivor in the above classes, to the parent or parents wholly or partly dependent for support on the decedent, or to other wholly dependent relatives listed by section 8133 (a)(5) of this title, or to both in proportions provided by regulation.

(v) If there is no survivor in the above classes and no burial allowance is payable under section 8134 of this title, an amount not exceeding that which would be expendable under section 8134 of this title if applicable shall be paid to reimburse a person equitably entitled thereto to the extent and in the proportion that he has paid the burial expenses, but a compensated insurer or other person obligated by law or contract to pay the burial expenses or a State or political subdivision or entity is deemed not equitably entitled.

(b) Payments under subsection (a) of this section, except for an amount payable for a period preceding the death of the individual, are at the basic rate of compensation for permanent disability specified by section 8107(a) of this title even if at the time of death the individual was entitled to the augmented rate specified by section 8110 of this title.

(c) A surviving beneficiary under subsection (a) of this section, except one under subsection (a)(D)(v), does not have a vested right to payment and must be alive to receive payment.

(d) A beneficiary under subsection (a) of this section, except one under subsection (a)(D)(v), ceases to be entitled to payment on the happening of an event which would terminate his right to compensation for death under section 8133 of this title. When that entitlement ceases, compensation remaining unpaid under subsection (a) of this section is payable to the surviving beneficiary in accordance with subsection (a) of this section.

§8110. Augmented compensation for dependents

(a) For the purpose of this section, "dependent" means—

(1) a wife, if—

(A) she is a member of the same household as the employee;

(B) she is receiving regular contributions from the employee for her support; or

(C) the employee has been ordered by a court to contribute to her support;

(2) a husband, if—

(A) he is a member of the same household as the employee; or

(B) he is receiving regular contributions from the employee for his support; or

(C) the employee has been ordered by a court to contribute to his support;

(3) an unmarried child, while living with the employee or receiving regular contributions from the employee toward his support, and who is—

(A) under 18 years of age; or

(B) over 18 years of age and incapable of self-support because of physical or mental disability; and

(4) a parent, while wholly dependent on and supported by the employee.

Notwithstanding paragraph (3) of this subsection, compensation payable for a child that would otherwise end because the child has reached 18 years of age shall continue if he is a student as defined by section 8101 of this title at the time he reaches 18 years of age for so long as he continues to be such a student or until he marries.

(b) A disabled employee with one or more dependents is entitled to have his basic compensation for disability augmented—

(1) at the rate of 8 1/3 percent of his monthly pay if that compensation is payable under section 8105 or 8107(a) of this title; and

(2) at the rate of 8 1/3 percent of the difference between his monthly pay and his monthly wage-earning capacity if that compensation is payable under section 8106(a) of this title.

§8111. Additional compensation for services of attendants or vocational rehabilitation

(a) The Secretary of Labor may pay an employee who has been awarded compensation an additional sum of not more than $1,500 a month, as the Secretary considers necessary, when the Secretary finds that the service of an attendant is necessary constantly because the employee is totally blind, or has lost the use of both hands or both feet, or is paralyzed and unable to walk, or because of other disability resulting from the injury making him so helpless as to require constant attendance.

(b) The Secretary may pay an individual undergoing vocational rehabilitation under section 8104 of this title additional compensation necessary for his maintenance, but not to exceed $200 a month.

8112. Maximum and minimum monthly payments

(a) Except as provided by section 8138 of this title, the monthly rate of compensation for disability, including augmented compensation under section 8110 of this title but not including additional compensation under section 8111 of this title, may not be more than 75 percent of the monthly pay of the maximum rate of basic pay for GS-15, and in case of total disability may not be less than 75 percent of the monthly pay of the minimum rate of basic pay for GS-2 or the amount of the monthly pay of the employee, whichever is less.

(b) The provisions of subsection (a) shall not apply to any employee whose disability is a result of an assault which occurs during an assassination or attempted assassination of a Federal official described under section 351(a) or 1751(a) of title 18, and was sustained in the performance of duty.

§8113. Increase or decrease of basic compensation

(a) If an individual—

(1) was a minor or employed in a learner's capacity at the time of injury; and

(2) was not physically or mentally handicapped before the injury; the Secretary of Labor, on review under section 8128 of this title after the time the wage-earning capacity of the individual would probably have increased but for the injury, shall recompute prospectively the monetary compensation payable for disability on the basis of an assumed monthly pay corresponding to the probable increased wage-earning capacity.

(b) If an individual without good cause fails to apply for and undergo vocational rehabilitation when so directed under section 8104 of this title, the Secretary, on review under section 8128 of this title and after finding that in the absence of the failure the wage-earning capacity of the individual would probably have substantially increased, may reduce prospectively the monetary compensation of the individual in accordance with what would probably have been his wage-earning capacity in the absence of the failure, until the individual in good faith complies with the direction of the Secretary.

§8114. Computation of pay

(a) For the purpose of this section—

(1) "overtime pay" means pay for hours of service in excess of a statutory or other basic workweek or other basic unit of worktime, as observed by the employing establishment; and

(2) "year" means a period of 12 calendar months, or the equivalent thereof as specified by regulations prescribed by the Secretary of Labor.

(b) In computing monetary compensation for disability or death on the basis of monthly pay, that pay is determined under this section.

(c) The monthly pay at the time of injury is deemed one-twelfth of the average annual earnings of the employee at that time. When compensation is paid on a weekly basis, the weekly equivalent of the monthly pay is deemed one-fifty-second of the average annual earnings. However, for so much of a period of total disability as does not exceed 90 calendar days from the date of the beginning of compensable disability, the compensation, in the discretion of the Secretary of Labor, may be computed on the basis of the actual daily wage of the employee at the time of injury in which event he may be paid compensation for the days he would have worked but for the injury.

(d) Average annual earnings are determined as follows:

(1) If the employee worked in the employment in which he was employed at the time of his injury during substantially the whole year immediately preceding the injury and the employment was in a position for which an annual rate of pay—

(A) was fixed, the average annual earnings are the annual rate of pay; or

(B) was not fixed, the average annual earnings are the product obtained by multiplying his daily wage for the particular employment, or the average thereof if the daily wage has fluctuated, by 300 if he was employed on the basis of a 6-day workweek, 280 if employed on the basis of a 5 1/2-day week, and 260 if employed on the basis of a 5-day week.

(2) If the employee did not work in employment in which he was employed at the time of his injury during substantially the whole year immediately preceding the injury, but the position was one which would have afforded employment for substantially a whole year, the average annual earnings are a sum equal to the average annual earnings of an employee of the same class working substantially the whole immediately preceding year in the same or similar employment by the United States in the same or neighboring place, as determined under paragraph (1) of this subsection.

(3) If either of the foregoing methods of determining the average annual earnings cannot be applied reasonably and fairly, the average annual earnings are a sum that reasonably represents the annual earning capacity of the injured employee in the employment in which

he was working at the time of the injury having regard to the previous earnings of the employee in Federal employment, and of other employees of the United States in the same or most similar class working in the same or most similar employment in the same or neighboring location, other previous employment of the employee, or other relevant factors. However, the average annual earnings may not be less than 150 times the average daily wage the employee earned in the employment during the days employed within 1 year immediately preceding his injury.

(4) If the employee served without pay or at nominal pay, paragraphs (1), (2), and (3) of this subsection apply as far as practicable, but the average annual earnings of the employee may not exceed the minimum rate of basic pay for GS-15. If the average annual earnings cannot be determined reasonably and fairly in the manner otherwise provided by this section, the average annual earnings shall be determined at the reasonable value of the service performed but not in excess of $3,600 a year.

(e) The value of subsistence and quarters, and of any other form of remuneration in kind for services if its value can be estimated in money, and premium pay under section 5545(c)(1) of this title are included as part of the pay, but account is not taken of—

(1) overtime pay;

(2) additional pay or allowance authorized outside the United States because of differential in cost of living or other special circumstances; or

(3) bonus or premium pay for extraordinary service including bonus or pay for particularly hazardous service in time of war.

§8115. Determination of wage-earning capacity

(a) In determining compensation for partial disability, except permanent partial disability compensable under sections 8107—8109 of this title, the wage-earning capacity of an employee is determined by his actual earnings if his actual earnings fairly and reasonably represent his wage-earning capacity. If the actual earnings of the employee do not fairly and reasonably represent his wage-earning capacity or if the employee has no actual earnings, his wage-earning capacity as appears reasonable under the circumstances is determined with due regard to—

(1) the nature of his injury;

(2) the degree of physical impairment;

(3) his usual employment;

(4) his age;

(5) his qualifications for other employment;

(6) the availability of suitable employment; and

(7) other factors or circumstances which may affect his wage-earning capacity in his disabled condition.

(b) Section 8114(d) of this title is applicable in determining the wage-earning capacity of an employee after the beginning of partial disability.

§8116. Limitations on right to receive compensation

(a) While an employee is receiving compensation under this subchapter, or if he has been paid a lump sum in commutation of installment payments until the expiration of the period during which the installment payments would have continued, he may not receive salary, pay, or remuneration of any type from the United States, except—

(1) in return for service actually performed;

(2) pension for service in the Army, Navy, or Air Force;

(3) other benefits administered by the Department of Veterans Affairs unless such benefits are payable for the same injury or the same death; and

(4) retired pay, retirement pay, retainer pay, or equivalent pay for service in the Armed Forces or other uniformed services, subject to the reduction of such pay in accordance with section 5532(b) of title 5, United States Code.

However, eligibility for or receipt of benefits under subchapter III of chapter 83 of this title, or another retirement system for employees of the Government, does not impair the right of the employee to compensation for scheduled disabilities specified by section 8107(c) of this title.

(b) An individual entitled to benefits under this subchapter because of his injury, or because of the death of an employee, who also is entitled to receive from the United States under a provision of statute other than this subchapter payments or benefits for that injury or death (except proceeds of an insurance policy), because of service by him (or in the case of death, by the deceased) as an employee or in the armed forces, shall elect which benefits he will receive. The individual shall make the election within 1 year after the injury or death or within a further time allowed for good cause by the Secretary of Labor. The election when made is irrevocable, except as otherwise provided by statute.

§8116. Limitations on right to receive compensation

(c) The liability of the United States or an instrumentality thereof under this subchapter or any extension thereof with respect to the injury or death of an employee is exclusive and instead of all other liability of the United States or the instrumentality to the employee, his legal representative, spouse, dependents, next of kin, and any other person otherwise entitled to recover damages from the United States or the instrumentality because of the injury or death in a direct judicial proceeding, in a civil action, or in admiralty, or by an administrative or judicial proceeding under a workmen's compensation statute or under a Federal tort liability statute. However, this subsection does not apply to a master or a member of a crew of a vessel.

(d) Notwithstanding the other provisions of this section, an individual receiving benefits for disability or death under this subchapter who is also receiving benefits under subchapter III of chapter 84 of this title or benefits under title II of the Social Security Act shall be entitled to all such benefits, except that—

(1) benefits received under section 223 of the Social Security Act (on account of disability) shall be subject to reduction on account of benefits paid under this subchapter pursuant to the provisions of section 224 of the Social Security Act; and

(2) in the case of benefits received on account of age or death under title II of the Social Security Act, compensation payable under this subchapter based on the Federal service of an employee shall be reduced by the amount of any such social security benefits payable that are attributable to Federal service of that employee covered by chapter 84 of this title. However, eligibility for or receipt of benefits under chapter 84 of this title, or benefits under title II of the Social Security Act by virtue of service covered by chapter 84 of this title, does not affect the right of the employee to compensation for scheduled disabilities specified by section 8107(c) of this title.

§8117. Time of accrual of right

An employee is not entitled to compensation for the first 3 days of temporary disability, except—

(1) when the disability exceeds 14 days;

(2) when the disability is followed by permanent disability; or

(3) as provided by sections 8103 and 8104 of this title.

§8118. Continuation of pay; election to use annual or sick leave

(a) The United States shall authorize the continuation of pay of an employee, as defined in section 8101(1) of this title (other than those referred to in clause (B) or (E)), who has filed a claim for a period of wage loss due to a traumatic injury with his immediate superior on a form approved by the Secretary of Labor within the time specified in section 8122(a)(2) of this title.

(b) Continuation of pay under this subchapter shall be furnished—

(1) without a break in time unless controverted under regulations of the Secretary;

(2) for a period not to exceed 45 days; and

(3) under accounting procedures and such other regulations as the Secretary may require.

(c) An employee may use annual or sick leave to his credit at the time the disability begins, but his compensation for disability does not begin, and the time periods specified by section 8117 of this title do not begin to run, until termination of pay as set forth in subsections (a) and (b) or the use of annual or sick leave ends.

(d) If a claim under subsection (a) is denied by the Secretary, payments under this section shall, at the option of the employee, be charged to sick or annual leave or shall be deemed overpayments of pay within the meaning of section 5584 of title 5, United States Code.

(e) Payments under this section shall not be considered as compensation as defined by section 8101(12) of this title.

§8119. Notice of injury or death

An employee injured in the performance of his duty, or someone on his behalf, shall give notice thereof. Notice of a death believed to be related to the employment shall be given by an eligible beneficiary specified in section 8133 of this title, or someone on his behalf. A notice of injury or death shall—

(a) be given within 30 days after the injury or death;

(b) be given to the immediate superior of the employee by personal delivery or by depositing it in the mail properly stamped and addressed;

(c) be in writing;

(d) state the name and address of the employee;

(e) state the year, month, day, and hour when and the particular locality where the injury or death occurred;

(f) state the cause and nature of the injury, or, in the case of death, the employment factors believed to be the cause; and

(g) be signed by and contain the address of the individual giving the notice.

§8120. Report of injury

Immediately after an injury to an employee which results in his death or probable disability, his immediate superior shall report to the Secretary of Labor. The Secretary may—

(1) prescribe the information that the report shall contain;

(2) require the immediate superior to make supplemental reports; and

(3) obtain such additional reports and information from employees as are agreed on by the Secretary and the head of the employing agency.

§8121. Claim

Compensation under this subchapter may be allowed only if an individual or someone on his behalf makes claim therefor. The claim shall—

(1) be made in writing within the time specified by section 8122 of this title;

(2) be delivered to the office of the Secretary of Labor or to an individual whom the Secretary may designate by regulation, or deposited in the mail properly stamped and addressed to the Secretary or his designee;

(3) be on a form approved by the Secretary;

(4) contain all information required by the Secretary;

(5) be sworn to by the individual entitled to compensation or someone on his behalf; and

(6) except in case of death, be accompanied by a certificate of the physician of the employee stating the nature of the injury and the nature and probable extent of the disability.

The Secretary may waive paragraphs (3)—(6) of this section for reasonable cause shown.

§8122. Time for making claim

(a) An original claim for compensation for disability or death must be filed within 3 years after the injury or death. Compensation for disability or death, including medical care in disability cases, may not be allowed if claim is not filed within that time unless—

(1) the immediate superior had actual knowledge of the injury or death within 30 days. The knowledge must be such to put the immediate superior reasonably on notice of an on-the-job injury or death; or

(2) written notice of injury or death as specified in section 8119 of this title was given within 30 days.

(b) In a case of latent disability, the time for filing claim does not begin to run until the employee has a compensable disability and is aware, or by the exercise of reasonable diligence should have been aware, of the causal relationship of the compensable disability to his employment. In such a case, the time for giving notice of injury begins to run when the employee is aware, or by the exercise of reasonable diligence should have been aware, that his condition is causally related to his employment, whether or not there is a compensable disability.

(c) The timely filing of a disability claim because of injury will satisfy the time requirements for a death claim based on the same injury.

(d) The time limitations in subsections (a) and (b) of this section do not—

(1) begin to run against a minor until he reaches 21 years of age or has had a legal representative appointed; or

(2) run against an incompetent individual while he is incompetent and has no duly appointed legal representative; or

(3) run against any individual whose failure to comply is excused by the Secretary on the ground that such notice could not be given because of exceptional circumstances.

§8123. Physical examinations

(a) An employee shall submit to examination by a medical officer of the United States, or by a physician designated or approved by the Secretary of Labor, after the injury and as frequently and at the times and places as may be reasonably required. The employee may have a physician designated and paid by him present to participate in the examination. If there is disagreement between the physician making the examination for the United States and the physician of the employee, the Secretary shall appoint a third physician who shall make an examination.

(b) An employee is entitled to be paid expenses incident to an examination required by the Secretary which in the opinion of the Secretary are necessary and reasonable, including transportation and loss of wages incurred in order to be examined. The expenses, when authorized or approved by the Secretary, are paid from the Employees' Compensation Fund.

(c) The Secretary shall fix the fees for examinations held under this section by physicians not employed by or under contract to the United States to furnish medical services to employees. The fees, when authorized or approved by the Secretary, are paid from the Employees' Compensation Fund.

(d) If an employee refuses to submit to or obstructs an examination, his right to compensation under this subchapter is suspended until the refusal or obstruction stops. Compensation is not payable while a refusal or obstruction continues, and the period of the refusal or obstruction is deducted from the period for which compensation is payable to the employee.

§8124. Findings and award; hearings

(a) The Secretary of Labor shall determine and make a finding of facts and make an award for or against payment of compensation under this subchapter after—

(1) considering the claim presented by the beneficiary and the report furnished by the immediate superior; and

(2) completing such investigation as he considers necessary.

(b)(1) Before review under section 8128(a) of this title, a claimant for compensation not satisfied with a decision of the Secretary under subsection (a) of this section is entitled, on request made within 30 days after the date of the issuance of the decision, to a hearing on his claim before a representative of the Secretary. At the hearing, the claimant is entitled to present evidence in further support of his claim. Within 30 days after the hearing ends, the Secretary shall notify the claimant in writing of his further decision and any modifications of the award he may make and of the basis of his decision.

(2) In conducting the hearing, the representative of the Secretary is not bound by common law or statutory rules of evidence, by technical or formal rules of procedure, or by section 554 of this title except as provided by this subchapter, but may conduct the hearing in such manner as to best ascertain the rights of the claimant. For this purpose, he shall receive such relevant evidence as the claimant adduces and such other evidence as he determines necessary or useful in evaluating the claim.

§8133. Compensation in case of death

(a) If death results from an injury sustained in the performance of duty, the United States shall pay a monthly compensation equal to a percentage of the monthly pay of the deceased employee in accordance with the following schedule:

(1) To the widow or widower, if there is no child, 50 percent.

(2) To the widow or widower, if there is a child, 45 percent and in addition 15 percent for each child not to exceed a total of 75 percent for the widow or widower and children.

(3) To the children, if there is no widow or widower, 40 percent for one child and 15 percent additional for each additional child not to exceed a total of 75 percent, divided among the children share and share alike.

(4) To the parents, if there is no widow, widower, or child, as follows:

(A) 25 percent if one parent was wholly dependent on the employee at the time of death and the other was not dependent to any extent;

(B) 20 percent to each if both were wholly dependent; or

(C) a proportionate amount in the discretion of the Secretary of Labor if one or both were partly dependent.

If there is a widow, widower, or child, so much of the percentages are payable as, when added to the total percentages payable to the widow, widower, and children, will not exceed a total of 75 percent.

(5) To the brothers, sisters, grandparents, and grandchildren, if there is no widow, widower, child, or dependent parent as follows:

(A) 20 percent if one was wholly dependent on the employee at the time of death;

(B) 30 percent if more than one was wholly dependent, divided among the dependents share and share alike; or

(C) 10 percent if no one is wholly dependent but one or more is partly dependent, divided among the dependents share and share alike.

If there is a widow, widower, or child, or dependent parent, so much of the percentages are payable as, when added to the total percentages payable to the widow, widower, children, and dependent parents, will not exceed a total of 75 percent.

(b) The compensation payable under subsection (a) of this section is paid from the time of death until—

(1) a widow, or widower dies or remarries before reaching age 55;

(2) a child, a brother, a sister, or a grandchild dies, marries, or becomes 18 years of age, or if over age 18 and incapable of self-support becomes capable of self-support; or

(3) a parent or grandparent dies, marries, or ceases to be dependent.

Notwithstanding paragraph (2) of this subsection, compensation payable to or for a child, a brother or sister, or grandchild that would otherwise end because the child, brother or sister, or grandchild has reached 18 years of age shall continue if he is a student as defined by section 8101 of this title at the time he reaches 18 years of age for so long as he continues to be such a student or until he marries. A widow or widower who has entitlements to benefits under this title derived from more than one husband or wife shall elect one entitlement to be utilized.

(c) On the cessation of compensation under this section to or on account of an individual, the compensation of the remaining individuals entitled to compensation for the unexpired part of the period during which their compensation is payable, is that which they would have received if they had been the only individuals entitled to compensation at the time of the death of the employee.

(d) When there are two or more classes of individuals entitled to compensation under this section and the apportionment of compensation under this section would result in injustice, the Secretary may modify the apportionment to meet the requirements of the case.

(e) In computing compensation under this section, the monthly pay is deemed not less than the minimum rate of basic pay for GS-2. However, the total monthly compensation may not exceed—

(1) the monthly pay computed under section 8114 of this title, except for increases authorized by section 8146a of this title; or

(2) 75 percent of the monthly pay of the maximum rate of basic pay for GS-15.

(f) Notwithstanding any funeral and burial expenses paid under section 8134, there shall be paid a sum of $200 to the personal representative of a deceased employee within the meaning of section 8101(1) of this title for reimbursement of the costs of termination of the decedent's status as an employee of the United States.

§8134. Funeral expenses; transportation of body

(a) If death results from an injury sustained in the performance of duty, the United States shall pay, to the personal representative of the deceased or otherwise, funeral and burial expenses not to exceed $800, in the discretion of the Secretary of Labor.

(b) The body of an employee whose home is in the United States, in the discretion of the Secretary, may be embalmed and transported in a hermetically sealed casket to his home or last place of residence at the expense of the Employees' Compensation Fund if—

(1) the employee dies from—

(A) the injury while away from his home or official station or outside the United States; or

(B) from other causes while away from his home or official station for the purpose of receiving medical or other services, appliances, supplies, or examination under this subchapter; and

(2) the relatives of the employee request the return of his body.

If the relatives do not request the return of the body of the employee, the Secretary may provide for its disposition and incur and pay from the Employees' Compensation Fund the necessary and reasonable transportation, funeral, and burial expenses.

§8135. Lump-sum payment

(a) The liability of the United States for compensation to a beneficiary in the case of death or of permanent total or permanent partial disability may be discharged by a lump-sum payment equal to the present value of all future payments of compensation computed at 4 percent true discount compounded annually if—

(1) the monthly payment to the beneficiary is less than $50 a month;

(2) the beneficiary is or is about to become a nonresident of the United States; or

(3) the Secretary of Labor determines that it is for the best interest of the beneficiary.

The probability of the death of the beneficiary before the expiration of the period during which he is entitled to compensation shall be determined according to the most current United States Life Tables, as developed by the United States Department of Health, Education, and Welfare, which shall be updated from time to time, but the lump-sum payment to a widow or widower of the deceased employee may not exceed 60 months' compensation. The probability of the happening of any other contingency affecting the amount or duration of compensation shall be disregarded.

(b) On remarriage before reaching age 55, a widow or widower entitled to compensation under section 8133 of this title, shall be paid a lump sum equal to twenty-four times the monthly compensation payment (excluding compensation on account of another individual) to which he was entitled immediately before the remarriage.

§8151. Civil service retention rights

(a) In the event the individual resumes employment with the Federal Government, the entire time during which the employee was receiving compensation under this chapter shall be credited to the employee for the purposes of within-grade step increases, retention purposes, and other rights and benefits based upon length of service.

APPENDIX 4:
SELECTED PROVISIONS OF THE LONGSHORE AND HARBOR WORKERS' COMPENSATION ACT [33 U.S.C. §§901-950]

SEC. 901. SHORT TITLE; THIS ACT MAY BE CITED AS THE "LONGSHORE AND HARBOR WORKERS' COMPENSATION ACT".

SEC. 903. COVERAGE

(a) Disability or death; injuries occurring upon navigable waters of United States

Except as otherwise provided in this section, compensation shall be payable under this chapter in respect of disability or death of an employee, but only if the disability or death results from an injury occurring upon the navigable waters of the United States (including any adjoining pier, wharf, dry dock, terminal, building way, marine railway, or other adjoining area customarily used by an employer in loading, unloading, repairing, dismantling, or building a vessel).

(b) Governmental officers and employees

No compensation shall be payable in respect of the disability or death of an officer or employee of the United States, or any agency thereof, or of any State or foreign government, or any subdivision thereof.

(c) Intoxication; willful intention to kill

No compensation shall be payable if the injury was occasioned solely by the intoxication of the employee or by the willful intention of the employee to injure or kill himself or another.

(d) Small vessels

(1) No compensation shall be payable to an employee employed at a facility of an employer if, as certified by the Secretary, the facility is engaged in the business of building, repairing, or dismantling exclusively small vessels (as defined in paragraph (3) of this subsection), unless the injury occurs while upon the navigable waters of the United States or while upon any adjoining pier, wharf, dock, facility over land for launching vessels, or facility over land for hauling, lifting, or drydocking vessels.

(2) Notwithstanding paragraph (1), compensation shall be payable to an employee—

(A) who is employed at a facility which is used in the business of building, repairing, or dismantling small vessels if such facility receives Federal maritime subsidies; or

(B) if the employee is not subject to coverage under a State workers' compensation law.

(3) For purposes of this subsection, a small vessel means—

(A) a commercial barge which is under 900 lightship displacement tons; or

(B) a commercial tugboat, towboat, crew boat, supply boat, fishing vessel, or other work vessel which is under 1,600 tons gross as measured under section 14502 of title 46, or an alternate tonnage measured under section 14302 of that title as prescribed by the Secretary under section 14104 of that title.

(e) Credit for benefits paid under other laws

Notwithstanding any other provision of law, any amounts paid to an employee for the same injury, disability, or death for which benefits are claimed under this chapter pursuant to any other workers' compensation law or section 688 of title 46, Appendix (relating to recovery for injury to or death of seamen), shall be credited against any liability imposed by this chapter.

SEC. 904. LIABILITY FOR COMPENSATION

(a) Every employer shall be liable for and shall secure the payment to his employees of the compensation payable under sections 907, 908, and 909 of this title. In the case of an employer who is a subcontractor, only if such subcontractor fails to secure the payment of compensation shall the contractor be liable for and be required to secure the payment of compensation. A subcontractor shall not be deemed to have failed to secure the payment of compensation if the contractor has provided insurance for such compensation for the benefit of the subcontractor.

(b) Compensation shall be payable irrespective of fault as a cause for the injury.

SEC. 905. EXCLUSIVENESS OF LIABILITY

(a) Employer liability; failure of employer to secure payment of compensation

The liability of an employer prescribed in section 904 of this title shall be exclusive and in place of all other liability of such employer to the employee, his legal representative, husband or wife, parents, dependents, next of kin, and anyone otherwise entitled to recover damages from such employer at law or in admiralty on account of such injury or death, except that if an employer fails to secure payment of compensation as required by this chapter, an injured employee, or his legal representative in case death results from the injury, may elect to claim compensation under the chapter, or to maintain an action at law or in admiralty for damages on account of such injury or death. In such action the defendant may not plead as a defense that the injury was caused by the negligence of a fellow servant, or that the employee assumed the risk of his employment, or that the injury was due to the contributory negligence of the employee. For purposes of this subsection, a contractor shall be deemed the employer of a subcontractor's employees only if the subcontractor fails to secure the payment of compensation as required by section 904 of this title.

(b) Negligence of vessel

In the event of injury to a person covered under this chapter caused by the negligence of a vessel, then such person, or anyone otherwise entitled to recover damages by reason thereof, may bring an action against such vessel as a third party in accordance with the provisions of section 933 of this title, and the employer shall not be liable to the vessel for such damages directly or indirectly and any agreements or warranties to the contrary shall be void. If such person was employed by the vessel to provide stevedoring services, no such action shall be permitted if the injury was caused by the negligence of persons engaged in providing stevedoring services to the vessel. If such person was employed to provide shipbuilding, repairing, or breaking services and such person's employer was the owner, owner pro hac vice, agent, operator, or charterer of the vessel, no such action shall be permitted, in whole or in part or directly or indirectly, against the injured person's employer (in any capacity, including as the vessel's owner, owner pro hac vice, agent, operator, or charterer) or against the employees of the employer. The liability of the vessel under this subsection shall not be based upon the warranty of seaworthiness or a breach thereof at the time the injury occurred. The remedy provided in this subsection shall be exclusive of all other remedies against the vessel except remedies available under this chapter.

(c) Outer Continental Shelf

In the event that the negligence of a vessel causes injury to a person entitled to receive benefits under this Act by virtue of section 1333 of title 43, then such person, or anyone otherwise entitled to recover damages by reason thereof, may bring an action against such vessel in accordance with the provisions of subsection (b) of this section. Nothing contained in subsection (b) of this section shall preclude the enforcement according to its terms of any reciprocal indemnity provision whereby the employer of a person entitled to receive benefits under this chapter by virtue of section 1333 of title 43 and the vessel agree to defend and indemnify the other for cost of defense and loss or liability for damages arising out of or resulting from death or bodily injury to their employees.

SEC. 906. COMPENSATION

(a) Time for commencement

No compensation shall be allowed for the first three days of the disability, except the benefits provided for in section 907 of this title: Provided, however, That in case the injury results in disability of more than fourteen days the compensation shall be allowed from the date of the disability.

(b) Maximum rate of compensation

(1) Compensation for disability or death (other than compensation for death required by this chapter to be paid in a lump sum) shall not exceed an amount equal to 200 per centum of the applicable national average weekly wage, as determined by the Secretary under paragraph (3).

(2) Compensation for total disability shall not be less than 50 per centum of the applicable national average weekly wage determined by the Secretary under paragraph (3), except that if the employee's average weekly wages as computed under section 910 of this title are less than 50 per centum of such national average weekly wage, he shall receive his average weekly wages as compensation for total disability.

(3) As soon as practicable after June 30 of each year, and in any event prior to October 1 of such year, the Secretary shall determine the national average weekly wage for the three consecutive calendar quarters ending June 30. Such determination shall be the applicable national

average weekly wage for the period beginning with October 1 of that year and ending with September 30 of the next year. The initial determination under this paragraph shall be made as soon as practicable after October 27, 1972.

(c) Applicability of determinations

Determinations under subsection (b)(3) of this section with respect to a period shall apply to employees or survivors currently receiving compensation for permanent total disability or death benefits during such period, as well as those newly awarded compensation during such period.

SEC. 907. MEDICAL SERVICES AND SUPPLIES

(a) General requirement

The employer shall furnish such medical, surgical, and other attendance or treatment, nurse and hospital service, medicine, crutches, and apparatus, for such period as the nature of the injury or the process of recovery may require.

(b) Physician selection; administrative supervision; change of physicians and hospitals

The employee shall have the right to choose an attending physician authorized by the Secretary to provide medical care under this chapter as hereinafter provided. If, due to the nature of the injury, the employee is unable to select his physician and the nature of the injury requires immediate medical treatment and care, the employer shall select a physician for him. The Secretary shall actively supervise the medical care rendered to injured employees, shall require periodic reports as to the medical care being rendered to injured employees, shall have authority to determine the necessity, character, and sufficiency of any medical aid furnished or to be furnished, and may, on his own initiative or at the request of the employer, order a change of physicians or hospitals when in his judgment such change is desirable or necessary in the interest of the employee or where the charges exceed those prevailing within the community for the same or similar services or exceed the provider's customary charges. Change of physicians at the request of employees shall be permitted in accordance with regulations of the Secretary.

(c) Physicians and health care providers not authorized to render medical care or provide medical services

(1)(A) The Secretary shall annually prepare a list of physicians and health care providers in each compensation district who are not authorized to render medical care or provide medical services under this chapter. The names of physicians and health care providers contained on the list required under this subparagraph shall be made available to employees and employers in each compensation district through posting and in such other forms as the Secretary may prescribe.

(B) Physicians and health care providers shall be included on the list of those not authorized to provide medical care and medical services pursuant to subparagraph (A) when the Secretary determines under this section, in accordance with the procedures provided in subsection (j) of this section, that such physician or health care provider—

(i) has knowingly and willfully made, or caused to be made, any false statement or misrepresentation of a material fact for use in a claim for compensation or claim for reimbursement of medical expenses under this chapter;

(ii) has knowingly and willfully submitted, or caused to be submitted, a bill or request for payment under this chapter containing a charge which the Secretary finds to be substantially in excess of the charge for the service, appliance, or supply prevailing within the community or in excess of the provider's customary charges, unless the Secretary finds there is good cause for the bill or request containing the charge;

(iii) has knowingly and willfully furnished a service, appliance, or supply which is determined by the Secretary to be substantially in excess of the need of the recipient thereof or to be of a quality which substantially fails to meet professionally recognized standards;

(iv) has been convicted under any criminal statute (without regard to pending appeal thereof) for fraudulent activities in connection with any Federal or State program for which payments are made to physicians or providers of similar services, appliances, or supplies; or

(v) has otherwise been excluded from participation in such program.

(C) Medical services provided by physicians or health care providers who are named on the list published by the Secretary pursuant to subparagraph (A) of this section shall not be reimbursable under this chapter; except that the Secretary shall direct the reimbursement of medical claims for services rendered by such physicians or health care providers in cases where the services were rendered in an emergency.

(D) A determination under subparagraph (B) shall remain in effect for a period of not less than three years and until the Secretary finds and gives notice to the public that there is reasonable assurance that the basis for the determination will not reoccur.

(E) A provider of a service, appliance, or supply shall provide to the Secretary such information and certification as the Secretary may require to assure that this subsection is enforced.

(2) Whenever the employer or carrier acquires knowledge of the employee's injury, through written notice or otherwise as prescribed by the chapter, the employer or carrier shall forthwith authorize medical treatment and care from a physician selected by an employee pursuant to subsection (b) of this section. An employee may not select a physician who is on the list required by paragraph (1) of this subsection. An employee may not change physicians after his initial choice unless the employer, carrier, or deputy commissioner has given prior consent for such change. Such consent shall be given in cases where an employee's initial choice was not of a specialist whose services are necessary for and appropriate to the proper care and treatment of the compensable injury or disease. In all other cases, consent may be given upon a showing of good cause for change.

(d) Request of treatment or services prerequisite to recovery of expenses; formal report of injury and treatment; suspension of compensation for refusal of treatment or examination; justification

(1) An employee shall not be entitled to recover any amount expended by him for medical or other treatment or services unless—

(A) the employer shall have refused or neglected a request to furnish such services and the employee has complied with subsections (b) and (c) of this section and the applicable regulations; or

(B) the nature of the injury required such treatment and services and the employer or his superintendent or foreman having knowledge of such injury shall have neglected to provide or authorize same.

(2) No claim for medical or surgical treatment shall be valid and enforceable against such employer unless, within ten days following the first treatment, the physician giving such treatment furnishes to the employer and the deputy commissioner a report of such injury or treatment, on a form prescribed by the Secretary. The Secretary may excuse the failure to furnish such report within the ten-day period whenever he finds it to be in the interest of justice to do so.

(3) The Secretary may, upon application by a party in interest, make an award for the reasonable value of such medical or surgical treatment so obtained by the employee.

(4) If at any time the employee unreasonably refuses to submit to medical or surgical treatment, or to an examination by a physician selected by the employer, the Secretary or administrative law judge may, by order, suspend the payment of further compensation during such time as

such refusal continues, and no compensation shall be paid at any time during the period of such suspension, unless the circumstances justified the refusal.

(e) Physical examination; medical questions; report of physical impairment; review or reexamination; costs

In the event that medical questions are raised in any case, the Secretary shall have the power to cause the employee to be examined by a physician employed or selected by the Secretary and to obtain from such physician a report containing his estimate of the employee's physical impairment and such other information as may be appropriate. Any party who is dissatisfied with such report may request a review or reexamination of the employee by one or more different physicians employed or selected by the Secretary. The Secretary shall order such review or reexamination unless he finds that it is clearly unwarranted. Such review or reexamination shall be completed within two weeks from the date ordered unless the Secretary finds that because of extraordinary circumstances a longer period is required. The Secretary shall have the power in his discretion to charge the cost of examination or review under this subsection to the employer, if he is a self-insurer, or to the insurance company which is carrying the risk, in appropriate cases, or to the special fund in section 944 of this title.

(f) Place of examination; exclusion of physicians other than examining physician of Secretary; good cause for conclusions of other physicians respecting impairment; examination by employer's physician; suspension of proceedings and compensation for refusal of examination

An employee shall submit to a physical examination under subsection (e) of this section at such place as the Secretary may require. The place, or places, shall be designated by the Secretary and shall be reasonably convenient for the employee. No physician selected by the employer, carrier, or employee shall be present at or participate in any manner in such examination, nor shall conclusions of such physicians as to the nature or extent of impairment or the cause of impairment be available to the examining physician unless otherwise ordered, for good cause, by the Secretary. Such employer or carrier shall, upon request, be entitled to have the employee examined immediately thereafter and upon the same premises by a qualified physician or physicians in the presence of such physician as the employee may select, if any. Proceedings shall be suspended and no compensation shall be payable for any period during which the employee may refuse to submit to examination.

(g) Fees and charges for examinations, treatment, or service; limitation; regulations

All fees and other charges for medical examinations, treatment, or service shall be limited to such charges as prevail in the community for such treatment, and shall be subject to regulation by the Secretary. The Secretary shall issue regulations limiting the nature and extent of medical expenses chargeable against the employer without authorization by the employer or the Secretary.

(h) Third party liability

The liability of an employer for medical treatment as herein provided shall not be affected by the fact that his employee was injured through the fault or negligence of a third party not in the same employ, or that suit has been brought against such third party. The employer shall, however, have a cause of action against such third party to recover any amounts paid by him for such medical treatment in like manner as provided in section 933 (b) of this title.

(i) Physicians' ineligibility for subsection (e) physical examinations and reviews because of workmen's compensation claim employment or fee acceptance or participation

Unless the parties to the claim agree, the Secretary shall not employ or select any physician for the purpose of making examinations or reviews under subsection (e) of this section who, during such employment, or during the period of two years prior to such employment, has been employed by, or accepted or participated in any fee relating to a workmen's compensation claim from any insurance carrier or any self-insurer.

(j) Procedure; judicial review

(1) The Secretary shall have the authority to make rules and regulations and to establish procedures, not inconsistent with the provisions of this chapter, which are necessary or appropriate to carry out the provisions of subsection (c) of this section, including the nature and extent of the proof and evidence necessary for actions under this section and the methods of taking and furnishing such proof and evidence.

(2) Any decision to take action with respect to a physician or health care provider under this section shall be based on specific findings of fact by the Secretary. The Secretary shall provide notice of these findings and an opportunity for a hearing pursuant to section 556 of title 5 for a provider who would be affected by a decision under this section. A request for a hearing must be filed with the Secretary within thirty days after notice of the findings is received by the provider making such request. If a hearing is held, the Secretary shall, on the basis of

evidence adduced at the hearing, affirm, modify, or reverse the findings of fact and proposed action under this section.

(3) For the purpose of any hearing, investigation, or other proceeding authorized or directed under this section, the provisions of section [1] 49 and 50 of title 15 (relating to the attendance of witnesses and the production of books, papers, and documents) shall apply to the jurisdiction, powers, and duties of the Secretary or any officer designated by him.

(4) Any physician or health care provider, after any final decision of the Secretary made after a hearing to which he was a party, irrespective of the amount in controversy, may obtain a review of such decision by a civil action commenced within sixty days after the mailing to him of notice of such decision, but the pendency of such review shall not operate as a stay upon the effect of such decision. Such action shall be brought in the court of appeals of the United States for the judicial circuit in which the plaintiff resides or has his principal place of business, or the Court of Appeals for the District of Columbia. As part of his answer, the Secretary shall file a certified copy of the transcript of the record of the hearing, including all evidence submitted in connection therewith. The findings of fact of the Secretary, if based on substantial evidence in the record as a whole, shall be conclusive.

(k) Refusal of treatment on religious grounds

(1) Nothing in this chapter prevents an employee whose injury or disability has been established under this chapter from relying in good faith on treatment by prayer or spiritual means alone, in accordance with the tenets and practice of a recognized church or religious denomination, by an accredited practitioner of such recognized church or religious denomination, and on nursing services rendered in accordance with such tenets and practice, without suffering loss or diminution of the compensation or benefits under this chapter. Nothing in this subsection shall be construed to except an employee from all physical examinations required by this chapter.

(2) If an employee refuses to submit to medical or surgical services solely because, in adherence to the tenets and practice of a recognized church or religious denomination, the employee relies upon prayer or spiritual means alone for healing, such employee shall not be considered to have unreasonably refused medical or surgical treatment under subsection (d) of this section.

SEC. 908. COMPENSATION FOR DISABILITY

Compensation for disability shall be paid to the employee as follows:

(a) Permanent total disability: In case of total disability adjudged to be permanent 662/3 per centum of the average weekly wages shall be paid to the employee during the continuance of such total disability. Loss of both hands, or both arms, or both feet, or both legs, or both eyes, or of any two thereof shall, in the absence of conclusive proof to the contrary, constitute permanent total disability. In all other cases permanent total disability shall be determined in accordance with the facts.

(b) Temporary total disability: In case of disability total in character but temporary in quality 662/3 per centum of the average weekly wages shall be paid to the employee during the continuance thereof.

(c) Permanent partial disability: In case of disability partial in character but permanent in quality the compensation shall be 662/3 per centum of the average weekly wages, which shall be in addition to compensation for temporary total disability or temporary partial disability paid in accordance with subsection (b) or subsection (e) of this section, respectively, and shall be paid to the employee, as follows:

(1) Arm lost, three hundred and twelve weeks' compensation.

(2) Leg lost, two hundred and eighty-eight weeks' compensation.

(3) Hand lost, two hundred and forty-four weeks' compensation.

(4) Foot lost, two hundred and five weeks' compensation.

(5) Eye lost, one hundred and sixty weeks' compensation.

(6) Thumb lost, seventy-five weeks' compensation.

(7) First finger lost, forty-six weeks' compensation.

(8) Great toe lost, thirty-eight weeks' compensation.

(9) Second finger lost, thirty weeks' compensation.

(10) Third finger lost, twenty-five weeks' compensation.

(11) Toe other than great toe lost, sixteen weeks' compensation.

(12) Fourth finger lost, fifteen weeks' compensation.

(13) Loss of hearing:

(A) Compensation for loss of hearing in one ear, fifty-two weeks.

(B) Compensation for loss of hearing in both ears, two-hundred weeks.

(C) An audiogram shall be presumptive evidence of the amount of hearing loss sustained as of the date thereof, only if

(i) such audiogram was administered by a licensed or certified audiologist or a physician who is certified in otolaryngology,

(ii) such audiogram, with the report thereon, was provided to the employee at the time it was administered, and

(iii) no contrary audiogram made at that time is produced.

(D) The time for filing a notice of injury, under section 912 of this title, or a claim for compensation, under section 913 of this title, shall not begin to run in connection with any claim for loss of hearing under this section, until the employee has received an audiogram, with the accompanying report thereon, which indicates that the employee has suffered a loss of hearing.

(E) Determinations of loss of hearing shall be made in accordance with the guides for the evaluation of permanent impairment as promulgated and modified from time to time by the American Medical Association.

(14) Phalanges: Compensation for loss of more than one phalange of a digit shall be the same as for loss of the entire digit. Compensation for loss of the first phalange shall be one-half of the compensation for loss of the entire digit.

(15) Amputated arm or leg: Compensation for an arm or a leg, if amputated at or above the elbow or the knee, shall be the same as for a loss of the arm or leg; but, if amputated between the elbow and the wrist or the knee and the ankle, shall be the same as for loss of a hand or foot.

(16) Binocular vision or per centum of vision: Compensation for loss of binocular vision or for 80 per centum or more of the vision of an eye shall be the same as for loss of the eye.

(17) Two or more digits: Compensation for loss of two or more digits, or one or more phalanges of two or more digits, of a hand or foot may be proportioned to the loss of use of the hand or foot occasioned thereby, but shall not exceed the compensation for loss of a hand or foot.

(18) Total loss of use: Compensation for permanent total loss of use of a member shall be the same as for loss of the member.

(19) Partial loss or partial loss of use: Compensation for permanent partial loss or loss of use of a member may be for proportionate loss or loss of use of the member.

(20) Disfigurement: Proper and equitable compensation not to exceed $7,500 shall be awarded for serious disfigurement of the face, head, or neck or of other normally exposed areas likely to handicap the employee in securing or maintaining employment.

(21) Other cases: In all other cases in the class of disability, the compensation shall be 66 2/3 per centum of the difference between the average weekly wages of the employee and the employee's wage-earning capacity thereafter in the same employment or otherwise, payable during the continuance of partial disability.

(22) In any case in which there shall be a loss of, or loss of use of, more than one member or parts of more than one member set forth in paragraphs (1) to (19) of this subsection, not amounting to permanent total disability, the award of compensation shall be for the loss of, or loss of use of, each such member or part thereof, which awards shall run consecutively, except that where the injury affects only two or more digits of the same hand or foot, paragraph (17) of this subsection shall apply.

(23) Notwithstanding paragraphs (1) through (22), with respect to a claim for permanent partial disability for which the average weekly wages are determined under section 910 (d)(2) of this title, the compensation shall be 66 2/3 per centum of such average weekly wages multiplied by the percentage of permanent impairment, as determined under the guides referred to in section 902 (10) of this title, payable during the continuance of such impairment.

(d)(1) If an employee who is receiving compensation for permanent partial disability pursuant to subsection (c)(1)–(20) of this section dies from causes other than the injury, the total amount of the award unpaid at the time of death shall be payable to or for the benefit of his survivors, as follows:

(A) if the employee is survived only by a widow or widower, such unpaid amount of the award shall be payable to such widow or widower,

(B) if the employee is survived only by a child or children, such unpaid amount of the award shall be paid to such child or children in equal shares,

(C) if the employee is survived by a widow or widower and a child or children, such unpaid amount of the award shall be payable to such survivors in equal shares,

(D) if there be no widow or widower and no surviving child or children, such unpaid amount of the award shall be paid to the survivors specified in section 909 (d) of this title (other than a wife, husband, or child); and the amount to be paid each such survivor shall be determined by multiplying such unpaid amount of the award by the appropriate percentage specified in section 909 (d) of this title, but if the aggregate amount to which all such survivors are entitled, as so determined, is less than such unpaid amount of the award, the excess amount shall be divided among such survivors pro rata according to the amount otherwise payable to each under this subparagraph.

(2) Notwithstanding any other limitation in section 909 of this title, the total amount of any award for permanent partial disability pursuant to subsection (c)(1)–(20) of this section unpaid at time of death shall be payable in full in the appropriate distribution.

(3) An award for disability may be made after the death of the injured employee. Except where compensation is payable under subsection (c)(21) of this section if there be no survivors as prescribed in this section, then the compensation payable under this subsection shall be paid to the special fund established under section 944 (a) of this title.

(e) Temporary partial disability:

In case of temporary partial disability resulting in decrease of earning capacity the compensation shall be two-thirds of the difference between the injured employee's average weekly wages before the injury and his wage-earning capacity after the injury in the same or another employment, to be paid during the continuance of such disability, but shall not be paid for a period exceeding five years.

(f) Injury increasing disability:

(1) In any case in which an employee having an existing permanent partial disability suffers injury, the employer shall provide compensation for such disability as is found to be attributable to that injury based upon the average weekly wages of the employee at the time of the injury. If following an injury falling within the provisions of subsection (c)(1)–(20) of this section, the employee is totally and permanently disabled, and the disability is found not to be due solely to that injury, the employer shall provide compensation for the applicable prescribed period of weeks provided for in that section for the subsequent injury, or for one hundred and four weeks, whichever is the greater, except that, in the case of an injury falling within the provisions of subsection (c)(13) of this section, the employer shall provide compensation for the lesser of such periods. In all other cases of total permanent disability or of death, found not to be due solely to that injury, of an employee having an existing permanent partial disability, the employer shall provide in addition to compensation under subsections (b) and (e) of this section, compensation payments or death benefits for one hundred and four weeks only. If following an injury falling within the provisions of subsection (c)(1)–(20) of this section, the em-

ployee has a permanent partial disability and the disability is found not to be due solely to that injury, and such disability is materially and substantially greater than that which would have resulted from the subsequent injury alone, the employer shall provide compensation for the applicable period of weeks provided for in that section for the subsequent injury, or for one hundred and four weeks, whichever is the greater, except that, in the case of an injury falling within the provisions of subsection (c)(13) of this section, the employer shall provide compensation for the lesser of such periods.

In all other cases in which the employee has a permanent partial disability, found not to be due solely to that injury, and such disability is materially and substantially greater than that which would have resulted from the subsequent injury alone, the employer shall provide in addition to compensation under subsections (b) and (e) of this section, compensation for one hundred and four weeks only.

(2)(A) After cessation of the payments for the period of weeks provided for herein, the employee or his survivor entitled to benefits shall be paid the remainder of the compensation that would be due out of the special fund established in section 944 of this title, except that the special fund shall not assume responsibility with respect to such benefits (and such payments shall not be subject to cessation) in the case of any employer who fails to comply with section 932 (a) of this title.

(B) After cessation of payments for the period of weeks provided for in this subsection, the employer or carrier responsible for payment of compensation shall remain a party to the claim, retain access to all records relating to the claim, and in all other respects retain all rights granted under this chapter prior to cessation of such payments.

(3) Any request, filed after September 28, 1984, for apportionment of liability to the special fund established under section 944 of this title for the payment of compensation benefits, and a statement of the grounds therefore, shall be presented to the deputy commissioner prior to the consideration of the claim by the deputy commissioner. Failure to present such request prior to such consideration shall be an absolute defense to the special fund's liability for the payment of any benefits in connection with such claim, unless the employer could not have reasonably anticipated the liability of the special fund prior to the issuance of a compensation order.

(g) Maintenance for employees undergoing vocational rehabilitation:

An employee who as a result of injury is or may be expected to be totally or partially incapacitated for a remunerative occupation and who, under the direction of the Secretary as provided by section 939 (c) of this title, is being rendered fit to engage in a remunerative occupation, shall receive additional compensation necessary for his maintenance, but such additional compensation shall not exceed $25 a week. The expense shall be paid out of the special fund established in section 944 of this title.

(h) The wage-earning capacity of an injured employee in cases of partial disability under subsection (c)(21) of this section or under subsection (e) of this section shall be determined by his actual earnings if such actual earnings fairly and reasonably represent his wage-earning capacity: Provided, however, That if the employee has no actual earnings or his actual earnings do not fairly and reasonably represent his wage-earning capacity, the deputy commissioner may, in the interest of justice, fix such wage-earning capacity as shall be reasonable, having due regard to the nature of his injury, the degree of physical impairment, his usual employment, and any other factors or circumstances in the case which may affect his capacity to earn wages in his disabled condition, including the effect of disability as it may naturally extend into the future.

(i)(1) Whenever the parties to any claim for compensation under this chapter, including survivors benefits, agree to a settlement, the deputy commissioner or administrative law judge shall approve the settlement within thirty days unless it is found to be inadequate or procured by duress. Such settlement may include future medical benefits if the parties so agree. No liability of any employer, carrier, or both for medical, disability, or death benefits shall be discharged unless the application for settlement is approved by the deputy commissioner or administrative law judge. If the parties to the settlement are represented by counsel, then agreements shall be deemed approved unless specifically disapproved within thirty days after submission for approval.

(2) If the deputy commissioner disapproves an application for settlement under paragraph (1), the deputy commissioner shall issue a written statement within thirty days containing the reasons for disapproval. Any party to the settlement may request a hearing before an administrative law judge in the manner prescribed by this chapter. Following such hearing, the administrative law judge shall enter an order approving or rejecting the settlement.

(3) A settlement approved under this section shall discharge the liability of the employer or carrier, or both. Settlements may be agreed upon at any stage of the proceeding including after entry of a final compensation order.

(4) The special fund shall not be liable for reimbursement of any sums paid or payable to an employee or any beneficiary under such

settlement, or otherwise voluntarily paid prior to such settlement by the employer or carrier, or both.

(j)(1) The employer may inform a disabled employee of his obligation to report to the employer not less than semiannually any earnings from employment or self-employment, on such forms as the Secretary shall specify in regulations.

(2) An employee who—

(A) fails to report the employee's earnings under paragraph (1) when requested, or

(B) knowingly and willfully omits or understates any part of such earnings, and who is determined by the deputy commissioner to have violated clause (A) or (B) of this paragraph, forfeits his right to compensation with respect to any period during which the employee was required to file such report.

(3) Compensation forfeited under this subsection, if already paid, shall be recovered by a deduction from the compensation payable to the employee in any amount and on such schedule as determined by the deputy commissioner.

SEC. 909. COMPENSATION FOR DEATH

If the injury causes death, the compensation therefore shall be known as a death benefit and shall be payable in the amount and to or for the benefit of the persons following:

(a) Reasonable funeral expenses not exceeding $3,000.

(b) If there be a widow or widower and no child of the deceased, to such widow or widower 50 per centum of the average wages of the deceased, during widowhood, or dependent widowerhood, with two years' compensation in one sum upon remarriage; and if there be a surviving child or children of the deceased, the additional amount of 16 2/3 per centum of such wages for each such child; in case of the death or remarriage of such widow or widower, if there be one surviving child of the deceased employee, such child shall have his compensation increased to 50 per centum of such wages, and if there be more than one surviving child of the deceased employee, to such children, in equal parts, 50 per centum of such wages increased by 16 2/3 per centum of such wages for each child in excess of one: Provided, That the total amount payable shall in no case exceed 66 2/3 per centum of such wages. The deputy commissioner having jurisdiction over the claim may, in his discretion, require the appointment of a guardian for the purpose of receiving the compensation of a minor child. In the absence of such a requirement the appointment of a guardian for such purposes shall not be necessary.

(c) If there be one surviving child of the deceased, but no widow or widower, then for the support of such child 50 per centum of the wages of the deceased; and if there be more than one surviving child of the deceased, but no widow or dependent husband, then for the support of such children, in equal parts 50 per centum of such wages increased by 16 2/3 per centum of such wages for each child in excess of one: Provided, That the total amount payable shall in no case exceed 66 2/3 per centum of such wages.

(d) If there be no surviving wife or husband or child, or if the amount payable to a surviving wife or husband and to children shall be less in the aggregate than 66 2/3 per centum of the average wages of the deceased; then for the support of grandchildren or brothers and sisters, if dependent upon the deceased at the time of the injury, and any other persons who satisfy the definition of the term "dependent" in section 152 of title 26, but are not otherwise eligible under this section, 20 per centum of such wages for the support of each such person during such dependency and for the support of each parent, or grandparent, of the deceased if dependent upon him at the time of the injury, 25 per centum of such wages during such dependency. But in no case shall the aggregate amount payable under this subsection exceed the difference between 66 2/3 per centum of such wages and the amount payable as hereinbefore provided to widow or widower and for the support of surviving child or children.

(e) In computing death benefits, the average weekly wages of the deceased shall not be less than the national average weekly wage as prescribed in section 906 (b) of this title, but—

(1) the total weekly benefits shall not exceed the lesser of the average weekly wages of the deceased or the benefit which the deceased employee would have been eligible to receive under section 906 (b)(1) of this title; and

(2) in the case of a claim based on death due to an occupational disease for which the time of injury (as determined under section 910 (i) of this title) occurs after the employee has retired, the total weekly benefits shall not exceed one fifty-second part of the employee's average annual earnings during the 52-week period preceding retirement.

(f) All questions of dependency shall be determined as of the time of the injury.

(g) Aliens: Compensation under this chapter to aliens not residents (or about to become nonresidents) of the United States or Canada shall be the same in amount as provided for residents, except that dependents in any foreign country shall be limited to surviving wife and child or children, or if there be no surviving wife or child or children, to surviving father or mother whom the employee has supported, either wholly or in part, for the period of one year prior to the date of the injury, and except that the Secretary may, at his option or upon the application of the insurance carrier shall, commute all future installments of compensation to be paid to such aliens by paying or causing to be paid to them one-half of the commuted amount of such future installments of compensation as determined by the Secretary.

SEC. 913. FILING OF CLAIMS

(a) Time to file

Except as otherwise provided in this section, the right to compensation for disability or death under this chapter shall be barred unless a claim therefore is filed within one year after the injury or death. If payment of compensation has been made without an award on account of such injury or death, a claim may be filed within one year after the date of the last payment. Such claim shall be filed with the deputy commissioner in the compensation district in which such injury or death occurred. The time for filing a claim shall not begin to run until the employee or beneficiary is aware, or by the exercise of reasonable diligence should have been aware, of the relationship between the injury or death and the employment.

(b) Failure to file

(1) Notwithstanding the provisions of subsection (a) of this section failure to file a claim within the period prescribed in such subsection shall not be a bar to such right unless objection to such failure is made at the first hearing of such claim in which all parties in interest are given reasonable notice and opportunity to be heard.

(2) Notwithstanding the provisions of subsection (a) of this section, a claim for compensation for death or disability due to an occupational disease which does not immediately result in such death or disability shall be timely if filed within two years after the employee or claimant becomes aware, or in the exercise of reasonable diligence or by reason of medical advice should have been aware, of the relationship between the employment, the disease, and the death or disability, or within one year of the date of the last payment of compensation, whichever is later.

(c) Effect on incompetents and minors

If a person who is entitled to compensation under this chapter is mentally incompetent or a minor, the provisions of subsection (a) of this section shall not be applicable so long as such person has no guardian or other authorized representative, but shall be applicable in the case of a person who is mentally incompetent or a minor from the date of appointment of such guardian or other representative, or in the case of a minor, if no guardian is appointed before he becomes of age, from the date he becomes of age.

(d) Tolling provision

Where recovery is denied to any person, in a suit brought at law or in admiralty to recover damages in respect of injury or death, on the ground that such person was an employee and that the defendant was an employer within the meaning of this chapter and that such employer had secured compensation to such employee under this chapter, the limitation of time prescribed in subsection (a) of this section shall begin to run only from the date of termination of such suit.

SEC. 914. PAYMENT OF COMPENSATION

(a) Manner of payment

Compensation under this chapter shall be paid periodically, promptly, and directly to the person entitled thereto, without an award, except where liability to pay compensation is controverted by the employer.

(b) Period of installment payments

The first installment of compensation shall become due on the fourteenth day after the employer has been notified pursuant to section 912 of this title, or the employer has knowledge of the injury or death, on which date all compensation then due shall be paid. Thereafter compensation shall be paid in installments, semimonthly, except where the deputy commissioner determines that payment in installments should be made monthly or at some other period.

(c) Notification of commencement or suspension of payment

Upon making the first payment, and upon suspension of payment for any cause, the employer shall immediately notify the deputy commissioner, in accordance with a form prescribed by the Secretary, that payment of compensation has begun or has been suspended, as the case may be.

(d) Right to compensation controverted

If the employer controverts the right to compensation he shall file with the deputy commissioner on or before the fourteenth day after he has knowledge of the alleged injury or death, a notice, in accordance with a form prescribed by the Secretary stating that the right to compensation is controverted, the name of the claimant, the name of the employer, the date of the alleged injury or death, and the grounds upon which the right to compensation is controverted.

(e) Additional compensation for overdue installment payments payable without award

If any installment of compensation payable without an award is not paid within fourteen days after it becomes due, as provided in subsection (b) of this section, there shall be added to such unpaid installment an amount equal to 10 per centum thereof, which shall be paid at the same time as, but in addition to, such installment, unless notice is filed under subsection (d) of this section, or unless such nonpayment is excused by the deputy commissioner after a showing by the employer that owing to conditions over which he had no control such installment could not be paid within the period prescribed for the payment.

(f) Additional compensation for overdue installment payments payable under terms of award

If any compensation, payable under the terms of an award, is not paid within ten days after it becomes due, there shall be added to such unpaid compensation an amount equal to 20 per centum thereof, which shall be paid at the same time as, but in addition to, such compensation, unless review of the compensation order making such award is had as provided in section 921 of this title and an order staying payment has been issued by the Board or court.

(g) Notice of payment; penalty

Within sixteen days after final payment of compensation has been made, the employer shall send to the deputy commissioner a notice, in accordance with a form prescribed by the Secretary, stating that such final payment has been made, the total amount of compensation paid, the name of the employee and of any other person to whom compensation has been paid, the date of the injury or death, and the date to which compensation has been paid. If the employer fails to so notify the deputy commissioner within such time the Secretary shall assess against such employer a civil penalty in the amount of $100.

(h) Investigations, examinations, and hearings for controverted, stopped, or suspended payments

The deputy commissioner

(1) may upon his own initiative at any time in a case in which payments are being made without an award, and

(2) shall in any case where right to compensation is controverted, or where payments of compensation have been stopped or suspended, upon receipt of notice from any person entitled to compensation, or from the employer, that the right to compensation is controverted, or that payments of compensation have been stopped or suspended, make such investigations, cause such medical examinations to be made, or hold such hearings, and take such further action as he considers will properly protect the rights of all parties.

(i) Deposit by employer

Whenever the deputy commissioner deems it advisable he may require any employer to make a deposit with the Treasurer of the United States to secure the prompt and convenient payment of such compensation, and payments therefrom upon any awards shall be made upon order of the deputy commissioner.

(j) Reimbursement for advance payments

If the employer has made advance payments of compensation, he shall be entitled to be reimbursed out of any unpaid installment or installments of compensation due.

(k) Receipt for payment

An injured employee, or in case of death his dependents or personal representative, shall give receipts for payment of compensation to the employer paying the same and such employer shall produce the same for inspection by the deputy commissioner, whenever required.

SEC. 934. COMPENSATION NOTICE

Every employer who has secured compensation under the provisions of this chapter shall keep posted in a conspicuous place or places in and about his place or places of business typewritten or printed notices, in accordance with a form prescribed by the Secretary, stating that such employer has secured the payment of compensation in accordance with the provisions of this chapter. Such notices shall contain the name and address of the carrier, if any, with whom the employer has secured payment of compensation and the date of the expiration of the policy.

APPENDIX 5:
SELECTED PROVISIONS OF THE BLACK
LUNG BENEFITS ACT [30 U.S.C. §§901-945]

SEC. 901. CONGRESSIONAL FINDINGS AND DECLARATION OF PURPOSE; SHORT TITLE

(a) Congress finds and declares that there are a significant number of coal miners living today who are totally disabled due to pneumoconiosis arising out of employment in one or more of the Nation's coal mines; that there are a number of survivors of coal miners whose deaths were due to this disease; and that few States provide benefits for death or disability due to this disease to coal miners or their surviving dependents. It is, therefore, the purpose of this subchapter to provide benefits, in cooperation with the States, to coal miners who are totally disabled due to pneumoconiosis and to the surviving dependents of miners whose death was due to such disease; and to ensure that in the future adequate benefits are provided to coal miners and their dependents in the event of their death or total disability due to pneumoconiosis.

(b) This subchapter may be cited as the "Black Lung Benefits Act".

SEC. 922. PAYMENT OF BENEFITS

(a) Schedules

Subject to the provisions of subsection (b) of this section, benefit payments shall be made by the Secretary under this part as follows:

(1) In the case of total disability of a miner due to pneumoconiosis, the disabled miner shall be paid benefits during the disability at a rate equal to 37 1/2 per centum of the monthly pay rate for Federal employees in grade GS-2, step 1.

(2) In the case of death of a miner due to pneumoconiosis or, except with respect to a claim filed under part C of this subchapter on or after the effective date of the Black Lung Benefits Amendments of 1981, of a miner receiving benefits under this part, benefits shall be paid to his widow (if any) at the rate the deceased miner would receive such benefits if he were totally disabled.

(3) In the case of the child or children of a miner whose death is due to pneumoconiosis or, except with respect to a claim filed under part C of this subchapter on or after the effective date of the Black Lung Benefits Amendments of 1981, of a miner who is receiving benefits under this part at the time of his death or who was totally disabled by pneumoconiosis at the time of his death, in the case of the child or children of a widow who is receiving benefits under this part at the time of her death, and in the case of any child or children entitled to the payment of benefits under paragraph (5) of section 921(c) of this title, benefits shall be paid to such child or children as follows: If there is one such child, he shall be paid benefits at the rate specified in paragraph (1). If there is more than one such child, the benefits paid shall be divided equally among them and shall be paid at a rate equal to the rate specified in paragraph (1), increased by 50 per centum of such rate if there are two such children, by 75 per centum of such rate if there are three such children, and by 100 per centum of such rate if there are more than three such children: Provided, That benefits shall only be paid to a child for so long as he meets the criteria for the term 'child' contained in section 902(g) of this title: And provided further, That no entitlement to benefits as a child shall be established under this paragraph (3) for any month for which entitlement to benefits as a widow is established under paragraph (2).

(4) In the case of an individual entitled to benefit payments under clause (1) or (2) of this subsection who has one or more dependents, the benefit payments shall be increased at the rate of 50 per centum of such benefit payments, if such individual has one dependent, 75 per centum if such individual has two dependents, and 100 per centum if such individual has three or more dependents.

(5) In the case of the dependent parent or parents of a miner whose death is due to pneumoconiosis, or, except with respect to a claim filed under part C of this subchapter on or after the effective date of the Black Lung Benefits Amendments of 1981, of a miner who is receiving benefits under this part at the time of his death or who was totally disabled by pneumoconiosis at the time of death, and who is not survived at the time of his death by a widow or a child, in the case of the dependent surviving brother(s) or sister(s) of such a miner

who is not survived at the time of his death by a widow, child, or parent, in the case of the dependent parent or parents of a miner (who is not survived at the time of his or her death by a widow or a child) who are entitled to the payment of benefits under paragraph (5) of section 921(c) of this title, or in the case of the dependent surviving brother(s) or sister(s) of a miner (who is not survived at the time of his or her death by a widow, child, or parent) who are entitled to the payment of benefits under paragraph (5) of section 921(c) of this title, benefits shall be paid under this part to such parent(s), or to such brother(s), or sister(s), at the rate specified in paragraph (3) (as if such parent(s) or such brother(s) or sister(s), were the children of such miner). In determining for purposes of this paragraph whether a claimant bears the relationship as the miner's parent, brother, or sister, the Secretary shall apply legal standards consistent with those applicable to relationship determination under title II of the Social Security Act (42 U.S.C. 401 et seq.). No benefits to a sister or brother shall be payable under this paragraph for any month beginning with the month in which he or she receives support from his or her spouse, or marries. Benefits shall be payable under this paragraph to a brother only if he is -

(1)(A) under eighteen years of age, or

(B) under a disability as defined in section 223(d) of the Social Security Act 423(d)) which began before the age specified in section 202(d)(1)(B)(ii) of such Act (42 U.S.C. 402(d)(1)(B)(ii)), or in the case of a student, before he ceased to be a student, or

(C) a student as defined in section 902(g) of this title; or

(2) who is, at the time of the miner's death, disabled as determined in accordance with section 223(d) of the Social Security Act (42 U.S.C. 423(d)), during such disability. Any benefit under this paragraph for a month prior to the month in which a claim for such benefit is filed shall be reduced to any extent that may be necessary, so that it will not render erroneous any benefit which, before the filing of such claim, the Secretary has certified for payment for such prior months. As used in this paragraph, 'dependent' means that during the one year period prior to and ending with such miner's death, such parent, brother, or sister was living in the miner's household, and was, during such period, totally dependent on the miner for support. Proof of such support shall be filed by such claimant within two years after May 1972, or within two years after the miner's death, whichever is the later. Any such proof which is filed after the expiration of such period shall be deemed to have been filed within such period if it is shown to the

satisfaction of the Secretary that there was good cause for failure to file such proof within such period. The determination of what constitutes 'living in the miner's household', 'totally dependent upon the miner for support,' and 'good cause,' shall for purposes of this paragraph be made in accordance with regulations of the Secretary. Benefit payments under this paragraph to a parent, brother, or sister, shall be reduced by the amount by which such payments would be reduced on account of excess earnings of such parent, brother, or sister, respectively, under section 203(b)-(l) of the Social Security Act (42 U.S.C. 403(b)-(l)), as if the benefit under this paragraph were a benefit under section 202 of such Act (42 U.S.C. 402).

. . . .

(6) If an individual's benefits would be increased under paragraph (4) of this subsection because he or she has one or more dependents, and it appears to the Secretary that it would be in the interest of any such dependent to have the amount of such increase in benefits (to the extent attributable to such dependent) certified to a person other than such individual, then the Secretary may, under regulations prescribed by him, certify the amount of such increase in benefits (to the extent so attributable) not to such individual but directly to such dependent or to another person for the use and benefit of such dependent; and any payment made under this clause, if otherwise valid under this subchapter, shall be a complete settlement and satisfaction of all claims, rights, and interests in and to such payment.

(b) Reduction of benefits

Notwithstanding subsection (a) of this section, benefit payments under this section to a miner or his widow, child, parent, brother, or sister shall be reduced, on a monthly or other appropriate basis, by an amount equal to any payment received by such miner or his widow, child, parent, brother, or sister under the workmen's compensation, unemployment compensation, or disability insurance laws of his State on account of the disability of such miner due to pneumoconiosis, and the amount by which such payment would be reduced on account of excess earnings of such miner under section 203(b) through (l) of the Social Security Act (42 U.S.C. 403(b) to (l)) if the amount paid were a benefit payable under section 202 of such Act (42 U.S.C. 402). This part shall not be considered a workmen's compensation law or plan for purposes of section 224 of such Act (42 U.S.C. 424a).

(c) Reporting of income

Benefits payable under this part shall be deemed not to be income for purposes of the Internal Revenue Code of 1986.

SEC. 923. FILING OF NOTICE OF CLAIM

(a) Promulgation of regulations; time requirement

Except as otherwise provided in section 924 of this title, no payment of benefits shall be made under this part except pursuant to a claim filed therefor on or before December 31, 1973, in such manner, in such form, and containing such information, as the Secretary shall by regulation prescribe.

(b) Utilization of personnel and procedures; evidence required to establish claim; medical evidence; affidavits; autopsy reports; reimbursement of expenses

In carrying out the provisions of this part, the Secretary shall to the maximum extent feasible (and consistent with the provisions of this part) utilize the personnel and procedures he uses in determining entitlement to disability insurance benefit payments under section 223 of the Social Security Act (42 U.S.C. 423), but no claim for benefits under this part shall be denied solely on the basis of the results of a chest roentgenogram. In determining the validity of claims under this part, all relevant evidence shall be considered, including, where relevant, medical tests such as blood gas studies, X-ray examination, electrocardiogram, pulmonary function studies, or physical performance tests, and any medical history, evidence submitted by the claimant's physician, or his wife's affidavits, and in the case of a deceased miner, other appropriate affidavits of persons with knowledge of the miner's physical condition, and other supportive materials. Where there is no medical or other relevant evidence in the case of a deceased miner, such affidavits, from persons not eligible for benefits in such case with respect to claims filed on or after the effective date of the Black Lung Benefits Amendments of 1981, shall be considered to be sufficient to establish that the miner was totally disabled due to pneumoconiosis or that his or her death was due to pneumoconiosis. In any case, other than that involving a claim filed on or after the effective date of the Black Lung Benefits Amendments of 1981, in which there is other evidence that a miner has a pulmonary or respiratory impairment, the Secretary shall accept a board certified or board eligible radiologist's interpretation of a chest roentgenogram which is of a quality sufficient to demonstrate the presence of pneumoconiosis submitted in support of a claim for benefits under this subchapter if such roentgenogram has been taken by a radiologist or qualified technician, except where the Secretary has reason to believe that the claim has been fraudulently represented. In order to insure that any such roentgenogram is of adequate quality to demonstrate the presence of pneumoconiosis, and in order to provide for uniform quality in the roentgenograms, the

Secretary of Labor may, by regulation, establish specific requirements for the techniques used to take roentgenograms of the chest. Unless the Secretary has good cause to believe that an autopsy report is not accurate, or that the condition of the miner is being fraudulently misrepresented, the Secretary shall accept such autopsy report concerning the presence of pneumoconiosis and the stage of advancement of pneumoconiosis. Claimants under this part shall be reimbursed for reasonable medical expenses incurred by them in establishing their claims. For purposes of determining total disability under this part, the provisions of subsections (a), (b), (c), (d), and (g) of section 221 of such Act (42 U.S.C. 421(a) to (d), (g)) shall be applicable. The provisions of sections 204, 205(a), (b), (d), (e),

(c) Filing of claim for workmen's compensation; necessity; exceptions

No claim for benefits under this section shall be considered unless the claimant has also filed a claim under the applicable State workmen's compensation law prior to or at the same time his claim was filed for benefits under this section; except that the foregoing provisions of this paragraph shall not apply in any case in which the filing of a claim under such law would clearly be futile because the period within which such a claim may be filed thereunder has expired or because pneumoconiosis is not compensable under such law, or in any other situation in which, in the opinion of the Secretary, the filing of a claim would clearly be futile.

(d) Employment termination and benefits entitlement

No miner who is engaged in coal mine employment shall (except as provided in section 921(c)(3) of this title) be entitled to any benefits under this part while so employed. Any miner who has been determined to be eligible for benefits pursuant to a claim filed while such miner was engaged in coal mine employment shall be entitled to such benefits if his or her employment terminates within one year after the date such determination becomes final.

SEC. 924. TIME FOR FILING CLAIMS

(a) Claims filed before December 31, 1973

(1) No claim for benefits under this part on account of total disability of a miner shall be considered unless it is filed on or before December 31, 1973, or, in the case of a claimant who is a widow, within six months after the death of her husband or by December 31, 1973, whichever is the later.

(2) In the case of a claim by a child this paragraph shall apply, notwithstanding any other provision of this part.

(A) If such claim is filed within six months following May 1972, and if entitlement to benefits is established pursuant to such claim, such entitlement shall be effective retroactively from December 30, 1969, or from the date such child would have been first eligible for such benefit payments had section 922(a)(3) of this title been applicable since December 30, 1969, whichever is the lesser period. If on the date such claim is filed the claimant is not eligible for benefit payments, but was eligible at any period of time during the period from December 30, 1969, to the date such claim is filed, entitlement shall be effective for the duration of eligibility during such period.

(B) If such claim is filed after six months following May 1972, and if entitlement to benefits is established pursuant to such claim, such entitlement shall be effective retroactively from a date twelve months preceding the date such claim is filed, or from the date such child would have been first eligible for such benefit payments had section 922(a)(3) of this title been applicable since December 30, 1969, whichever is the lesser period. If on the date such claim is filed the claimant is not eligible for benefit payments, but was eligible at any period of time during the period from a date twelve months preceding the date such claim is filed, to the date such claim is filed, entitlement shall be effective for the duration of eligibility during such period.

(C) No claim for benefits under this part, in the case of a claimant who is a child, shall be considered unless it is filed within six months after the death of his father or mother (whichever last occurred) or by December 31, 1973, whichever is the later.

(D) Any benefit under subparagraph (A) or (B) for a month prior to the month in which a claim is filed shall be reduced, to any extent that may be necessary, so that it will not render erroneous any benefit which, before the filing of such claim, the Secretary has certified for payment for such prior month.

(3) No claim for benefits under this part, in the case of a claimant who is a parent, brother, or sister shall be considered unless it is filed within six months after the death of the miner or by December 31, 1973, whichever is the later.

(b) Filing of claims after June 30, 1973

No benefits shall be paid under this part after December 31, 1973, if the claim therefor was filed after June 30, 1973.

(c) Effective date of claims

No benefits under this part shall be payable for any period prior to the date a claim therefor is filed.

(d) Reduction of State benefits

No benefits shall be paid under this part to the residents of any State which, after December 30, 1969, reduces the benefits payable to persons eligible to receive benefits under this part, under its State laws which are applicable to its general work force with regard to workmen's compensation, unemployment compensation, or disability insurance.

(e) Conditions upon payment

No benefits shall be payable to a widow, child, parent, brother, or sister under this part on account of the death of a miner unless

(1) benefits under this part were being paid to such miner with respect to disability due to pneumoconiosis prior to his death,

(2) the death of such miner occurred prior to January 1, 1974, or

(3) any such individual is entitled to benefits under paragraph (5) of section 921(c) of this title.

SEC. 924A. NOTIFICATION TO MINERS OF ELIGIBILITY FOR MEDICAL SERVICES AND SUPPLIES; PERIOD FOR FILING CLAIM

The Secretary of Health and Human Services shall notify each miner receiving benefits under this part on account of his or her total disability who such Secretary has reason to believe became eligible for medical services and supplies on January 1, 1974, of his or her possible eligibility for such benefits. Where such Secretary so notifies a miner, the period during which he or she may file a claim for medical services and supplies under part C of this subchapter shall not terminate before six months after such notification is made.

943. Black lung insurance program

(a) Authorization to establish and carry out

The Secretary is authorized to establish and carry out a black lung insurance program which will enable operators of coal mines to purchase insurance covering their obligations under section 932 of this title.

(b) Non-availability of other insurance coverage

The Secretary may exercise his or her authority under this section only if, and to the extent that, insurance coverage is not otherwise available, at reasonable cost, to operators of coal mines.

(c) Agreements with coal mine operators; reinsurance agreements

(1) The Secretary may enter into agreements with operators of coal mines who may be liable for the payment of benefits under section 932 of this title, under which the Black Lung Compensation Insurance Fund established under subsection (a) of this section (hereinafter in this section referred to as the 'insurance fund') shall assume all or part of the liability of such operator in return for the payment of premiums to the insurance fund, and on such terms and conditions as will fully protect the financial solvency of the insurance fund. During any period in which such agreement is in effect the operator shall be deemed in compliance with the requirements of section 933 of this title with respect to the risks covered by such agreement.

(2) The Secretary may also enter into reinsurance agreements with one or more insurers or pools of insurers under which, in return for the payment of premiums to the insurance fund, and on such terms and conditions as will fully protect the financial solvency of the insurance fund, the insurance fund shall provide reinsurance coverage for benefits required to be paid under section 932 of this title.

(d) Terms and conditions of insurability

The Secretary may by regulation provide for general terms and conditions of insurability as applicable to operators of coal mines or insurers eligible for insurance or reinsurance under this section, including -

(1) the types, classes, and locations of operators or facilities which shall be eligible for such insurance or reinsurance;

(2) the classification, limitation, and rejection of any operator or facility which may be advisable;

(3) appropriate premiums for different classifications of operators or facilities;

(4) appropriate loss deductibles;

(5) experience rating; and

(6) any other terms and conditions relating to insurance or reinsurance coverage or exclusion which may be appropriate to carry out the purposes of this section.

(e) Premium schedule studies and investigations

The Secretary may undertake and carry out such studies and investigations, and receive or exchange such information, as may be necessary to formulate a premium schedule which will enable the insurance and reinsurance authorized by this section to be provided on a basis which is (1) in accordance with accepted actuarial principles; and (2) fair and equitable.

(f) Regulations relating to premium rates

(1) On the basis of estimates made by the Secretary in formulating a premium schedule under subsection (e) of this section, and such other information as may be available, the Secretary shall from time to time prescribe by regulation the chargeable premium rates for types and classes of insurers, operators of coal mines, and facilities for which insurance or reinsurance coverage shall be available under this section and the terms and conditions under which, and the area within which, such insurance or reinsurance shall be available and such rates shall apply.

(2) Such premium rates shall be (A) based on a consideration of the risks involved, taking into account differences, if any, in risks based on location, type of operations, facilities, type of coal, experience, and any other matter which may be considered under accepted actuarial principles; and (B) adequate, on the basis of accepted actuarial principles, to provide reserves for anticipated losses.

(3) All premiums received by the Secretary shall be paid into the insurance fund.

(g) Black Lung Compensation Insurance Fund

(1) The Secretary may establish in the Department of Labor a Black Lung Compensation Insurance Fund which shall be available, without fiscal year limitation -

(A) to pay claims of miners for benefits covered by insurance or reinsurance issued under this section;

(B) to pay the administrative expenses of carrying out the black lung compensation insurance program under this section; and

(C) to repay to the Secretary of the Treasury such sums as may be borrowed in accordance with the authority provided in subsection (i) of this section.

(2) The insurance fund shall be credited with—

(A) premiums, fees, or other charges which may be collected in connection with insurance or reinsurance coverage provided under this section;

(B) such amounts as may be advanced to the insurance fund from appropriations in order to maintain the insurance fund in an operative condition adequate to meet its liabilities; and

(C) income which may be earned on investments of the insurance fund pursuant to paragraph (3).

(3) If, after all outstanding current obligations of the insurance fund have been liquidated and any outstanding amounts which may have been advanced to the insurance fund from appropriations authorized under subsection (i) of this section have been credited to the appropriation from which advanced, the Secretary determines that the moneys of the insurance fund are in excess of current needs, he or she may request the investment of such amounts as he or she deems advisable by the Secretary of the Treasury in public debt securities with maturities suitable for the needs of the insurance fund and bearing interest at prevailing market rates.

(h) Annual report to Congress

The Secretary shall report to the Congress not later than the first day of April of each year on the financial condition of the insurance fund and the results of the operations of the insurance fund during the preceding fiscal year and on its expected condition and operations during the fiscal year in which the report is made.

(i) Authorization of appropriations

There are authorized to be appropriated to the insurance fund, as repayable advances, such sums as may be necessary to meet obligations incurred under subsection (g) of this section. All such sums shall remain available without fiscal year limitation. Advances made pursuant to this subsection shall be repaid, with interest, to the general fund of the Treasury when the Secretary determines that moneys are available in the insurance fund for such repayments. Interest on such advances shall be computed in the same manner as provided in subsection (b)(2) of section 934a of this title.

APPENDIX 6:
THE FEDERAL EMPLOYMENT LIABILITY ACT
[45 U.S.C. §§ 51 – 60]

§ 51. LIABILITY OF COMMON CARRIERS BY RAILROAD, IN INTERSTATE OR FOREIGN COMMERCE, FOR INJURIES TO EMPLOYEES FROM NEGLIGENCE; EMPLOYEE DEFINED

Every common carrier by railroad while engaging in commerce between any of the several States or Territories, or between any of the States and Territories, or between the District of Columbia and any of the States or Territories, or between the District of Columbia or any of the States or Territories and any foreign nation or nations, shall be liable in damages to any person suffering injury while he is employed by such carrier in such commerce, or, in case of the death of such employee, to his or her personal representative, for the benefit of the surviving widow or husband and children of such employee; and, if none, then of such employee's parents; and, if none, then of the next of kin dependent upon such employee, for such injury or death resulting in whole or in part from the negligence of any of the officers, agents, or employees of such carrier, or by reason of any defect or insufficiency, due to its negligence, in its cars, engines, appliances, machinery, track, roadbed, works, boats, wharves, or other equipment.

Any employee of a carrier, any part of whose duties as such employee shall be the furtherance of interstate or foreign commerce; or shall, in any way directly or closely and substantially, affect such commerce as above set forth shall, for the purposes of this chapter, be considered as being employed by such carrier in such commerce and shall be considered as entitled to the benefits of this chapter.

§ 52. CARRIERS IN TERRITORIES OR OTHER POSSESSIONS OF UNITED STATES

Every common carrier by railroad in the Territories, the District of Columbia, the Panama Canal Zone, or other possessions of the United States shall be liable in damages to any person suffering injury while he is employed by such carrier in any of said jurisdictions, or, in case of the death of such employee, to his or her personal representative, for the benefit of the surviving widow or husband and children of such employee; and, if none, then of such employee's parents; and, if none, then of the next of kin dependent upon such employee, for such injury or death resulting in whole or in part from the negligence of any of the officers, agents, or employees of such carrier, or by reason of any defect or insufficiency, due to its negligence, in its cars, engines, appliances, machinery, track, roadbed, works, boats, wharves, or other equipment.

§ 53. CONTRIBUTORY NEGLIGENCE; DIMINUTION OF DAMAGES

In all actions on and after April 22, 1908 brought against any such common carrier by railroad under or by virtue of any of the provisions of this chapter to recover damages for personal injuries to an employee, or where such injuries have resulted in his death, the fact that the employee may have been guilty of contributory negligence shall not bar a recovery, but the damages shall be diminished by the jury in proportion to the amount of negligence attributable to such employee: Provided, That no such employee who may be injured or killed shall be held to have been guilty of contributory negligence in any case where the violation by such common carrier of any statute enacted for the safety of employees contributed to the injury or death of such employee.

§ 54. ASSUMPTION OF RISKS OF EMPLOYMENT

In any action brought against any common carrier under or by virtue of any of the provisions of this chapter to recover damages for injuries to, or the death of, any of its employees, such employee shall not be held to have assumed the risks of his employment in any case where such injury or death resulted in whole or in part from the negligence of any of the officers, agents, or employees of such carrier; and no employee shall be held to have assumed the risks of his employment in any case where the violation by such common carrier of any statute enacted for the safety of employees contributed to the injury or death of such employee.

§ 54A. CERTAIN FEDERAL AND STATE REGULATIONS DEEMED STATUTORY AUTHORITY

A regulation, standard, or requirement in force, or prescribed by the Secretary of Transportation under chapter 201 of title 49 or by a State agency that is participating in investigative and surveillance activities under section 20105 of title 49, is deemed to be a statute under sections 53 and 54 of this title.

§ 55. CONTRACT, RULE, REGULATION, OR DEVICE EXEMPTING FROM LIABILITY; SET-OFF

Any contract, rule, regulation, or device whatsoever, the purpose or intent of which shall be to enable any common carrier to exempt itself from any liability created by this chapter, shall to that extent be void: Provided, That in any action brought against any such common carrier under or by virtue of any of the provisions of this chapter, such common carrier may set off therein any sum it has contributed or paid to any insurance, relief benefit, or indemnity that may have been paid to the injured employee or the person entitled thereto on account of the injury or death for which said action was brought.

§ 56. ACTIONS; LIMITATION; CONCURRENT JURISDICTION OF COURTS

No action shall be maintained under this chapter unless commenced within three years from the day the cause of action accrued.

Under this chapter an action may be brought in a district court of the United States, in the district of the residence of the defendant, or in which the cause of action arose, or in which the defendant shall be doing business at the time of commencing such action. The jurisdiction of the courts of the United States under this chapter shall be concurrent with that of the courts of the several States.

§ 57. WHO INCLUDED IN TERM "COMMON CARRIER"

The term "common carrier" as used in this chapter shall include the receiver or receivers or other persons or corporations charged with the duty of the management and operation of the business of a common carrier.

§ 58. DUTY OR LIABILITY OF COMMON CARRIERS AND RIGHTS OF EMPLOYEES UNDER OTHER ACTS NOT IMPAIRED

Nothing in this chapter shall be held to limit the duty or liability of common carriers or to impair the rights of their employees under any other Act or Acts of Congress.

§ 59. SURVIVAL OF RIGHT OF ACTION OF PERSON INJURED

Any right of action given by this chapter to a person suffering injury shall survive to his or her personal representative, for the benefit of the surviving widow or husband and children of such employee, and, if none, then of such employee's parents; and, if none, then of the next of kin dependent upon such employee, but in such cases there shall be only one recovery for the same injury.

§ 60. PENALTY FOR SUPPRESSION OF VOLUNTARY INFORMATION INCIDENT TO ACCIDENTS; SEPARABILITY

Any contract, rule, regulation, or device whatsoever, the purpose, intent, or effect of which shall be to prevent employees of any common carrier from furnishing voluntarily information to a person in interest as to the facts incident to the injury or death of any employee, shall be void, and whoever, by threat, intimidation, order, rule, contract, regulation, or device whatsoever, shall attempt to prevent any person from furnishing voluntarily such information to a person in interest, or whoever discharges or otherwise disciplines or attempts to discipline any employee for furnishing voluntarily such information to a person in interest, shall, upon conviction thereof, be punished by a fine of not more than $1,000 or imprisoned for not more than one year, or by both such fine and imprisonment, for each offense: Provided, That nothing herein contained shall be construed to void any contract, rule, or regulation with respect to any information contained in the files of the carrier, or other privileged or confidential reports.

If any provision of this chapter is declared unconstitutional or the applicability thereof to any person or circumstances is held invalid, the validity of the remainder of the chapter and the applicability of such provision to other persons and circumstances shall not be affected thereby.

APPENDIX 7:
THE MERCHANT MARINE ACT [46 U.S.C. § 688]

§ 688. RECOVERY FOR INJURY TO OR DEATH OF SEAMAN

(a) Application of railway employee statutes; jurisdiction

Any seaman who shall suffer personal injury in the course of his employment may, at his election, maintain an action for damages at law, with the right of trial by jury, and in such action all statutes of the United States modifying or extending the common-law right or remedy in cases of personal injury to railway employees shall apply; and in case of the death of any seaman as a result of any such personal injury the personal representative of such seaman may maintain an action for damages at law with the right of trial by jury, and in such action all statutes of the United States conferring or regulating the right of action for death in the case of railway employees shall be applicable. Jurisdiction in such actions shall be under the court of the district in which the defendant employer resides or in which his principal office is located.

(b) Limitation for certain aliens; applicability in lieu of other remedy

(1) No action may be maintained under subsection (a) of this section or under any other maritime law of the United States for maintenance and cure or for damages for the injury or death of a person who was not a citizen or permanent resident alien of the United States at the time of the incident giving rise to the action if the incident occurred—

(A) while that person was in the employ of an enterprise engaged in the exploration, development, or production of offshore mineral or energy resources—including but not limited to drilling, mapping, surveying, diving, pipe laying, maintaining, repairing, constructing, or transporting supplies, equipment or personnel, but not including transporting those resources by a vessel constructed or adapted primarily to carry oil in bulk in the cargo spaces; and

(B) in the territorial waters or waters overlaying the continental shelf of a nation other than the United States, its territories, or possessions. As used in this paragraph, the term "continental shelf" has the meaning stated in article I of the 1958 Convention on the Continental Shelf.

(2) The provisions of paragraph (1) of this subsection shall not be applicable if the person bringing the action establishes that no remedy was available to that person—

(A) under the laws of the nation asserting jurisdiction over the area in which the incident occurred; or

(B) under the laws of the nation in which, at the time of the incident, the person for whose injury or death a remedy is sought maintained citizenship or residency.

APPENDIX 8:
DIRECTORY OF OCCUPATIONAL SAFETY AND HEALTH ADMINISTRATION OFFICES

STATE	ADDRESS	TELEPHONE NUMBER	FAX NUMBER
Alabama	432 Martha Parham West P.O. Box 870388 Tuscaloosa, AL 35487	205-348-7138	205-348-3049
Alaska	3301 Eagle Street P.O. Box 107022 Anchorage, AL 99510	907-269-4954	907-269-4950
Arizona	800 West Washington Phoenix, AZ 85007	602-542-5795	602-542-1614
Arkansas	10421 West Markham Little Rock, AR 72205	501-682-4522	501-682-4532
California	455 Golden Gate Avenue Room 5246 San Francisco, CA 94102	415-703-4441	415-972-8513
Colorado	110 Veterinary Science Building Fort Collins, CO 80523	303-491-6151	303-491-7778
Connecticut	200 Folly Brook Boulevard Wethersfield, CT 06109	203-566-4550	203-566-6916
Delaware	4425 Market Street Wilmington, DE 19802	302-761-8219	302-761-6601
District of Columbia	950 Upshur Street N.W. Washington, DC 20011	202-576-6339	202-576-7282
Florida	2002 St. Augustine Road Building E, Suite 45 Tallahassee, FL 32399	904-488-3044	904-922-4538

STATE	ADDRESS	TELEPHONE NUMBER	FAX NUMBER
Georgia	Georgia Institute of Technology O'Keefe Building Room 22 Atlanta, GA 30332	404-894-2646	404-894-8275
Hawaii	830 Punchbowl Street Honolulu, HI 96813	808-586-9100	808-586-9099
Idaho	1910 University Drive Boise, ID 83725	208-385-3283	208-385-4411
Illinois	State of Illinois Center 100 West Randolph Street Suite 3-400 Chicago, IL 60601	312-814-2337	312-814-7238
Indiana	402 West Washington, Indianapolis, IN 46204	317-232-2688	317-2320748
Iowa	1000 East Grand Avenue, Des Moines, IA 50319	515-281-5352	515-281-4831
Kansas	512 South West 6th Street, Topeka, KS 66603	913-296-7476	913-206-1775
Kentucky	1049 U.S. Highway 127 South Frankfort, KY 40601	502-564-6895	502-564-4769
Louisiana	P.O. Box 94094 Baton Rouge, LA 70804	504-342-9601	504-342-5158
Maine	State House Station #82 Augusta, ME 04333	207-624-6460	207-624-6449
Maryland	501 St. Paul Place 3rd Floor Baltimore, MD 21202	410-333-4210	410-333-8308
Massachusetts	1001 Watertown Street West Newton Massachusetts 02165	617-969-7177	617-969-4581
Michigan	3423 North Martin Luther King Boulevard Lansing, MI 48909	517-335-8250	517-335-8010
Minnesota	443 Lafayette Road Saint Paul, MN 55155	612-297-2393	612-297-1953
Mississippi	2906 North State Street Suite 201 Jackson, MS 39216	601-987-3981	601-987-3890

STATE	ADDRESS	TELEPHONE NUMBER	FAX NUMBER
Missouri	3315 West Truman Boulevard Jefferson City, MO 65109	573-751-3403	573-751-3721
Montana	P.O. Box 1728 Helena, MT 59624	406-444-6418	406-444-4140
Nebraska	State Office Building 301 Centennial Mall South Lower Level Lincoln, NE 68509	402-471-4717	402-471-5039
Nevada	2500 West Washington, Las Vegas, NV 89106	702486-5016	702-486-5331
New Hampshire	6 Hazen Drive Concord, NH 03301	603-271-2024	603-271-2667
New Jersey	Station Plaza 4, CN953 22 South Clinton Avenue Trenton, NJ 08625	609-292-2424	609-292-4409
New Mexico	525 Camino de Los Marquez, Suite 3 P.O. Box 26110 Santa Fe, NM 87502	505-827-4230	505-827-4422
New York	State Office Campus Building 12, Room 457 Albany, NY 12240	518-457-2481	518-457-5545
North Carolina	319 Chapanoke Road Suite 105 Raleigh, NC 27603	919-662-4644	919-662-4671
North Dakota	1200 Missouri Avenue Room 304 Bismarck, ND 58506	701-328-5188	701-328-5200
Ohio	145 S. Front Street Columbus, OH 43216	614-644-2246	614-644-3133
Oklahoma	4001 North Lincoln Boulevard Oklahoma City, OK 73105	405-528-1500	405-528-5751
Oregon	350 Winter Street NE Room 430 Salem, OR 97310	503-378-3272	503-378-5729
Pennsylvania	Indiana University of Pennsylvania Safety Sciences Department 205 Uhler Hall Indiana, PA 15705	412-357-2561	412-357-2385

STATE	ADDRESS	TELEPHONE NUMBER	FAX NUMBER
Rhode Island	3 Capital Hill Providence, RI 02908	401-277-2438	401-277-6953
South Carolina	3600 Forest Drive P.O. Box 11329 Columbia, SC 29211	803-734-9614	803-734-9741
South Dakota	South Dakota State University, West Hall Box 510 907 Harvey Dunn Street Brookings, SD 57007	605-688-4101	605-688-6290
Tennessee	710 James Robertson Parkway, 3rd Floor Nashville, TN 37243	615-741-7036	615-741-3325
Texas	4000 South I H 35 Austin, TX 78704	512-440-3834	512-440-3831
Utah	160 East 300 South Salt Lake City, UT 84114	801-530-6868	801-530-6992
Vermont	National Life Building, Drawer 20 Montpelier, VT 05602	802-828-2765	802-828-2748
Virginia	13 South 13th Street Richmond, VA 23219	804-786-6539	804-786-8418
Washington	P.O. Box 44643 Olympia, WA 98504	360-902-5638	360-902-5459
West Virginia	Capitol Complex Building #3 1800 East Washington Street, Room 319 Charleston, WV 25305	304-558-7890	304-558-3797
Wisconsin	1414 East Washington Avenue Madison, WI 53703	608-266-8579	608-266-9711
Wyoming	Herschler Building 2 East 122 West 25th Street Cheyenne, WY 82008	307-777-7786	307-777-3646

APPENDIX 9:
NOTICE TO OSHA OF ALLEGED
SAFETY OR HEALTH HAZARDS

U. S. Department of Labor
Occupational Safety and Health Administration

Notice of Alleged Safety or Health Hazards

For the General Public:

This form is provided for the assistance of any complainant and is not intended to constitute the exclusive means by which a complaint may be registered with the U.S. Department of Labor.

Sec 8(f)(1) of the Williams-Steiger Occupational Safety and Health Act, 29 U.S.C. 651, provides as follows: Any employees or representative of employees who believe that a violation of a safety or health standard exists that threatens physical harm, or that an imminent danger exists, may request an inspection by giving notice to the Secretary or his authorized representative of such violation or danger. Any such notice shall be reduced to writing, shall set forth with reasonable particularity the grounds for the notice, and shall be signed by the employee or representative of employees, and a copy shall be provided the employer or his agent no later than at the time of inspection, except that, upon request of the person giving such notice, his name and the names of individual employees referred to therein shall not appear in such copy or on any record published, released, or made available pursuant to subsection (g) of this section. If upon receipt of such notification the Secretary determines there are reasonable grounds to believe that such violation or danger exists, he shall make a special inspection in accordance with the provisions of this section as soon as practicable to determine if such violation or danger exists. If the Secretary determines there are no reasonable grounds to believe that a violation or danger exists, he shall notify the employees or representative of the employees in writing of such determination.

NOTE: Section 11(c) of the Act provides explicit protection for employees exercising their rights, including making safety and health complaints.

For Federal Employees:

This report format is provided to assist Federal employees or authorized representatives in registering a report of unsafe or unhealthful working conditions with the U.S.Department of Labor.

The Secretary of Labor may conduct unannounced inspection of agency workplaces when deemed necessary if an agency does not have occupational safety and health committees established in accordance with Subpart F, 29 CFR 1960; or in response to the reports of unsafe or unhealthful working conditions upon request of such agency committees under Sec. 1-3, Executive Order 12196; or in the case of a report of imminent danger when such a committee has not responded to the report as required in Sec. 1-201(h).

INSTRUCTIONS:

Open the form and complete the front page as accurately and completely as possible. Describe each hazard you think exists in as much detail as you can. If the hazards described in your complaint are not all in the same area, please identify where each hazard can be found at the worksite. If there is any particular evidence that supports your suspicion that a hazard exists (for instance, a recent accident or physical symptoms of employees at your site) include the information in your description. If you need more space than is provided on the form, continue on any other sheet of paper.

After you have completed the form, return it to your local OSHA office.

NOTE: It is unlawful to make any false statement, representation or certification in any document filed pursuant to the Occupational Safety and Health Act of 1970. Violations can be punished by a fine of not more than $10,000. or by imprisonment of not more than six months, or by both. (Section 17(g))

Public reporting burden for this voluntary collection of information is estimated to vary from 15 to 25 minutes per response with an average of 17 minutes per response, including the time for reviewing instructions, searching existing data sources, gathering and maintaining the data needed, and completing and reviewing the collection of information. An Agency may not conduct or sponsor, and persons are not required to respond to the collection of information unless it displays a valid OMB Control Number. Send comment regarding this burden estimate or any other aspect of this collection of information, including suggestions for reducing this burden to the Directorate of Enforcement Programs, Department of Labor, Room N-3119, 200 Constitution Ave., NW, Washington, DC; 20210.

OMB Approval# 1218-0064; Expires: 2-29-2008

Do not send the completed form to this Office.

U. S. Department of Labor
Occupational Safety and Health Administration

Notice of Alleged Safety or Health Hazards

	Complaint Number	

Establishment Name				
Site Address				
	Site Phone		Site FAX	
Mailing Address				
	Mail Phone		Mail FAX	
Management Official			Telephone	
Type of Business				

HAZARD DESCRIPTION/LOCATION. Describe briefly the hazard(s) which you believe exist. Include the approximate number of employees exposed to or threatened by each hazard. Specify the particular building or worksite where the alleged violation exists.

Has this condition been brought to the attention of:	☐ Employer ☐ Other Government Agency(specify)
Please Indicate Your Desire:	☐ Do NOT reveal my name to my Employer ☐ My name may be revealed to the Employer
The Undersigned believes that a violation of an Occupational Safety or Health standard exists which is a job safety or health hazard at the establishment named on this form.	(Mark "X" in ONE box) ☐ Employee ☐ Federal Safety and Health Committee ☐ Representative of Employees ☐ Other (specify)

Complainant Name		Telephone	
Address(Street,City,State,Zip)			
Signature		Date	

If you are an authorized representative of employees affected by this complaint, please state the name of the organization that you represent and your title:

Organization Name: Your Title:

APPENDIX 10:
WORKERS' COMPENSATION INSURANCE COVERAGE REQUIREMENTS FOR AGRICULTURAL AND DOMESTIC WORKERS

STATE	AGRICULTURAL WORKERS	DOMESTIC WORKERS
Alabama	voluntary	voluntary
Alaska	compulsory	compulsory
Arizona	compulsory	voluntary
Arkansas	voluntary	voluntary
California	compulsory	compulsory
Colorado	compulsory	compulsory
Connecticut	compulsory	compulsory
Delaware	elective	compulsory
District of Columbia	compulsory	compulsory
Florida	compulsory	voluntary
Georgia	elective	voluntary
Hawaii	compulsory	compulsory
Idaho	compulsory	voluntary
Illinois	compulsory	compulsory
Indiana	voluntary	voluntary
Iowa	compulsory	compulsory
Kansas	voluntary	compulsory
Kentucky	voluntary	compulsory
Louisiana	compulsory	excluded
Maine	compulsory	voluntary

STATE	AGRICULTURAL WORKERS	DOMESTIC WORKERS
Maryland	compulsory	compulsory
Massachusetts	compulsory	compulsory
Michigan	compulsory	compulsory
Minnesota	compulsory	compulsory
Mississippi	voluntary	voluntary
Missouri	elective	excluded
Montana	compulsory	voluntary
Nebraska	elective	voluntary
Nevada	voluntary	excluded
New Hampshire	compulsory	compulsory
New Jersey	elective	compulsory
New Mexico	voluntary	voluntary
New York	compulsory	compulsory
North Carolina	compulsory	compulsory
North Dakota	voluntary	voluntary
Ohio	compulsory	compulsory
Oklahoma	compulsory	compulsory
Oregon	compulsory	voluntary
Pennsylvania	compulsory	voluntary
Rhode Island	compulsory	voluntary
South Carolina	voluntary	compulsory
South Dakota	compulsory	compulsory
Tennessee	voluntary	voluntary
Texas	elective	voluntary
Utah	compulsory	compulsory
Vermont	compulsory	voluntary
Virginia	compulsory	excluded
Washington	compulsory	compulsory
West Virginia	compulsory	voluntary
Wisconsin	compulsory	voluntary
Wyoming	compulsory	excluded

APPENDIX 11:
DIRECTORY OF STATE WORKERS' COMPENSATION BOARDS

STATE	ADDRESS	TELEPHONE
ALABAMA	Workers' Compensation Division Department of Industrial Relations Industrial Relations Building Montgomery, AL 36131	(334) 242-2868
ALASKA	Workers' Compensation Division Department of Labor 1111 West 8th Street, Suite 307 P.O. Box 25512 Juneau, AK 99802-5512	(907) 465-2790
ARIZONA	Industrial Commission 800 West Washington Street, P. O. Box 19070, Phoenix, AZ 85005-9070	(602) 542-4411
ARKANSAS	Workers' Compensation Commission 4th and Spring Streets P. O. Box 950 Little Rock, AR 72203-9050	(501) 682-3930
CALIFORNIA	Division of Workers' Compensation 45 Fremont Street, Suite 3160 P. O. Box 420603 San Francisco, CA 94142	(415) 975-0700
COLORADO	Division of Workers' Compensation 1515 Arapahoe Street Denver, CO 80202	(303) 575-8700
CONNECTICUT	Workers' Compensation Commission 21 Oak Street Hartford,CT 06106	(860) 493-1500
DELAWARE	Industrial Accident Board 4425 N. Market Street, 3rd Floor Wilmington, DE 19802	(302) 761-8200

STATE	ADDRESS	TELEPHONE
DISTRICT OF COLUMBIA	Office of Workers' Compensation 1200 Upshur St. NW, 2nd Floor Washington, DC 20011	(202) 576-6265
FLORIDA	Division of Workers' Compensation 301 Forrest Building 2728 Centerview Drive Tallahassee, FL 32399-0680	(904) 488-2514
GEORGIA	Board of Workers' Compensation 270 Peachtree Street NW Atlanta, GA 30303-1205	(404) 656-3875
HAWAII	Disability Compensation Division Department of Labor and Industrial Relations 830 Punchbowl Street, Room 211 P. O. Box 3769, Honolulu, HI 96812	(808) 586-9151
IDAHO	Industrial Commission Statehouse Mail 317 Main Street P. O. Box 83720 Boise, ID 83720-0041	(208) 334-6000
ILLINOIS	Industrial Commission, 100 West Randolph Street, Suite 8-200, Chicago, IL 60601	(312) 814-6500
INDIANA	Workers' Compensation Board Room W-196 402 West Washington Street Indianapolis, IN 46204	(317) 232-3808
IOWA	Division of Industrial Services Iowa Workforce Development 1000 East Grand Avenue Des Moines, IA 50319	(515) 281-5934
KANSAS	Division of Workers' Compensation Department of Human Resources, 800 SW Jackson Street, Suite 600 Topeka, KS 66612-1227	(913) 296-3441
KENTUCKY	Department of Workers Claims 1270 Louisville Road Perimeter Park West, Bldg. C Frankfort, KY 40601	(502) 564-5550
LOUISIANA	Office of Workers' Compensation, 1001 North 23rd Street P. O. Box 94040 Baton Rouge, LA 70802-9040	(504) 342-7555
MAINE	Workers' Compensation Board 27 State House Station Augusta, ME 04333	(207) 287-3751

STATE	ADDRESS	TELEPHONE
MARYLAND	Workers' Compensation Commission 6 North Liberty Street Baltimore, MD 21201-3785	(410) 767-0900
MASSACHUSETTS	Dept. of Industrial Accidents 600 Washington Street, 7th Floor Boston, MA 02111	(617) 727-4900
MICHIGAN	Bureau of Workers' Disability Compensation 201 North Washington Square P. O. Box 30016 Lansing, MI 48909	(517) 322-1296
MINNESOTA	Division of Workers' Compensation Department of Labor and Industry 443 Lafayette Road North St. Paul, MN 55155-4319	(612) 296-6490
MISSISSIPPI	Workers' Compensation Commission 1428 Lakeland Drive P. O. Box 5300 Jackson, MS 39296-5300	(601) 987-4200
MISSOURI	Division of Workers' Compensation Department of Labor and Industrial Relations P. O. Box 58 Jefferson City, MO 65102	(573) 751-4231
MONTANA	Employment Relations Division Department of Labor and Industry 1805 Prospect Avenue P. O. Box 8011 Helena, MT 59604-8011	(406) 444-6530
NEBRASKA	Workers' Compensation Court Capitol Building P. O. Box 98908 Lincoln, NE 68509-8908	(402) 471-2568
NEVADA	State Industrial Insurance System 515 East Musser Street Carson City, NV 89714	(702) 687-5220
NEW HAMPSHIRE	Workers' Compensation Division Department of Labor 95 Pleasant Street Concord, NH 03301	(603) 271-3176
NEW JERSEY	Division of Workers' Compensation Department of Labor, C. N. 381 Trenton, NJ 08625-0381	(609) 292-2414

STATE	ADDRESS	TELEPHONE
NEW MEXICO	Workers' Compensation Admin. 2410 Centre Drive SE P. O. Box 27198 Albuquerque, NM 87125-7198	(505) 841-6000
NEW YORK	Workers' Compensation Board 100 Broadway-Menands Albany, NY 12241	(518) 474-6670
NORTH CAROLINA	Industrial Commission Dobbs Building 430 North Salisbury Street Raleigh, NC 27611	(919) 733-4820
NORTH DAKOTA	Workers' Compensation Bureau 500 East Front Avenue Bismarck, ND 58504-5685	(701) 328-3800
OHIO	Bureau of Workers' Compensation 30 West Spring Street Columbus, OH 43266-0581	(614) 466-8751
OKLAHOMA	Workers' Compensation Court 1915 North Stiles Avenue Oklahoma City, OK 73105-4904	(405) 557-7600
OREGON	Workers' Compensation Division 350 Winter Street NE, Salem, OR 97310	(503) 945-7881
PENNSYLVANIA	Bureau of Workers' Compensation Department of Labor and Industr 1171 So. Cameron Street, Rm. 103 Harrisburg, PA 17104-2501	(717) 783-5421
PUERTO RICO	Industrial Commission G.P.O. Box 364466 San Juan, PR 00936-4466	(809) 783-2028
RHODE ISLAND	Division of Workers' Compensation Department of Labor 610 Manton Avenue P.O. Box 3500 Providence, RI 02909	(401) 457-1800
SOUTH CAROLINA	Workers' Compensation Commission 1612 Marion Street P. O. Box 1715 Columbia, SC 29202-1715	(803) 737-5700
SOUTH DAKOTA	Division of Labor & Management Department of Labor 700 Governors Dr., Kneip Bldg. Pierre, SD 57501-2291	(605) 773-3681

STATE	ADDRESS	TELEPHONE
TENNESSEE	Division of Workers' Compensation Department of Labor Gateway Plaza, 2nd Floor 710 James Robertson Parkway Nashville,. TN 37243-0661	(615) 741-2395
TEXAS	Workers' Compensation Commission Southfield Building 4000 South IH-35 Austin, TX 78704-7491	(512) 448-7900
UTAH	Industrial Accident Division Industrial Commission 160 East 300 South, 3rd Floor P. O. Box 146610, Salt Lake City, UT 84114-6610	(800) 530-5090
VERMONT	Workers' Compensation Board National Life Bldg. Montpelier, VT 05620	(802) 828-2286
VIRGINIA	Worker's Compensation Board 1000 DMV Drive Richmond, VA 23220	(804) 367-8699
WASHINGTON	Workers' Compensation Trust 601 McPhee Rd SW Olympia, WA 98502	(360) 586-0441
WEST VIRGINIA	Worker's Compensation Division 4700 Maccorkle Ave. Charleston, WV 25304	(304) 926-3400
WISCONSIN	Worker's Compensation Division 201 E. Washington Ave. Madison, WI 53703	(608) 266-1340
WYOMING	Division of Worker's Compensation 1510 E. Persing Blvd. Cheyenne, WY 82002	(307) 777-7441

APPENDIX 12:
TYPE OF INSURANCE REQUIRED UNDER STATE WORKERS' COMPENSATION LAWS

STATE	TYPE OF LAW	STATE FUND	PRIVATE CARRIER	SELF-INSURANCE
Alabama	compulsory	no	yes	yes
Alaska	compulsory	no	yes	yes
Arizona	compulsory	competitive	yes	yes
Arkansas	compulsory	no	yes	yes
California	compulsory	competitive	yes	yes
Colorado	compulsory	competitive	yes	yes
Connecticut	compulsory	no	yes	yes
Delaware	compulsory	no	yes	yes
District of Columbia	compulsory	no	yes	yes
Florida	compulsory	no	yes	yes
Georgia	compulsory	no	yes	yes
Hawaii	compulsory	competitive	yes	yes
Idaho	compulsory	competitive	yes	yes
Illinois	compulsory	no	yes	yes
Indiana	compulsory	no	yes	yes
Iowa	compulsory	no	yes	yes
Kansas	compulsory	no	yes	yes
Kentucky	compulsory	competitive	yes	yes
Louisiana	compulsory	competitive	yes	yes
Maine	compulsory	competitive	yes	yes
Maryland	compulsory	competitive	yes	yes

STATE	TYPE OF LAW	STATE FUND	PRIVATE CARRIER	SELF-INSURANCE
Massachusetts	compulsory	no	yes	yes
Michigan	compulsory	no	yes	yes
Minnesota	compulsory	competitive	yes	yes
Mississippi	compulsory	no	yes	yes
Missouri	compulsory	no	yes	yes
Montana	compulsory	competitive	yes	yes
Nebraska	compulsory	no	yes	yes
Nevada	compulsory	no	yes	yes
New Hampshire	compulsory	no	yes	yes
New Jersey	elective	no	yes	yes
New Mexico	compulsory	competitive	yes	yes
New York	compulsory	competitive	yes	yes
North Carolina	compulsory	no	yes	yes
North Dakota	compulsory	exclusive	no	no
Ohio	compulsory	exclusive	no	yes
Oklahoma	compulsory	competitive	yes	yes
Oregon	compulsory	competitive	yes	yes
Pennsylvania	compulsory	competitive	yes	yes
Rhode Island	compulsory	competitive	yes	yes
South Carolina	compulsory	no	yes	yes
South Dakota	compulsory	no	yes	yes
Tennessee	compulsory	no	yes	yes
Texas	elective	competitive	yes	yes
Utah	compulsory	competitive	yes	yes
Vermont	compulsory	no	yes	yes
Virginia	compulsory	no	yes	yes
Washington	compulsory	exclusive	no	yes
West Virginia	compulsory	exclusive	no	yes
Wisconsin	compulsory	no	yes	yes
Wyoming	compulsory	no	yes	yes

APPENDIX 13:
WORKERS' AND PHYSICIAN'S REPORT
FOR WORKERS' COMPENSATION CLAIM

OREGON
DEPARTMENT OF
CONSUMER
& BUSINESS
& SERVICES
Workers' Compensation Division

Worker s and Physician s Report for Workers Compensation Claim Form 827

NOTES to physician or nurse practitioner

Ask the worker to complete this form ONLY in the following circumstances:
- First report of injury or disease
- Report of aggravation of original injury
- Notice of change of attending physician or nurse practitioner

Give the worker a copy immediately. You must file Form 827 with the workers' compensation insurer if the worker has indicated any of the above reasons for filing in the Worker's Section of the 827.

The worker should NOT complete this form for the following:
- Progress report
- Closing report
- Palliative care request

For these reports, you have the *option* of filing Form 827, submitting chart notes, or submitting a report that includes data gathered on Form 827.

If the worker completes and signs this form, give the worker a copy immediately.

When you file Form 827 as required (or by election) you can simplify your filing by attaching thorough chart notes. Simply check the box(es) next to your filing reason(s) and the box in Section C, affirming that chart notes are attached, and complete the signature block.

If you have questions about completion of Form 827, contact a benefit consultant:	If you don't know the name and address of the insurer, call the Workers' Compensation Division Employer Index:
(800) 452-0288	(503) 947-7814 or find it at: www4.cbs.state.or.us/ex/wcd/cov/search/index.cfm

To order supplies of this form, call (503) 947-7627. This form may also be downloaded from WCD's Web site, http://oregonwcd.org/policy/forms/formsbyno.html, in MS Word 97 or PDF format.

440-827 (2/04/DCBS/WCD/WEB)

827

Notice to Worker and Physician or Nurse Practitioner

Do not use Form 827 as "notice of change of attending physician or nurse practitioner, **unless** the new medical service provider will be **primarily responsible** for the treatment of the injured worker due to a compensable occupational injury or disease.

Being "primarily responsible" for the treatment does *not* include:

- Treatment on an emergency basis
- Treatment on an "on-call" basis
- Consulting
- Specialist care
- Exams done at the request of the insurer or Workers' Compensation Division.
- Exams done as "worker requested medical examinations under ORS 656.325 (compensability).

Do NOT use Form 827 for the above circumstances.

Incorrect use of this form may result in *delay of benefits* to the worker.

Worker s and Physician s Report for Workers Compensation Claims

| | WCD employer no.: |
| Policy no.: |

Note to Physician or Nurse Practitioner: Ask the worker to complete this form ONLY for the three filing reasons in the worker's section; do not have the worker complete or sign form if this is a progress report or palliative-care request.

Worker or physician

Worker's legal name, street address, and mailing address:

Worker's language preference: ☐ English ☐ Spanish ☐ Russian ☐ Vietnamese ☐ Other (please specify):

Claim no. (if known): Social Security no. (see back of form):

Date of birth: Male/female ☐ ☐ Date/time of original injury:

Phone:

Employer at time of original injury — name and street address: Occupation: Last date worked:

Workers' compensation insurer's name, address:

Phone:

Worker
Worker: Check reason for filing this form, answer questions (if any), and sign below.

☐ **First report of injury or disease** (Do not complete or sign if you do not intend to make a claim.) **Describe accident:**

Has the same body part been injured before? ☐ Yes ☐ No (If yes, describe when and how.)

By my signature I authorize the use of my SSN as described in paragraph 2 on the back. If you do not authorize use of your SSN as described in paragraph 2 on the back, check here ☐.

☐ **Report of aggravation of original injury**
☐ **Notice of change of attending physician or nurse practitioner**

Reason for change:

By my signature I am giving NOTICE OF CLAIM or CHANGING MY ATTENDING PHYSICIAN OR NURSE PRACTITIONER. I authorize medical providers and other custodians of claim records to release relevant medical records. I certify that the above information is true to the best of my knowledge and belief. (See #3 and 4 on back.)

Check here if you have more than one employer ☐

X

Worker's signature Date

Physician
Physician: If worker initiated this report, give worker a copy immediately.

☐ **First report of injury or disease** (Mail this form to the workers' compensation insurer within 72 hours of visit.)
☐ **Change of attending physician or nurse practitioner** (I accept responsibility for the care and treatment of the above named worker.)
 ☐ Prior medical records have been requested from the previous attending physician or nurse practitioner.
 ☐ Insurer is hereby requested to send its records.
☐ **Progress report OR** ☐ **Closing report** (See instructions in Bulletin 239.)
☐ **Aggravation: actual worsening of underlying condition** (Mail 827 to insurer within five days of visit, along with written report/chart notes, describing actual worsening, as supported by objective findings.)
☐ **Palliative care request** — Complete remainder of form, except Section b. (Worker must be currently employed or in vocational training to be eligible.) Attach a palliative care plan or describe in "NOTES" below. See back of form.

If you don't know the name and address of the insurer, call the Workers' Compensation Division's Employer Index (503) 947-7814, or visit on-line: www4.cbs.state.or.us/ex/wcd/cov/search/index.cfm

To order supplies of this form, call (503) 947-7627.

a Date/time of first treatment: Last date treated: Hospitalized as inpatient? ☐ Yes ☐ No If yes, name hospital:

Next appointment date: Est. length of further treatment: Current diagnosis per ICD-9-CM code(s):

b Has the injury or illness caused permanent impairment? ☐ Yes ☐ No ☐ Impairment expected ☐ Unknown Medically stationary? ☐ Yes (date): ☐ No (anticipated date): (Attach findings of impairment, if any.)

Work ability status: ☐ Regular work authorized start (date): ☐ Modified work authorized from (date): through (date, if known): ☐ No work authorized from (date): through (date, if known):

c NOTES: Describe the following or check if chart notes are attached. ☐ (Chart notes should *specifically* describe items below.)

Symptoms:
Objective findings:
Type of treatment:
Lab/X-Ray results (if any):
Impairment findings (if any): ☐ Temporary ☐ Permanent
Physical limitations (if any):
Palliative care plan/justification:
If referred to another physician give name/address:
Surgery:
History (if closing report):
Remarks:

Health insurance provider name and phone: (print or type)

Physician's or nurse practitioner's name, degree, address, and phone: (print, type, or use stamp)

X

Physician's or nurse practitioner's signature Date

This form replaces and satisfies reporting requirements for Forms 827, 828, 829, 2215, and 2837. See Bulletin 292.

— Original and one copy to insurer
— Retain copy for your records
— Copy to worker immediately if initial claim, aggravation claim, or change of physician

827

440-827 (2-04/DCBS/WCD/WEB)

Notice to worker

Important information about your social security number (SSN)

1. You must provide your SSN. The Workers' Compensation Division (WCD) of the Department of Consumer and Business Services (DCBS) has authority to request your SSN under the Privacy Act of 1974, 5 USC & 552a (West 1977), Section 7(a)(2)(B). Authority under state law is provided in Oregon Revised Statutes 656.254 and 656.265. Your SSN will be used by DCBS to carry out its duties under ORS Chapter 656, which include compliance, research, claims processing, and injured-worker program administration. The workers' compensation insurer will use your SSN to obtain records related to your claim.

2. If you are filing this 827 form as a "First report of injury or disease," your authorization for the use of your SSN is also requested for use by various government agencies to carry out their statutory duties, including, but not limited to, planning, research, child support enforcement, employment assistance, benefit coordination, child labor law enforcement, risk management, hazard identification, rate setting, and training programs. If you do not authorize this use, please check the box on the front of this form under "First report of injury or disease." Checking this box will not interfere with the processing of your workers' compensation claim.

Authorization to release medical records

3. By signing this 827, you are authorizing medical providers and other custodians of claim records to release records related to the injury or disease claimed on this 827 per ORS 656 and OAR 436. Medical information relevant to the claim includes a past history of the complaints of, or treatment of, a condition similar to that presented in the claim or other conditions related to the same body part.

Caution against making false statements

4. Any person who knowingly makes any false statement or representation for the purpose of obtaining any benefit or payment is punishable, upon conviction, by imprisonment for a term of not more than one year or by a fine of not more than $1,000, or by both per ORS 656.990(1).

If you have questions about your claim that are not resolved by your employer or insurer, you may contact:

(Si Ud. tiene alguna pregunta acerca de su reclamacion que no haya sido resuelta por su empleador o compan a aseguradora, puede ponerse en contacto con):

Workers' Compensation Division	**Ombudsman for Injured Workers**
(Division de Compensacion para Trabajadores)	**(Ombudsman para Trabajadores Lastimados)**
P.O. Box 14480, Salem, OR 97309-0405	350 Winter Street NE, Salem, OR 97301-3878
Call Salem: (503) 947-7585 or (503) 947-7993 TTY OR	(503) 378-3351 or (503) 947-7189 TTY
Toll-free in Oregon: 1-800-452-0288	or toll-free, 1-800-927-1271

Notice to worker and physician or nurse practitioner

Aggravation is the actual worsening of a condition resulting from the original injury. Form 827 must be sent to the insurer along with a written report/chart notes, describing actual worsening, if any, as supported by objective findings.

A medical service provider who can be *primarily responsible* for the treatment of an injured worker may either be a doctor, physician, or an authorized nurse practitioner.

Primarily responsible medical service provider does not mean a person who provides emergency-room treatment, "on-call" treatment, a consultation or second opinion; specialist care; exams done at the request of the insurer or Workers' Compensation Division; or exams done as "worker-requested medical examinations" under ORS 656.325 (compensability).

Palliative care is a medical service that may reduce or moderate temporarily the intensity of an otherwise stable (medically stationary) condition. The physician must attach a palliative care plan, which must include the name of the provider who will render the care, modalities ordered, frequency, and duration **(not to exceed 180 days)**; and a description of how the requested care relates to the compensable condition, how it will enable the worker to continue current employment or vocational training, and any possible adverse effects on the worker if the requested care is not approved. The insurer has **30 days** to respond in writing to the request. With the approval of the insurer, palliative care is compensable if it is necessary to enable the worker to continue current employment or a vocational training program. If the insurer does not approve, the medical service provider or the worker may request approval from the director of the Department of Consumer and Business Services; such request must be made within **90 days** of the insurer's disapproval, or within **120 days** of the date the request was first submitted to the insurer if the insurer did not respond within **30 days**. Palliative treatment may begin prior to insurer approval; however, if the requested care is ultimately disapproved, insurer payment for such treatment may be disallowed. The following types of medical care are NOT palliative care and ARE compensable after the worker is medically stationary, without the insurer's prior approval: services provided to a permanently and totally disabled worker; administration and monitoring of prescription medications; services necessary to provide or monitor prosthetic devices, braces, and supports; services provided under an aggravation claim (ORS 656.273); services provided for claims reopened under the board's own motion (ORS 656.278); diagnostic services; life-preserving treatments; and curative care to stabilize a temporary and acute waxing and waning of symptoms of the accepted conditions.

Regular work means the job the worker held at the time of injury.

440-827 (2/04/DCBS/WCD/WEB)   **Additional supplies of this form** may be obtained by calling (503) 947-7627.

827

Notice to worker
(continued)

Claim acceptance or denial

You will receive written notice from your employer's insurer of the acceptance or denial of your claim. If your employer is self-insured, the notice will be sent by your employer or the company your employer has hired to process its workers' compensation claims. If your claim is denied, the reason for the denial and your rights will be explained.

Medical care

You must tell your doctor or hospital on your first visit that your injury or illness is work-related. The doctor must tell you if there are any limits to the medical services he or she may provide to you under the Oregon workers' compensation system.

If your claim is accepted, the insurer or self-insured employer will pay medical bills due to medical conditions the insurer accepts in writing, including reimbursement for prescription medications, transportation, meals, lodging, and other expenses, up to a maximum established rate. Your request for reimbursement must be made in writing and accompanied by copies of receipts. Medical bills are not paid before claim acceptance. Bills are not paid if your claim is denied, with some exceptions. Contact the insurer if you have questions about who will pay your medical bills.

Payments for time lost from work

In order for you to receive payments for time lost from work, your attending physician must notify the insurer or self-insured employer of your inability to work. After the original injury, you will not be paid for the first three calendar days you are unable to work unless you are totally disabled for at least 14 consecutive calendar days or you are admitted to a hospital as an inpatient within 14 days of the first onset of total disability.

You will receive a compensation check every two weeks during your recovery period as long as your attending physician verifies your inability to work. These checks will continue until you return to work or it is determined further treatment is not expected to improve your condition. Your time-loss benefits will be two-thirds of your gross weekly wage at the time of injury up to a maximum set by Oregon law.

440-827 (2/04/DCBS/WCD/WEB)

APPENDIX 14:
CALIFORNIA STATE WORKERS' COMPENSATION CLAIM FORM

HOW TO FILE A CLAIM FORM

A claim form is how you report a work injury or illness to your employer.

Enclosed is the Employee's Claim for Workers' Compensation Benefits. Please read the instructions on the top of the form.

Complete **only** the "Employee" section. Be sure to SIGN and DATE the claim form. It is important that you keep a copy of the claim form for your records.

Return the claim form to your employer. You may hand-deliver or mail it to your employer. If you choose to mail the claim form, we recommend you use certified mail—return receipt requested.

Your employer should then complete the "Employer" section and forward the completed claim form to his workers' compensation insurance company. Your employer should give you a copy of the completed claim form. You should request a copy from your employer in the event you do not receive one.

Keep a copy for your records.

Generally the insurance company has fourteen (14) days to mail you a status letter about your claim. If you don't receive this letter, you should call the insurance company.

If you need help, you may call an Information & Assistance Office. The local I & A phone numbers are listed on the back of this guide.

> *The information contained in this guide is general in nature and is not intended as a substitute for legal advice. Changes in the law or the specific facts of your case may result in legal interpretations which are different than presented here.*

I & A 01
Rev. 6/99

WORKERS' COMPENSATION APPEALS BOARD
DISTRICT OFFICES

ANAHEIM, 92801-1162
1661 N. Raymond Ave., Suite 202
Information & Assistance Unit (714) 738-4038

BAKERSFIELD, 93301-1929
1800 30th Street, Suite 100
Information & Assistance Unit (661) 395-2514

EUREKA, 95501-0481
100 "H" Street, Suite 202
Information & Assistance Unit (707) 441-5723

FRESNO, 93721-2280
2550 Mariposa Street, Suite 4078
Information & Assistance Unit (559) 445-5355

GOLETA, 93117-3018
6755 Hollister Avenue
Information & Assistance Unit (805) 968-4158

GROVER BEACH, 93433-2261
1562 Grand Avenue
Information & Assistance Unit (805) 481-3380

LONG BEACH, 90802-4339
300 Oceangate Street, Suite 200
Information & Assistance Unit (562) 590-5240

LOS ANGELES, 90013-1105
320 West 4th Street, 9th Floor
Information & Assistance Unit (213) 576-7389

OAKLAND, 94612-1402
1515 Clay Street, 6th Floor
Information & Assistance Unit (510) 622-2861

OXNARD, 93030
2220 East Gonzales Road, Suite 100
Information & Assistance Unit (805) 485-3528

POMONA, 91766-1601
435 West Mission Blvd., Suite 300
Information & Assistance Unit (909) 623-8568

REDDING, 96001-2796
2115 Civic Center Drive, Suite 15
Information & Assistance Unit (530) 225-2047

RIVERSIDE, 92501-3337
3737 Main Street, Suite 300
Information & Assistance Unit (951) 782-4347

SACRAMENTO, 95825-2403
2424 Arden Way, Suite 230
Information & Assistance Unit (916) 263-2741

SALINAS, 93906-2016
1880 North Main Street, Suites 100 & 200
Information & Assistance Unit (831) 443-3058

SAN BERNARDINO, 92401-1411
464 West Fourth Street, Suite 239
Information & Assistance Unit (909) 383-4522

SAN DIEGO, 92108
7575 Metropolitan Road, Suite 202
Information & Assistance Unit (619) 767-2170

SAN FRANCISCO, 94102-7002
455 Golden Gate Avenue, 2nd Floor
Information & Assistance Unit (415) 703-5020

SAN JOSE, 95113-1482
100 Paseo de San Antonio, Suite 241
Information & Assistance Unit (408) 277-1292

SANTA ANA, 92701-4070
28 Civic Center Plaza, Suite 451
Information & Assistance Unit (714) 558-4597

SANTA MONICA, 90405-5219
2701 Ocean Park Blvd., Suite 220
Information & Assistance Unit (310) 452-1188

SANTA ROSA, 95404-4760
50 "D" Street, Suite 420
Information & Assistance Unit (707) 576-2452

STOCKTON, 95202-2393
31 East Channel Street, Suite 344
Information & Assistance Unit (209) 948-7980

VAN NUYS, 91401-3373
6150 Van Nuys Blvd., Suite 105
Information & Assistance Unit (818) 901-5374

Rev. 11/04

Workers' Compensation Claim Form (DWC 1) & Notice of Potential Eligibility
Formulario de Reclamo de Compensacion para Trabajadores (DWC 1) y Notificacion de Posible Elegibilidad

Return to Work: To help you to return to work as soon as possible, you should actively communicate with your treating doctor, claims administrator, and employer about the kinds of work you can do while recovering. They may coordinate efforts to return you to modified duty or other work that is medically appropriate. This modified or other duty may be temporary or may be extended depending on the nature of your injury or illness.

Payment for Permanent Disability: If a doctor says your injury or illness results in a permanent disability, you may receive additional payments. The amount will depend on the type of injury, your age, occupation, and date of injury.

Vocational Rehabilitation (VR): If a doctor says your injury or illness prevents you from returning to the same type of job and your employer doesn't offer modified or alternative work, you may qualify for VR. If you qualify, your claims administrator will pay the costs, up to a maximum set by state law. VR is a benefit for injuries that occurred prior to 2004.

Supplemental Job Displacement Benefit (SJDB): If you do not return to work within 60 days after your temporary disability ends, and your employer does not offer modified or alternative work, you may qualify for a nontransferable voucher payable to a school for retraining and/or skill enhancement. If you qualify, the claims administrator will pay the costs up to the maximum set by state law based on your percentage of permanent disability. SJDB is a benefit for injuries occurring on or after 1/1/04.

Death Benefits: If the injury or illness causes death, payments may be made to relatives or household members who were financially dependent on the deceased worker.

It is illegal for your employer to punish or fire you for having a job injury or illness, for filing a claim, or testifying in another person's workers' compensation case (Labor Code 132a). If proven, you may receive lost wages, job reinstatement, increased benefits, and costs and expenses up to limits set by the state.

You have the right to disagree with decisions affecting your claim. If you have a disagreement, contact your claims administrator first to see if you can resolve it. If you are not receiving benefits, you may be able to get State Disability Insurance (SDI) benefits. Call State Employment Development Department at (800) 480-3287.

You can obtain free information from an information and assistance officer of the State Division of Workers' Compensation, or you can hear recorded information and a list of local offices by calling **(800) 736-7401.** You may also go to the DWC web site at **www.dir.ca.gov.** Link to Workers' Compensation.

You can consult with an attorney. Most attorneys offer one free consultation. If you decide to hire an attorney, his or her fee will be taken out of some of your benefits. For names of workers' compensation attorneys, call the State Bar of California at (415) 538-2120 or go to their web site at **www.californiaspecialist.org.**

impuestos. Los pagos por incapacidad temporal son dos tercios de su pago semanal promedio, con cantidades m'nimas y maximas establecidas por las leyes estatales. Los pagos no se hacen durante los primeros tres d'as en que Ud. no trabaje, a menos que Ud. sea hospitalizado(a) de noche, o no pueda trabajar durante mas de 14 d'as.

Regreso al Trabajo: Para ayudarle a regresar a trabajar lo antes posible, Ud. debe comunicarse de manera activa con el medico que le atienda, el/la administrador(a) de reclamos y el empleador, con respecto a las clases de trabajo que Ud. puede hacer mientras se recupera. Es posible que ellos coordinen esfuerzos para regresarle a un trabajo modificado, o a otro trabajo, que sea apropiado desde el punto de vista medico. Este trabajo modificado, u otro trabajo, podr'a extenderse o no temporalmente, dependiendo de la 'ndole de su lesion o enfermedad.

Pago por Incapacidad Permanente: Si el doctor dice que su lesion o enfermedad resulta en una incapacidad permanente, es posible que Ud. reciba pagos adicionales. La cantidad dependera de la clase de lesion, su edad, su ocupacion y la fecha de la lesion.

Rehabilitacion Vocacional: Si el doctor dice que su lesion o enfermedad no le permite regresar a la misma clase de trabajo, y su empleador no le ofrece trabajo modificado o alterno, es posible que usted reuna los requisitos para rehabilitacion vocacional. Si Ud. reune los requisitios, su administrador(a) de reclamos pagara los costos, hasta un maximo establecido por las leyes estatales. Este es un beneficio para lesiones que ocurrieron antes de 2004.

Beneficio Suplementario por Desplazamiento de Trabajo: Si Ud. no vuelve al trabajo en un plazo de 60 d'as despues que los pagos por incapcidad temporal terminan, y su empleador no ofrece un trabajo modificado o alterno, es posible que usted reune los requisitos para recibir un vale no-transferible pagadero a una escuela para recibir un nuevo entrenamiento y/o mejorar su habilidad. Si Ud. reune los requisitios, el administrador(a) de reclamos pagara los costos hasta un maximo establecido por las leyes estatales basado en su porcentaje del incapicidad permanente. Este es un beneficio para lesiones que ocurren en o despues de 1/1/04.

Beneficios por Muerte: Si la lesion o enfermedad causa la muerte, es posible que los pagos se hagan a los parientes o a las personas que vivan en el hogar, que depend'an economicamente del/de la trabajador(a) difunto(a).

Es ilegal que su empleador le castigue o despida, por sufrir una lesion o enfermedad en el trabajo, por presentar un reclamo o por atestiguar en el caso de compensacion para trabajadores de otra persona. (El Codigo Laboral seccion 132a). Si es probado, puede ser que usted reciba pagos por perdida de sueldos, reposicion del trabajo, aumento de beneficios, y gastos hasta un l'mite establecido por el estado.

Ud. tiene derecho a estar en desacuerdo con las decisiones que afecten su reclamo. Si Ud. tiene un desacuerdo, primero comun'quese con su administrador(a) de reclamos, para ver si usted puede resolverlo. Si usted no esta recibiendo beneficios, es posible que Ud. pueda obtener beneficios de Seguro Estatal de Incapacidad (SDI). Llame al Departamento Estatal del Desarrollo del Empleo (EDD) al (800) 480-3287.

Ud. puede obtener informacion gratis, de un oficial de informacion y asistencia, de la Division estatal de Compensacion al Trabajador *(Division of Workers' Compensation – DWC)*, o puede escuchar informacion grabada, as' como una lista de oficinas locales, llamando al **(800) 736-7401.** Ud. tambien puede ir al sitio electronico en el Internet de la DWC en **www.dir.ca.gov.** Enlacese a la seccion de Compensacion para Trabajadores.

Ud. puede consultar con un(a) abogado(a). La mayor'a de los abogados ofrecen una consulta gratis. Si Ud. decide contratar a un(a) abogado(a), sus honorarios se tomaran de sus beneficios. Para obtener nombres de abogados de compensacion para trabajadores, llame a la Asociacion Estatal de Abogados de California *(State Bar)* al (415) 538-2120, o vaya a su sitio electronico en el Internet en **www.californiaspecialist.org.**

State of California
Department of Industrial Relations
DIVISION OF WORKERS' COMPENSATION

Estado de California
Departamento de Relaciones Industriales
DIVISION DE COMPENSACIÓN AL TRABAJADOR

WORKERS' COMPENSATION CLAIM FORM (DWC 1)

PETITION DEL EMPLEADO PARA DE COMPENSACIÓ DEL
TRABAJADOR (DWC 1)

Employee: Complete the **"Employee"** section and give the form to your employer. Keep a copy and mark it **"Employee's Temporary Receipt"** until you receive the signed and dated copy from your employer. You may call the Division of Workers' Compensation and hear recorded information at **(800) 736-7401**. An explanation of workers' compensation benefits is included as the cover sheet of this form.

You should also have received a pamphlet from your employer describing workers' compensation benefits and the procedures to obtain them.

Empleado: Complete la sección ***"Empleado"*** *y entregue la forma a su empleador. Quédese con la copia designada* ***"Recibo Temporal del Empleado"*** *hasta que Ud. reciba la copia firmada y fechada de su empleador. Ud. puede llamar a la División de Compensación al Trabajador al (800) 736-7401 para oír información grabada. En la hoja cubierta de esta forma esta la explicación de los beneficios de compensación al trabajador.*

Ud. también deber'a haber recibido de su empleador un folleto describiendo los beneficios de compensación al trabajador lesionado y los procedimientos para obtenerlos.

Any person who makes or causes to be made any knowingly false or fraudulent material statement or material representation for the purpose of obtaining or denying workers' compensation benefits or payments is guilty of a felony.

Toda aquella persona que a propósito haga o cause que se produzca cualquier declaración o representación material falsa o fraudulenta con el fin de obtener o negar beneficios o pagos de compensación a trabajadores lesionados es culpable de un crimen mayor "felonía".

Employee—complete this section and see note above *Empleado—complete esta sección y note la notación arriba.*

1. Name. *Nombre.* _____   Today's Date. *Fecha de Hoy.* _____
2. Home Address. *Dirección Residencial.* _____
3. City. *Ciudad.* _____ State. *Estado.* _____ Zip. *Código Postal.* _____
4. Date of Injury. *Fecha de la lesión (accidente).* _____ Time of Injury. *Hora en que ocurrió.* ____ a.m. ____ p.m.
5. Address and description of where injury happened. *Dirección/lugar dónde occurió el accidente.* _____
6. Describe injury and part of body affected. *Describa la lesión y parte del cuerpo afectada.* _____
7. Social Security Number. *Número de Seguro Social del Empleado.* _____
8. Signature of employee. *Firma del empleado.* _____

Employer—complete this section and see note below. *Empleador—complete esta sección y note la notación aba jo.*

9. Name of employer. *Nombre del empleador.* _____
10. Address. *Dirección.* _____
11. Date employer first knew of injury. *Fecha en que el empleador supo por primera vez de la lesión o accidente.* _____
12. Date claim form was provided to employee. *Fecha en que se le entregó al empleado la petición.* _____
13. Date employer received claim form. *Fecha en que el empleado devolvió la petición al empleador.* _____
14. Name and address of insurance carrier or adjusting agency. *Nombre y dirección de la compañ'a de seguros o agencia administradora de seguros.* _____
15. Insurance Policy Number. *El número de la póliza de Seguro.* _____
16. Signature of employer representative. *Firma del representante del empleador.* _____
17. Title. *T'tulo.* _____   18. Telephone. *Teléfono.* _____

Employer: You are required to date this form and provide copies to your insurer or claims administrator and to the employee, dependent or representative who filed the claim within **one working day** of receipt of the form from the employee.

SIGNING THIS FORM IS NOT AN ADMISSION OF LIABILITY

Empleador: Se requiere que Ud. feche esta forma y que provéa copias a su compañ'a de seguros, administrador de reclamos, o dependiente/representante de reclamos y al empleado que hayan presentado esta petición dentro del plazo de ***un día hábil*** *desde el momento de haber sido recibida la forma del empleado.*

EL FIRMAR ESTA FORMA NO SIGNIFICA ADMISION DE RESPONSABILIDAD

❑ Employer copy/*Copia del Empleador* ❑ Employee copy/*Copia del Empleado* ❑ Claims Administrator/*Administrador de Reclamos* ❑ Temporary Receipt/*Recibo del Empleado*

7/1/04 Rev.

APPENDIX 15:
ATTORNEY FEES IN WORKERS'
COMPENSATION CASES

STATE	ATTORNEY FEE	APPROVAL BY
Alabama	15%	court
Alaska	no cap	agency
Arizona	25%	agency
Arkansas	25%	agency
California	individual case basis	agency
Colorado	20%	agency
Connecticut	individual case basis	agency
Delaware	30%	agency and court
District of Columbia	20%	agency
Florida	varies based on award amount	judge of compensation claims
Georgia	25%	agency
Hawaii	individual case basis	agency
Idaho	25% non-litigated claim-30% litigated claim	agency
Illinois	20%	agency
Indiana	individual case basis	agency
Iowa	individual case basis	agency
Kansas	25%	agency
Kentucky	varies based on award amount	agency
Louisiana	20%	court
Maine	individual case basis	agency
Maryland	varies according to disability type	agency

STATE	ATTORNEY FEE	APPROVAL BY
Massachusetts	varies	agency
Michigan	varies	agency
Minnesota	varies based on award amount	court
Mississippi	25% before agency; 33-1/3% before court	agency
Missouri	25%	agency
Montana	20%-25%	agency
Nebraska	reasonable fee	court
Nevada	no provision	n/a
New Hampshire	20%	agency
New Jersey	20%	court
New Mexico	statutory maximum	court
New York	individual case basis	agency
North Carolina	individual case basis	agency
North Dakota	varies	agency
Ohio	individual case basis	agency
Oklahoma	varies	court
Oregon	varies	agency
Pennsylvania	20%	agency
Rhode Island	individual case basis	court
South Carolina	individual case basis	agency
South Dakota	varies	agency
Tennessee	20%	agency and court
Texas	25%	agency
Utah	varies based on award amount	agency
Vermont	20%	agency
Virginia	individual case basis	agency
Washington	30%	agency
West Virginia	20%	n/a
Wisconsin	20% in disputed cases	agency
Wyoming	individual case basis	court

APPENDIX 16:
TABLE OF WAITING PERIODS FOR WORKERS' COMPENSATION BENEFITS BY STATE

STATE	WAITING PERIOD	COMPENSATION RETROACTIVE AFTER NUMBER OF DAYS OF DISABILITY
Alabama	3 days	21 days
Alaska	3 days	28 days
Arizona	7 days	14 days
Arkansas	7 days	2 weeks
California	3 days	14 days
Colorado	3 days	2 weeks
Connecticut	3 days	7 days
Delaware	3 days	7 days
District of Columbia	3 days	14 days
Florida	7 days	21 days
Georgia	7 days	21 days
Hawaii	3 days	none
Idaho	5 days	2 weeks
Illinois	3 days	14 days
Indiana	7 days	21 days
Iowa	3 days	14 days
Kansas	7 days	3 weeks
Kentucky	7 days	2 weeks
Louisiana	7 days	6 weeks
Maine	7 days	14 days
Maryland	3 days	14 days
Massachusetts	5 days	21 days

STATE	WAITING PERIOD	COMPENSATION RETROACTIVE AFTER NUMBER OF DAYS OF DISABILITY
Michigan	7 days	2 weeks
Minnesota	3 days	10 days
Mississippi	5 days	14 days
Missouri	3 days	14 days
Montana	4 days	none
Nebraska	7 days	6 weeks
Nevada	5 days	5 days
New Hampshire	3 days	14 days
New Jersey	7 days	7 days
New Mexico	7 days	4 weeks
New York	7 days	14 days
North Carolina	7 days	21 days
North Dakota	4 days	5 days
Ohio	7 days	2 weeks
Oklahoma	3 days	none
Oregon	3 days	21 days, 14 days
Pennsylvania	7 days	14 days
Rhode Island	3 days	none
South Carolina	7 days	14 days
South Dakota	7 days	7 days
Tennessee	7 days	14 days
Texas	7 days	4 weeks
Utah	3 days	14 days
Vermont	3 days	7 days
Virginia	7 days	3 weeks
Washington	3 days	14 days
West Virginia	3 days	7 days
Wisconsin	3 days	7 days

APPENDIX 17:
PERCENTAGE OF WAGES PAYABLE FOR TEMPORARY TOTAL DISABILITY UNDER STATE WORKERS' COMPENSATION LAWS

STATE	PERCENTAGE OF WAGES
Alabama	66-2/3%
Alaska	80%
Arizona	66-2/3%
Arkansas	66-2/3%
California	66-2/3%
Colorado	66-2/3%
Connecticut	75%
Delaware	66-2/3%
District of Columbia	66-2/3%
Florida	66-2/3%
Georgia	66-2/3%
Hawaii	66-2/3%
Idaho	67%
Illinois	66-2/3%
Indiana	66-2/3%
Iowa	80%
Kansas	66-2/3%
Kentucky	66-2/3%
Louisiana	66-2/3%
Maine	80%
Maryland	66-2/3%
Massachusetts	60%

STATE	PERCENTAGE OF WAGES
Michigan	80%
Minnesota	66-2/3%
Mississippi	66-2/3%
Missouri	66-2/3%
Montana	66-2/3%
Nebraska	66-2/3%
Nevada	66-2/3%
New Hampshire	60%
New Jersey	70%
New Mexico	66-2/3%
New York	66-2/3%
North Carolina	66-2/3%
North Dakota	66-2/3%
Ohio	72% reduced to 66.67% after 12 weeks
Oklahoma	70%
Oregon	66-2/3%
Pennsylvania	66-2/3%
Rhode Island	75%
South Carolina	66-2/3%
South Dakota	66-2/3%
Tennessee	66-2/3%
Texas	70%
Utah	66-2/3%
Vermont	66-2/3%
Virginia	66-2/3%
Washington	60-75% depending on marital status
West Virginia	66-2/3%
Wisconsin	66-2/3%
Wyoming	66-2/3%

APPENDIX 18:
PERCENTAGE OF WAGES PAYABLE FOR PERMANENT TOTAL DISABILITY UNDER STATE WORKERS' COMPENSATION LAWS

STATE	PERCENTAGE OF WAGES
Alabama	66-2/3%
Alaska	80%
Arizona	66-2/3%
Arkansas	66-2/3%
California	66-2/3%
Colorado	66-2/3%
Connecticut	75%
Delaware	66-2/3%
District of Columbia	66-2/3%
Florida	66-2/3%
Georgia	66-2/3%
Hawaii	66-2/3%
Idaho	67%
Illinois	66-2/3%
Indiana	66-2/3%
Iowa	80%
Kansas	66-2/3%
Kentucky	66-2/3%
Louisiana	66-2/3%
Maine	80%
Maryland	66-2/3%
Massachusetts	66-2/3%

Michigan	80%
Minnesota	66-2/3%
Mississippi	66-2/3%
Missouri	66-2/3%
Montana	66-2/3%
Nebraska	66-2/3%
Nevada	66-2/3%
New Hampshire	60%
New Jersey	70%
New Mexico	66-2/3%
New York	66-2/3%
North Carolina	66-2/3%
North Dakota	66-2/3%
Ohio	66-2/3%
Oklahoma	70%
Oregon	66-2/3%
Pennsylvania	66-2/3%
Rhode Island	75%
South Carolina	66-2/3%
South Dakota	66-2/3%
Tennessee	66-2/3%
Texas	75%
Utah	66-2/3%
Vermont	66-2/3%
Virginia	66-2/3%
Washington	60-75% depending on marital status
West Virginia	66-2/3%
Wisconsin	66-2/3%
Wyoming	66-2/3%

APPENDIX 19:
PERCENTAGE OF WAGES PAYABLE FOR PERMANENT PARTIAL DISABILITY UNDER STATE WORKERS' COMPENSATION LAWS

STATE	PERCENTAGE OF WAGES
Alabama	66-2/3%
Alaska	statutory computation
Arizona	55%
Arkansas	66-2/3%
California	66-2/3%
Colorado	statutory computation
Connecticut	75%
Delaware	66-2/3%
District of Columbia	66-2/3%
Florida	statutory computation
Georgia	66-2/3%
Hawaii	66-2/3%
Idaho	N/A
Illinois	60%
Indiana	66-2/3%
Iowa	80%
Kansas	66-2/3%
Kentucky	66-2/3%
Louisiana	66-2/3%
Maine	80%
Maryland	66-2/3%
Massachusetts	60%

STATE	PERCENTAGE OF WAGES
Michigan	80%
Minnesota	66-2/3%
Mississippi	66-2/3%
Missouri	66-2/3%
Montana	66-2/3%
Nebraska	66-2/3%
Nevada	statutory computation
New Hampshire	60%
New Jersey	70%
New Mexico	66-2/3%
New York	66-2/3%
North Carolina	66-2/3%
North Dakota	statutory computation
Ohio	statutory computation
Oklahoma	70%
Oregon	66-2/3%
Pennsylvania	66-2/3%
Rhode Island	75%
South Carolina	66-2/3%
South Dakota	66-2/3%
Tennessee	66-2/3%
Texas	70%
Utah	66-2/3%
Vermont	66-2/3%
Virginia	66-2/3%
Washington	statutory computation
West Virginia	66-2/3%
Wisconsin	66-2/3%
Wyoming	N/A

APPENDIX 20:
FEDERAL EMPLOYEE'S NOTICE OF TRAUMATIC INJURY AND CLAIM FOR CONTINUATION OF PAY/COMPENSATION

Federal Employee's Notice of Traumatic Injury and Claim for Continuation of Pay/Compensation	**U.S. Department of Labor** Employment Standards Administration Office of Workers' Compensation Programs

Employee: Please complete all boxes 1 - 15 below. Do not complete shaded areas.
Witness: Complete bottom section 16.
Employing Agency (Supervisor or Compensation Specialist): Complete shaded boxes a, b, and c.

Employee Data

1. Name of employee (Last, First, Middle)		2. Social Security Number

3. Date of birth Mo. Day Yr.	4. Sex ☐ Male ☐ Female	5. Home telephone	6. Grade as of date of injury Level Step

7. Employee's home mailing address (Include city, state, and ZIP code)	8. Dependents ☐ Wife, Husband ☐ Children under 18 years ☐ Other

Description of Injury

9. Place where injury occurred (e.g. 2nd floor, Main Post Office Bldg., 12th & Pine)

10. Date injury occurred Mo. Day Yr.	Time ☐ a.m. ☐ p.m.	11. Date of this notice Mo. Day Yr.	12. Employee's occupation

13. Cause of injury (Describe what happened and why)

	a. Occupation code
14. Nature of injury (Identify both the injury and the part of body, e.g., fracture of left leg)	b. Type code c. Source code
	OWCP Use - NOI Code

Employee Signature

15. I certify, under penalty of law, that the injury described above was sustained in performance of duty as an employee of the United States Government and that it was not caused by my willful misconduct, intent to injure myself or another person, nor by my intoxication. I hereby claim medical treatment, if needed, and the following, as checked below, while disabled for work:

☐ a. Continuation of regular pay (COP) not to exceed 45 days and compensation for wage loss if disability for work continues beyond 45 days. If my claim is denied, I understand that the continuation of my regular pay shall be charged to sick or annual leave, or be deemed an overpayment within the meaning of 5 USC 5584.

☐ b. Sick and/or Annual Leave

I hereby authorize any physician or hospital (or any other person, institution, corporation, or government agency) to furnish any desired information to the U.S. Department of Labor, Office of Workers' Compensation Programs (or to its official representative). This authorization also permits any official representative of the Office to examine and to copy any records concerning me.

Signature of employee or person acting on his/her behalf _____ **Date** _____

Any person who knowingly makes any false statement, misrepresentation, concealment of fact or any other act of fraud to obtain compensation as provided by the FECA or who knowingly accepts compensation to which that person is not entitled is subject to civil or administrative remedies as well as felony criminal prosecution and may, under appropriate criminal provisions, be punished by a fine or imprisonment or both.

Have your supervisor complete the receipt attached to this form and return it to you for your records.

Witness Statement

16. Statement of witness (Describe what you saw, heard, or know about this injury)

Name of witness	Signature of witness		Date signed
Address	City	State	ZIP Code

Form CA-1
Rev. Apr. 1999

FED. EMPLOYEE'S NOTICE OF TRAUMATIC INJURY/CLAIM FOR CONTINUATION OF PAY

Official Supervisor's Report: Please complete information requested below:

Supervisor's Report

17. Agency name and address of reporting office (include city, state, and zip code)

OWCP Agency Code

OSHA Site Code

ZIP Code

18. Employee's duty station (Street address and ZIP code)

19. Employee's retirement coverage ☐ CSRS ☐ FERS ☐ Other, (identify)

20. Regular work hours From: ☐ a.m. ☐ p.m. To: ☐ a.m. ☐ p.m. | 21. Regular work schedule ☐ Sun. ☐ Mon. ☐ Tues. ☐ Wed. ☐ Thurs. ☐ Fri. ☐ Sat.

22. Date of Injury Mo. Day Yr. | 23. Date notice received Mo. Day Yr. | 24. Date stopped work Mo. Day Yr. Time: ☐ a.m. ☐ p.m.

25. Date pay stopped Mo. Day Yr. | 26. Date 45 day period began Mo. Day Yr. | 27. Date returned to work Mo. Day Yr. Time: ☐ a.m. ☐ p.m.

28. Was employee injured in performance of duty? ☐ Yes ☐ No (If "No," explain)

29. Was injury caused by employee's willful misconduct, intoxication, or intent to injure self or another? ☐ Yes (If "Yes," explain) ☐ No

30. Was injury caused by third party? ☐ Yes ☐ No (If "No," go to item 32.) | 31. Name and address of third party (Include city, state, and ZIP code)

32. Name and address of physician first providing medical care (Include city, state, ZIP code) | 33. First date medical care received Mo. Day Yr.

34. Do medical reports show employee is disabled for work? ☐ Yes ☐ No

35. Does your knowledge of the facts about this injury agree with statements of the employee and/or witnesses? ☐ Yes ☐ No (If "No," explain)

36. If the employing agency controverts continuation of pay, state the reason in detail. | 37. Pay rate when employee stopped work $ ___ Per ___

Signature of Supervisor and Filing Instructions

38. A supervisor who knowingly certifies to any false statement, misrepresentation, concealment of fact, etc., in respect of this claim may also be subject to appropriate felony criminal prosecution.

I certify that the information given above and that furnished by the employee on the reverse of this form is true to the best of my knowledge with the following exception:

Name of supervisor (Type or print)

Signature of supervisor   Date

Supervisor's Title   Office phone

39. Filing instructions
☐ No lost time and no medical expense: Place this form in employee's medical folder (SF-66-D)
☐ No lost time, medical expense incurred or expected: forward this form to OWCP
☐ Lost time covered by leave, LWOP, or COP: forward this form to OWCP
☐ First Aid Injury

Form CA-1.

Rev. Apr. 1999

Instructions for Completing Form CA-1

Complete all items on your section of the form. If additional space is required to explain or clarify any point, attach a supplemental statement to the form. Some of the items on the form which may require further clarification are explained below.

Employee (Or person acting on the employees' behalf)

13) Cause of injury

Describe in detail how and why the injury occurred. Give appropriate details (e.g.: if you fell, how far did you fall and in what position did you land?)

14) Nature of Injury

Give a complete description of the condition(s) resulting from your injury. Specify the right or left side if applicable (e.g., fractured left leg: cut on right index finger).

15) Election of COP/Leave

If you are disabled for work as a result of this injury and filed CA-1 within thirty days of the injury, you may be entitled to receive continuation of pay (COP) from your employing agency. COP is paid for up to 45 calendar days of disability, and is not charged against sick or annual leave. If you elect sick or annual leave you may not claim compensation to repurchase leave used during the 45 days of COP entitlement.

Supervisor

At the time the form is received, complete the receipt of notice of injury and give it to the employee. In addition to completing items 17 through 39, the supervisor is responsible for obtaining the witness statement in Item 16 and for filling in the proper codes in shaded boxes a, b, and c on the front of the form. If medical expense or lost time is incurred or expected, the completed form should be sent to OWCP within 10 working days after it is received.

The supervisor should also submit any other information or evidence pertinent to the merits of this claim.

If the employing agency controverts COP, the employee should be notified and the reason for controversion explained to him or her.

17) Agency name and address of reporting office

The name and address of the office to which correspondence from OWCP should be sent (if applicable, the address of the personnel or compensation office).

18) Duty station street address and zip code

The address and zip code of the establishment where the employee actually works.

19) Employers Retirement Coverage.

Indicate which retirement system the employee is covered under.

30) Was injury caused by third party?

A third party is an individual or organization (other than the injured employee or the Federal government) who is liable for the injury. For instance, the driver of a vehicle causing an accident in which an employee is injured, the owner of a building where unsafe conditions cause an employee to fall, and a manufacturer whose defective product causes an employee's injury, could all be considered third parties to the injury.

32) Name and address of physician first providing medical care

The name and address of the physician who first provided medical care for this injury. If initial care was given by a nurse or other health professional (not a physician) in the employing agency's health unit or clinic, indicate this on a separate sheet of paper.

33) First date medical care received

The date of the first visit to the physician listed in item 31.

36) If the employing agency controverts continuation of pay, state the reason in detail.

COP may be controverted (disputed) for any reason; however, the employing agency may refuse to pay COP only if the controversion is based upon one of the nine reasons given below:

a) The disability was not caused by a traumatic injury.

b) The employee is a volunteer working without pay or for nominal pay, or a member of the office staff of a former President;

c) The employee is not a citizen or a resident of the United States or Canada;

d) The injury occurred off the employing agency's premises and the employee was not involved in official "off premise" duties;

e) The injury was proximately caused by the employee's willful misconduct, intent to bring about injury or death to self or another person, or intoxication;

f) The injury was not reported on Form CA-1 within 30 days following the injury;

g) Work stoppage first occurred 45 days or more following the injury;

h) The employee initially reported the injury after his or her employment was terminated; or

i) The employee is enrolled in the Civil Air Patrol, Peace Corps, Youth Conservation Corps, Work Study Programs, or other similar groups.

Employing Agency - Required Codes

Box a (Occupation Code), Box b (Type Code), Box c (Source Code), OSHA Site Code

The Occupational Safety and Health Administration (OSHA) requires all employing agencies to complete these items when reporting an injury. The proper codes may be found in OSHA Booklet 2014, "Recordkeeping and Reporting Guidelines.

OWCP Agency Code

This is a four-digit (or four digit plus two letter) code used by OWCP to identify the employing agency. The proper code may be obtained from your personnel or compensation office, or by contacting OWCP.

Form CA-1
Rev. Apr. 1999

FED. EMPLOYEE'S NOTICE OF TRAUMATIC INJURY/CLAIM FOR CONTINUATION OF PAY

Benefits for Employees under the Federal Employees' Compensation act (FECA)

The FECA, which is administered by the Office of Workers' Compensation Programs (OWCP), provides the following benefits for job-related traumatic injuries:

(1) Continuation of pay for disability resulting from traumatic, job-related injury, not to exceed 45 calendar days. (To be eligible for continuation of pay, the employee, or someone acting on his/her behalf, must file Form CA-1 within 30 days following the injury and provide medical evidence in support of disability within 10 days of submission of the CA-1. Where the employing agency continue's the employee's pay, the pay must not be interrupted unless one of the provision's outlined in 20 CFR 10.222 apply.

(2) Payment of compensation for wage loss after the expiration of COP, if disability extends beyond such point, or if COP is not payable. If disability continues after COP expires, Form CA-7, with supporting medical evidence, must be filed with OWCP. To avoid interruption of income, the form should be filed on the 40th day of the COP period.

(3) Payment of compensation for permanent impairment of certain organs, members, or functions of the body (such as loss or loss of use of an arm or kidney, loss of vision, etc.), or for serious defringement of the head, face, or neck.

(4) Vocational rehabilitation and related services where directed by OWCP.

(5) All necessary medical care from qualified medical providers. The injured employee may choose the physician who provides initial medical care. Generally, 25 miles from the place of injury, place of employment, or employee's home is a reasonable distance to travel for medical care.

An employee may use sick or annual leave rather than LWOP while disabled. The employee may repurchase leave used for approved periods. Form CA-7b, available from the personnel office, should be studied BEFORE a decision is made to use leave.

For additional information, review the regulations governing the administration of the FECA (Code of Federal Regulations, Chapter 20, Part 10) or pamphlet CA-810.

Privacy Act

In accordance with the Privacy Act of 1974, as amended (5 U.S.C. 552a), you are hereby notified that: (1) The Federal Employees' Compensation Act, as amended and extended (5 U.S.C. 8101, et seq.) (FECA) is administered by the Office of Workers' Compensation Programs of the U.S. Department of Labor, which receives and maintains personal information on claimants and their immediate families. (2) Information which the Office has will be used to determine eligibility for and the amount of benefits payable under the FECA, and may be verified through computer matches or other appropriate means. (3) Information may be given to the Federal agency which employed the claimant at the time of injury in order to verify statements made, answer questions concerning the status of the claim, verify billing, and to consider issues relating to retention, rehire, or other relevant matters. (4) Information may also be given to other Federal agencies, other government entities, and to private-sector agencies and/or employers as part of rehabilitative and other return-to-work programs and services. (5) Information may be disclosed to physicians and other health care providers for use in providing treatment or medical/vocational rehabilitation, making evaluations for the Office, and for other purposes related to the medical management of the claim. (6) Information may be given to Federal, state and local agencies for law enforcement purposes, to obtain information relevant to a decision under the FECA, to determine whether benefits are being paid properly, including whether prohibited dual payments are being made, and, where appropriate, to pursue salary/administrative offset and debt collection actions required or permitted by the FECA and/or the Debt Collection Act. (7) Disclosure of the claimant's social security number (SSN) or tax identifying number (TIN) on this form is mandatory. The SSN and/or TIN, and other information maintained by the Office, may be used for identification, to support debt collection efforts carried on by the Federal government, and for other purposes required or authorized by law. (8) Failure to disclose all requested information may delay the processing of the claim or the payment of benefits, or may result in an unfavorable decision or reduced level of benefits.

Note: This notice applies to all forms requesting information that you might receive from the Office in connection with the processing and adjudication of the claim you filed under the FECA.

Receipt of Notice of Injury

This acknowledges receipt of Notice of Injury sustained by (Name of injured employee)

Which occurred on (Mo., Day, Yr.)

At (Location)

Signature of Official Superior   Title   Date (Mo., Day, Yr.)

*U.S. GPO: 1999-454-845/12704

Form CA-1
Rev. Apr. 1999

APPENDIX 21:
FEDERAL EMPLOYEE'S NOTICE OF OCCUPATIONAL DISEASE AND CLAIM FOR COMPENSATION

Notice of Occupational Disease
and Claim for Compensation

U. S. Department of Labor
Employment Standards Administration
Office of Workers' Compensation Programs

Employee: Please complete all boxes 1 - 18 below. Do not complete shaded areas.
Employing Agency (Supervisor or Compensation Specialist): Complete shaded boxes a, b, and c.

Employee Data

1. Name of Employee (Last, First, Middle)

2. Social Security Number

3. Date of birth Mo. Day Yr.

4. Sex

5. Home telephone

6. Grade as of date of last exposure Level Step

7. Employee's home mailing address (Include city, state, and ZIP code)

8. Dependents
☐ Wife, Husband
☐ Children under 18 years
☐ Other

Claim Information

9. Employee's occupation

a. Occupation code

10. Location (address) where you worked when disease or illness occurred (include City, state, and ZIP code)

11. Date you first became aware of disease or illness Mo. Day Yr.

12. Date you first realized the disease or illness was caused or aggravated by your employment Mo. Day Yr.

13. Explain the relationship to your employment, and why you came to this realization

14. Nature of disease or illness

OWCP Use - NOI Code

b. Type code

c. Source code

15. If this notice and claim was not filed with the employing agency within 30 days after date shown above in item #12, explain the reason for the delay.

16. If the statement requested in item 1 of the attached instructions is not submitted with this form, explain reason for delay.

17. If the medical reports requested in item 2 of attached instructions are not submitted with this form, explain reason for delay.

Employee Signature

18. I certify, under penalty of law, that the disease or illness described above was the result of my employment with the United States Government, and that it was not caused by my willful misconduct, intent to injure myself or another person, nor by my intoxication. I hereby claim medical treatment, if needed, and other benefits provided by the Federal Employees' Compensation Act.

I hereby authorize any physician or hospital (or any other person, institution, corporation, or government, agency) to furnish any desired information to the U.S. Department of Labor, Office of Workers' Compensation Programs (or to its official representative). This authorization also permits any official representative of the Office to examine and to copy any records concerning me.

Signature of employee or person acting on his/her behalf

Date

Have your supervisor complete the receipt attached to this form and return it to you for your records.

Any person who knowingly makes any false statement, misrepresentation, concealment of fact or any other act of fraud to obtain compensation as provided by the FECA or who knowingly accepts compensation to which that person is not entitled is subject to civil or administrative remedies as well as felony criminal prosecution and may, under appropriate criminal provisions, be punished by a fine or imprisonment or both.

For sale by the Superintendent of Documents, U.S. Government Printing Office Washington, DC 20402

Form CA-2
Rev. Jan. 1997

FED EMPLOYEE'S NOTICE OF OCCUPATIONAL DISEASE & CLAIM FOR COMPENSATION

Official Supervisor's Report of Occupational Disease: Please complete information requested below

Supervisor's Report

19. Agency name and address of reporting office (include city, state, and ZIP Code)

OWCP Agency Code

OSHA Site Code

ZIP Code

20. Employee's duty station (Street address and ZIP Code)

ZIP Code

21. Regular work hours   From: ☐ a.m. ☐ p.m.   To: ☐ a.m. ☐ p.m.

22. Regular work schedule ☐ Sun. ☐ Mon. ☐ Tues. ☐ Wed. ☐ Thurs. ☐ Fri. ☐ Sat.

23. Name and address of physician first providing medical care (include city, state, ZIP code)

24. First date medical care received   Mo. Day Yr.

25. Do medical reports show employee is disabled for work? ☐ Yes ☐ No

26. Date employee first reported condition to supervisor   Mo. Day Yr.

27. Date and hour employee stopped work   Mo. Day Yr.   Time   ☐ a.m. ☐ p.m.

28. Date and hour employee's pay stopped   Mo. Day Yr.   Time   ☐ a.m. ☐ p.m.

29. Date employee was last exposed to conditions alleged to have caused disease or illness   Mo. Day Yr.

30. Date returned to work   Mo. Day Yr.   Time   ☐ a.m. ☐ p.m.

31. If employee has returned to work and work assignment has changed, describe new duties

32. Employee's Retirement Coverage ☐ CSRS ☐ FERS ☐ Other, (Specify)

33. Was injury caused by third party? ☐ Yes ☐ No   If "No," go to Item 34.

34. Name and address of third party (include city, state, and ZIP code)

Signature of Supervisor

35. A supervisor who knowingly certifies to any false statement, misrepresentation, concealment of fact, etc., in respect to this claim may also be subject to appropriate felony criminal prosecution.

I certify that the information given above and that furnished by the employee on the reverse of this form is true to the best of my knowledge with the following exception:

Name of Supervisor (Type or print)

Signature of Supervisor   Date

Supervisor's Title   Office phone

Form CA-2
Rev. Jan. 1997

Disability Benefits for Employees under the Federal Employees' Compensation Act (FECA)

The FECA, which is administered by the Office of Workers' Compensation Programs (OWCP), provides the following general benefits for employment-related occupational disease or illness:

(1) Full medical care from either Federal medical officers and hospitals, or private hospitals or physicians of the employee's choice.

(2) Payment of compensation for total or partial wage loss.

(3) Payment of compensation for permanent impairment of certain organs, members, or functions of the body (such as loss or loss of use of an arm or kidney, loss of vision, etc.), or for serious disfigurement of the head, face, or neck.

(4) Vocational rehabilitation and related services where necessary.

The first three days in a non-pay status are waiting days, and no compensation is paid for these days unless the period of disability exceeds 14 calendar days, or the employee has suffered a permanent disability. Compensation for total disability is generally paid at the rate of 2/3 of an employee's salary if there are no dependents, or 3/4 of salary if there are one or more dependents.

An employee may use sick or annual leave rather than LWOP while disabled. The employee may repurchase leave used for approved periods. Form CA-7b, available from the personnel off ice, should be studied BEFORE a decision is made to use leave.

If an employee is in doubt about compensation benefits, the OWCP District Office servicing the employing agency should be contacted. (Obtain the address from your employing agency.)

For additional information, review the regulations governing the administration of the FECA (Code of Federal Regulations, Title 20, Chapter 1) or Chapter 810 of the Office of Personnel Management's Federal Personnel Manual.

Privacy Act

In accordance with the Privacy Act of 1974, as amended (5 U.S.C. 552a), you are hereby notified that: (1) The Federal Employees' Compensation Act, as amended and extended (5 U.S.C. 8101, et seq.) (FECA) is administered by the Office of Workers' Compensation Programs of the U.S. Department of Labor, which receives and maintains personal information on claimants and their immediate families. (2) Information which the Office has will be used to determine eligibility for and the amount of benefits payable under the FECA, and may be verified through computer matches or other appropriate means. (3) Information may be given to the Federal agency which employed the claimant at the time of injury in order to verify statements made, answer questions concerning the status of the claim, verify billing, and to consider issues relating to retention, rehire, or other relevant matters. (4) Information may also be given to other Federal agencies, other government entities, and to private-sector agencies and/or employers as part of rehabilitative and other return-to-work programs and services. (5) Information may be disclosed to physicians and other health care providers for use in providing treatment or medical/vocational rehabilitation, making evaluations for the Office, and for other purposes related to the medical management of the claim. (6) Information may be given to Federal, state and local agencies for law enforcement purposes, to obtain information relevant to a decision under the FECA, to determine whether benefits are being paid properly, including whether prohibited dual Payments are being made, and, where appropriate, to pursue salary/administrative offset and debt collection actions required or permitted by the FECA and/or the Debt Collection Act. (7) Disclosure of the claimant's social security number (SSN) or tax identifying number (TIN) on this form is mandatory. The SSN and/or TIN, and other information maintained by the Office, may be used for identification, to support debt collection efforts carried on by the Federal government, and for other purposes required or authorized by law. (8) Failure to disclose all requested information may delay the processing of the claim or the payment of benefits, or may result in an unfavorable decision or reduced level of benefits.

Note: This notice applies to all forms requesting information that you might receive from the Office in connection with the processing and adjudication of the claim you filed under the FECA.

Receipt of Notice of Occupational Disease or Illness

This acknowledges receipt of notice of disease or illness sustained by:
(Name of injured employee)

I was first notified about this condition on (Mo., Day, Yr.)

At (Location)

Signature of Official Superior   Title   Date (Mo., Day, Yr.)

This receipt should be retained by the employee as a record that notice was filed.

Form CA-2

INSTRUCTIONS FOR COMPLETING FORM CA-2

Complete all items on your section of the form. If additional space is required to explain or clarify any point, attach a supplemental statement to the form, in addition to the information requested on the form, both the employee and the supervisor are required to submit additional evidence as described below. If this evidence is not submitted along with the form, the responsible party should explain the reason for the delay and state when the additional evidence will be submitted.

Employee (or person acting on the Employee's behalf)

Complete items 1 through 18 and submit the form to the employee's supervisor along with the statement and medical reports described below. Be sure to obtain the Receipt of Notice of Disease or Illness completed by the supervisor at the time the form is submitted.

1) Employee's statement

In a separate narrative statement attached to the form, the employee must submit the following information:

a) A detailed history of the disease or illness from the date it started.

b) Complete details of the conditions of employment which are believed to be responsible for the disease or illness.

c) A description of specific exposures to substances or stressful conditions causing the disease or illness, including locations where exposure or stress occurred, as well as the number of hours per day and days per week of such exposure or stress.

d) Identification of the part of the body affected. (If disability is due to a heart condition, give complete details of all activities for one week prior to the attack with particular attention to the final 24 hours of such period.)

e) A statement as to whether the employee ever suffered a similar condition. If so, provide full details of onset, history, and medical care received, along with names and addresses of physicians rendering treatment.

2) Medical report

a) Dates of examination or treatment.

b) History given to the physician by the employee.

c) Detailed description of the physician's findings.

d) Results of x-rays, laboratory tests, etc.

e) Diagnosis.

f) Clinical course of treatment.

g) Physician's opinion as to whether the disease or illness was caused or aggravated by the employment, along with an explanation of the basis for this opinion. (Medical reports that do not explain the basis for the physician's opinion are given very little weight in adjudicating the claim.)

3) Wage loss

If you have lost wages or used leave for this illness, Form CA-7 should also be submitted.

Supervisor (Or appropriate official in the employing agency)

At the time the form is received, complete the Receipt of Notice of Disease or Illness and give it to the employee. In addition to completing items 19 through 34, the supervisor is responsible for filling in the proper codes in shaded boxes a, b, and c on the front of the form. If medical expense or lost time is incurred or expected, the completed form must be sent to OWCP within ten working days after it is received. In a separate narrative statement attached to the form, the supervisor must:

a) Describe in detail the work performed by the employee. Identify fumes, chemicals, or other irritants or situations that the employee was exposed to which allegedly caused the condition. State the nature, extent, and duration of the exposure, including hours per days and days per week, requested above.

b) Attach copies of all medical reports (including x-ray reports and laboratory data) on file for the employee.

c) Attach a record of the employee's absence from work caused by any similar disease or illness. Have the employee state the reason for each absence.

d) Attach statements from each co-worker who has first-hand knowledge about the employee's condition and its cause. (The co-workers should state how such knowledge was obtained.)

e) Review and comment on the accuracy of the employee's statement requested above.

The supervisor should also submit any other information or evidence pertinent to the merits of this claim.

Item Explanation: Some of the items on the form which may require further clarification are explained below.

14. Nature of the disease or illness

Give a complete description of the disease or illness. Specify the left or right side if applicable (e.g., rash on left leg; carpal tunnel syndrome, right wrist).

19. Agency name and address of reporting office

The name and address of the office to which correspondence from OWCP should be sent (if applicable, the address of the personnel or compensation office).

23. Name and address of physician first providing medical care

The name and address of the physician who first provided medical care for this injury. If initial care was given by a nurse or other health professional (not a physician) in the employing agency's health unit or clinic, indicate this on a separate sheet of paper.

24. First date medical care received

The date of the first visit to the physician listed in item 23.

32. Employee's Retirement Coverage.

Indicate which retirement system the employee is covered under.

33. Was the injury caused by third party?

A third party is an individual or organization (other than the injured employee or the Federal government) who is liable for the disease. For instance, manufacturer of a chemical to which an employee was exposed might be considered a third party if improper instructions were given by the manufacturer for use of the chemical.

Employing Agency - Required Codes

Box a (Occupational Code), Box b. (Type Code), Box c (Source Code), OSHA Site Code

The Occupational Safety and Health Administration (OSHA) requires all employing agencies to complete these items when reporting an injury. The proper codes may be found in OSHA Booklet 2014, Record Keeping and Reporting Guidelines.

OWCP Agency Code

This is a four digit (or four digit two letter) code used by OWCP to identify the employing agency. The proper code may be obtained from your personnel or compensation office, or by contacting OWCP.

• U.S. GPO: 2001480-204/59062

Form CA-2
Rev. Jan. 1997

APPENDIX 22:
CLAIM FOR CONTINUATION OF COMPENSATION UNDER THE FEDERAL EMPLOYEE'S COMPENSATION ACT

Claim for Continuance of Compensation
Under the Federal Employees'
Compensation Act

U.S. Department of Labor
Employment Standards Administration
Office of Workers' Compensation Programs

INSTRUCTIONS TO BENEFICIARIES

OMB No. 1215-0154
Expires: 06-30-08

1. It is important that you carefully complete the other side of this form and return it to the OWCP within 30 days. Your failure to do so will result in suspension of the compensation you are receiving.

2. Complete Section A by printing the full name of the deceased employee and the OFFICE OF WORKERS' COMPENSATION PROGRAMS file number.

3. Answer all questions in the section or sections that apply to you. If you are receiving compensation as the:

   (A) WIDOW OR WIDOWER Complete Section B.
   (B) WIDOW OR WIDOWER RECEIVING COMPENSATION ON HER OR HIS ACCOUNT AND ON ACCOUNT OF A MINOR CHILD OR CHILDREN - Complete Sections B and C.
   (C) GUARDIAN OR CUSTODIAN OF A MINOR CHILD OR GRANDCHILD OR A PERSON INCAPABLE OF SELF-SUPPORT - Complete Section C.
   (D) PARENT, GRANDPARENT, OR A PERSON WHO IS PHYSICALLY INCAPABLE OF SELF-SUPPORT - Complete Section D.
   (E) Complete Block C if dependent is receiving educational benefits.

4. Carefully read and comply with directions in Section E.

5. Complete and sign the certificate in Section F.

6. Please return the completed form, in an envelope, to the address shown below.

The information on this form will be used to determine your eligibility for continuing benefits. Your response to this information is required to retain your compensation benefits. (20 CFR 10.126)

RETURN TO: U.S. DEPARTMENT OF LABOR, DFEC
CENTRAL MAILROOM
P.O. BOX 8300
LONDON, KY 40742-8300

CLAIM/CONTINUATION COMPENSATION UNDER FED EMPLOYEE'S COMPENSATION ACT

IMPORTANT: READ CAREFULLY THE INSTRUCTIONS ON THE OTHER SIDE OF THIS FORM BEFORE ANSWERING THE QUESTIONS BELOW

I HEREBY APPLY FOR CONTINUANCE OF COMPENSATION BENEFITS AWARDED TO ME (OR TO THE CLAIMANT ON WHOSE BEHALF I AM NOW ACTING) BY THE OFFICE OF WORKERS' COMPENSATION (OWCP) ON ACCOUNT OF THE DEATH OF:

A. Name of Deceased Employee	Employee's Federal Retirement Plan ☐ CSRS ☐ FERS ☐ Other	OWCP File No.

THIS BLOCK TO BE COMPLETED BY WIDOW/WIDOWER RECEIVING COMPENSATION

B. 1. Have You Married since the Death of Above Named Employee? ☐ Yes ☐ No (If "Yes" complete 10)

2. Do You Receive a Pension or Allowance from any other Federal Agency such as the Veterans' Administration, Social Security Administration or the Civil Service Commission on Account of the Death of this Employee? ☐ Yes ☐ No (If "Yes" complete 11)

THIS BLOCK TO BE COMPLETED BY ANY PERSON RECEIVING COMPENSATION ON BEHALF OF CHILD GRANDCHILD, OR DEPENDENT INCAPABLE OF SELF-SUPPORT

C. 3. Have any Dependents You Claim Compensation for Married Since the Death of the Above Named Employee? ☐ Yes ☐ No (If "Yes" complete 10)

4. Do Any Dependents You Claim Compensation for Receive a Pension or Allowance from Any Other Federal Agency Such as the Veterans' Administration, Social Security Administration, or the Civil Service Commission on Account of the Death of this Employee? ☐ Yes ☐ No (If "Yes" complete 11)

5. Give the Following Information for Each Person You Receive Compensation For:

NAME	AGE	IS PERSON IN YOUR CUSTODY? (Yes or No)	NAME, ADDRESS, AND RELATIONSHIP OF PERSON(S) HAVING CUSTODY IF NOT IN YOUR CUSTODY

THIS BLOCK IS TO BE COMPLETED BY PARENT, GRANDPARENT, OR DEPENDENT PHYSICALLY INCAPABLE OF SELF-SUPPORT

D. 6. Have You Married Since the Death of the Above Named Employee? ☐ Yes ☐ No (If "Yes" complete 10)

7. Do You Receive a Pension or Allowance from any other Federal Agency such as the Veterans' Administration or the Civil Service Commission on Account of the Death of this Employee? ☐ Yes ☐ No (If "Yes" complete 11)

8. Are You Capable of Self-Support? ☐ Yes ☐ No

9. Have You Been Employed Since Filing Your Last Claim Form? ☐ Yes ☐ No (If "Yes" complete 12)

ADDITIONAL INFORMATION: THIS BLOCK TO BE COMPLETED ONLY WHEN AN ANSWER TO 1, 2, 3, 4, 5, 6, 7, or 9 IS "YES."

E. 10. When and Where was the Marriage Performed and What was the Change in Name, If Any?

11. What Agency is Paying the Benefits and For What Reason Are They Being Paid?

12. State the Name of Your Employer, Nature of Employment, Dates Employed, and Amount Earned.

(Space for Answers to questions 10, 11, and 12)

CLAIMANT'S CERTIFICATION - TO BE COMPLETED IN ALL INSTANCES

F. I DECLARE UNDER THE PENALTIES OF PERJURY THAT THE INFORMATION CONTAINED ON THIS FORM IS TRUE AND CORRECT: AND THAT I WILL IMMEDIATELY NOTIFY THE OFFICE OF WORKERS' COMPENSATION PROGRAMS OF ANY CHANGES IN STATUS.

Signature of Claimant (or guardian)	Date (month, day, year)
Address of Claimant (or guardian)	Telephone Where You Can Be Reached ( ) --
Signature of Witness and Date Witnessed if Claimant Signs by Mark (X)	

APPENDIX 23:
LONGSHORE AND HARBOR WORKER'S
CLAIM FOR COMPENSATION CLAIM FORM

Employee's Claim for Compensation

U.S. Department of Labor
Employment Standards Administration
Office of Workers' Compensation Programs

See Instructions On Reverse	OMB No. 1215-0160

| 3. Name of person making claim (Type or print) | 1. OWCP No. |
| First   MI.   Last | 2. Carrier's No. |

5. Claimant's address (number, street, city, state, ZIP code)	4. Date of Injury
line 1:	6. Marital Status
line 2:	Married Single

| 7. Sex   Male   Female | 8. Date of Birth | 9. Social Security Number (Required by law) | 10. Did injury. cause loss of time beyond day or shift of accident?   Yes   No |

| 11. On date of injury give | a. Hour began work   AM   PM | b. Hour of accident   AM   PM | c. Did you stop work immediately?   yes   No | 12. Date and hour pay stopped? (mm/dd/yyyy) (hh:mm am/pm) |

| 13. Date and hour you returned to work (mm/dd/yyyy) (hh:mm am/pm) | 14. Occupation (Job title: longshore worker, welder, etc.) | 15. Injured while doing regular work?   Yes   No (if "No," explain in Item 24) |

| 16. Wages or earnings when injured (include overtime allowances, etc.)   a. Weekly | b. Total earnings during year immediately before injury. | 17. Has 3rd party or other claim been made because of this Injury?   Yes   No |

| 18. Number of years you worked for this employer | 19. Number of days usually worked per week | 20. Name of supervisor at time of accident? |

| 21. Earliest date supervisor or employer knew of accident (mm/dd/yyyy) | 22. Were you employed elsewhere during the week injured?   No   Yes   (If "Yes," state where and when on reverse.) |

23. Exact place where accident occurred (Street address, city, town, name of vessel, pier, terminal. etc.)

24. Describe in full how the accident occurred (Relate the events which resulted in the injury or occupational disease. Tell what the injured was doing at the time of the accident. Tell what happened and how it happened. Name any objects or substances involved and tell how they were involved. Give full details on all factors which led or contributed to the accident. If more space is needed, continue on reverse.)

| 25. Nature of injury (name part of body affected - fractured left leg, bruised right thumb, etc. If there was a loss or loss of use of a part of the body. describe.) | |

26. Have you received medical attention for this injury? (if "Yes," give name and address of doctor, clinic, hospital, etc.) Yes No	27. Were you treated by a physician of your choice? Yes No
	30. Have you worked during the period of disability? Yes No
28. Was such treatment provided by employer? Yes No	29. Are you still disabled on account of this injury? yes No	

| 31. Have you received any wages since becoming disabled?   Yes   No   (if "Yes," give dates on reverse) | 32. Has injury resulted in permanent disability, amputation or serious disfigurement?   Yes (Describe on reverse.)   No |

| 33. Name of employer (individual or firm name) | 34. Nature of employer's business |

| 35. Address of employer (Number, street, city, state, ZIP code) | 36. If accident occurred outside the U.S., state whether you are a U.S. Citizen   Yes   No |

| 37. I hereby make claim for compensation benefits, monetary and medical, under the _____ Act | 38. Date of this claim (mm/dd/yyyy) |
| Signature of claimant or person acting in his/her behalf | |

Section 31(a)(1) of the Longshore Act. 33 U.S.C. 931(a)(1) provides. as follows: Any claimant or representative of a claimant who knowingly and willfully makes a false statement or representation for the purpose of obtaining a benefit or payment under this Act shall be guilty of a felony, and on conviction thereof shall be punished by a fine not to exceed $10,000, by imprisonment not to exceed five years, or by both.

Form LS-203
Rev. Sept. 1998

Instructions

• Use this form to file a claim under any one of the following laws:

Longshore and Harbor Workers' Compensation Act
Defense Base Act
Outer Continental Shelf Lands Act
Nonappropriated Fund Instrumentalities Act

- Applicant may leave items 1. and 2. blank.

Except as noted below, a claim may be filed within one year after the injury or death (33 U.S.C. 913(a)). If compensation has been paid without an award, a claim may be filed within one year after the last payment. The time for filing a claim does not begin to run until the employee or beneficiary knows, or should have known by the exercise of reasonable diligence, of the relationship between the employment and the injury. Persons are not required to respond to this collection of information unless it displays a currently valid OMB control number. The information will be used to determine an injured worker's entitlement to compensation and medical benefits.

In case of hearing loss, a claim may be filed within one year after receipt by an employee of an audiogram, with the accompanying report thereon, indicating that the employee has suffered a loss of hearing.

In cases involving occupational disease which does not immediately result in death or disability, a claim may be filed within two years after the employee or claimant becomes aware, or in the exercise of reasonable diligence or by reason of medical advice should have been aware, of the relationship between the employment, the disease, and the death or disability.

To file a claim for compensation benefits, complete and sign two copies of this form and send or give both copies to the Office of Workers' Compensation Programs District Director in the city serving the district where the injury occurred. District Offices of OWCP are located In the following cities.

Baltimore	Honolulu	New Orleans	Philadelphia
Boston	Houston	New York	San Francisco
Chicago	Jacksonville	Norfolk	Seattle
	Long Beach		Washington, D.C.

Use the space below to continue answers. Please number each answer to correspond to the number of the item being continued.

PRIVACY ACT NOTICE

In accordance with the Privacy Act of 1974, as amended (5 U.S.C. 552a) you are hereby notified that (1) the Longshore and Harbor Workers' Compensation Act, as amended and extended (33 U.S.C. 901 et seq.) (LHWCA) is administered by the Office of Workers' Compensation Programs of the U.S. Department of Labor, which receives and maintains personal information on claimants and their immediate families. (2) Information which the Office has will be used to determine eligibility for and the amount of benefits payable under the LHWCA. (3) Information may be given to the employer which employed the claimant at the time of injury, or to the insurance carrier or other entity which secured the employer's compensation liability. (4) Information may be given to physicians and other medical service providers for use in providing treatment or medical/vocational rehabilitation, making evaluations and for other purposes relating to the medical management of the claim. (5) Information may be given to the Department of Labor's Office of Administrative Law Judges (OALJ), or other person, board or organization, which is authorized or required to render decisions with respect to the claim or other matter arising in connection with the claim. (6) Information may be given to Federal, state and local agencies for law enforcement purposes, to obtain information relevant to a decision under the LHWCA, to determine whether benefits are being or have been paid properly, and, where appropriate, to pursue salary/administrative offset and debt collection actions required or permitted by law. (7) Disclosure of the claimant's Social Security Number (SSN) or tax identifying number (TIN) on this form is mandatory. The SSN and/or TIN and other information maintained by the Office may be used for identification, and for other purposes authorized by law. (8) Failure to disclose all requested information may delay the processing of the claim, the payment of benefits, or may result in an unfavorable decision or reduced level of benefits.

Note: The notice applies to all forms requesting information that you might receive from the Office In connection with the processing and/or adjudication of the claim you filed under the LHWCA and related statutes.

Public Burden Statement

We estimate that it will take an average of 15 minutes to complete this collection of information, including time for reviewing instructions, searching existing data sources, gathering and maintaining the data needed, and completing and reviewing the collection of information. If you have any comments regarding this burden estimate or any other aspect of this collection of information, including suggestions for reducing this burden, send them to the U.S. Department of Labor, Division of Longshore and Harbor Workers' Compensation, 200 Constitution Avenue, NW, Washington, DC 20210. **DO NOT SEND THE COMPLETED FORM TO THIS OFFICE**

APPENDIX 24:
MINER'S CLAIM FOR BENEFITS UNDER THE BLACK LUNG BENEFITS ACT

Miner's Claim For Benefits Under
The Black Lung Benefits Act

U.S. Department of Labor
Employment Standards Administration
Office of Workers' Compensation Programs

I hereby claim all benefits which may be payable to me under the Black Lung Benefits Act. I also hereby apply on behalf of my family for any benefits that may be payable under the Act.

OMB No. 1215-0052
Expires: 08-31-08

IMPORTANT: No benefits may be paid under the Black Lung Benefits Act, unless a completed application form has been received. However, disclosure of your Social Security Number is voluntary; the failure to disclose such number will not result in the denial of any right, benefit or privilege to which an individual may be entitled. Collection of the information on this form is authorized by law (30 U.S.C. 901, et. seq.). This information is required to obtain a benefit.

(FOR DOL USE)

1. Miner's full name (First, middle, last)

2. Miner's Social Security Number

3. Miner's date of birth (Month, day, year)

4. Highest grade miner completed in school

5. Have you (or someone on your behalf) ever filed a claim for Federal Black Lung benefits before?

☐ Yes　　☐ No

6. Decision made (If more than one claim filed, identify and show disposition of each in item 18, "Remarks")

☐ Allowed　　☐ Denied
☐ Withdrawn　　☐ Pending

7. Are you still working in or around coal mines?

☐ Yes　　If "yes," answer only c.
☐ No　　If "no," answer a-c.

a. When did you stop working in or around coal mines or a coal preparation facility in the extraction, transportation or preparation of coal, or in coal mine construction or maintenance in or around a coal mine?

b. Why did you stop working in or around coal mines or in a coal preparation facility in the extraction, transportation or preparation of coal, or in coal mine construction or maintenance in or around a coal mine?

c. Have you ever been transferred from your regular coal mine job to lighter duty?

☐ Yes　☐ No　　if "yes," provide date and reasons why you were transferred. Use space in item 18, "Remarks".

8. How many years have you worked in or around coal mines, or in a coal preparation facility in the extraction or preparation of coal, or worked in coal mine construction or transportation in or around a coal mine? _____ To the best of your knowledge list your complete coal mine Employment History on Form CM-91 1 a.

NOTE: If available evidence is not sufficient to arrive at a determination, you may be requested to have an independent medical examination at no expense to you. Should the Department of Labor obtain information useful to your physician for treatment, such information may be furnished to that physician.

9. Describe briefly any disability you believe you have due to pneumoconiosis (Black Lung) or other respiratory or pulmonary disease resulting from coal mine employment. Specifically, what aspect(s) of your regular job in the coal mines are you physically unable to perform as a result of your disability?

NOTE: The amount of any state or Federal Workers' Compensation/Occupational Disease benefits you are receiving based on your disability due to coal workers' pneumoconiosis will be subtracted from your benefits under Part C of the Black Lung Benefits Act.

10. Have you filed a workers' compensation claim under any state or Federal law on account of your disability, due to coal workers' pneumoconiosis?

☐ Yes ☐ No (if "yes," complete items a through j).

a. With what State or Federal agency was the claim filed?	b. Approximate date of filing:	c. Claim No. (if known).

d. Decision made

☐ Allowed ☐ Denied ☐ Pending

e. Employer against whom Workers' Compensation Claim was filed?

f. Amount of payment:

Weekly: $ _____ per week

Other: $ _____ per _____

g. Date payment began:

Date payment ended:

h. Did you pay any attorney's fees or legal fees in securing your workers' compensation award? ☐ Yes ☐ No	i. If you have received a lump-sum payment based on you compensation claim, please indicate the following: Period covered (fill in below): Amount: $ From: To:

j. Do you receive any medical treatment benefits as part of your Workers' Compensation benefits? ☐ Yes ☐ No

NOTE- The amount of your earnings, either as an employee or from self-employment, will help us to determine the correct amount of black lung benefits to which you may be entitled. This information is required by the 1981 Amendment to the Black Lung Benefits Act.

11 a. Enter the names and addresses of all persons, companies, or government agencies for which you worked during the previous calendar year. If self-employed, so indicate.

Name and Address of Employer	Work Began Month, Year	Work Ended Month, Year	Approximate Earnings

b. How much do you expect your total earnings to be this year? (Count all of your earnings beginning with the first of the year and all expected earnings through the end of this year.) $ _____

12. Are you married now? ☐ Yes ☐ No (if "Yes" Complete items a-f.) (if "No" go to item 13).	a. Date of marriage

b. Your spouse's first and maiden name (Print) SSN:	c. Spouse's birth date	d. Do you and your spouse live together? ☐ Yes ☐ No (If "no", answer items e and f)

e. Are you under a court order to make support payments to your spouse?

☐ Yes ☐ No (if "yes" attach a copy of the order).

f. Do you make regular support payments to your spouse?

☐ Yes ☐ No (if "yes", indicate amount)

16. Do you have any **Unmarried** children who are:

	List All Such Children In Order Of Birth Beginning With The Oldest

Under age 18   ☐ Yes   ☐ No

Age 18-23 and attending school   ☐ Yes   ☐ No

Age 18 or older and disabled   ☐ Yes   ☐ No

(Use "Remarks' space Item 18 If space below Is insufficient.)

sex of child		Date of Birth (Mo., day, yr.)	Check (X) If child 18 or over Is student or disabled		Check (X) If that shows child's relationship to you			
M	F		STUDENT	DISABLED	LEGITIMATE	ADOPTED	STEPCHILD	OTHER
Full name of child:								
SSN:								
Full name of child:								
SSN:								
Full name of child:								
SSN:								
Full name of child:								
SSN:								

If Any Child Named Above Does Not Live With You, Enter The Name And Address Of The Person Or Organization With Whom The Child Lives in item 18, "Remarks".

17. The events listed below may affect the amount of your Federal Black Lung Benefits:

     your condition improves; or

     You become entitled to receive workers' compensation or occupational disease payments due to disability on account of pneumoconiosis; or

     The amount of any of the benefits described above to which you are entitled changes; or

     You work in or around coal mines or in any other employment, including self-employment.

The events listed below relating to your dependents may also affect the amount of your Federal Black Lung Benefits:

     A dependent marries, divorces, dies, or is adopted by someone else; or

     A child 18-23 stops attending school, or in the case of a disabled child 18 or older, the disabling condition improves.

It is **IMPORTANT** that you report **PROMPTLY** any of the above events which occur.

Do you agree to notify the Department of Labor if any of the above events occur?

18. Remarks: (You may use this space for any explanations. if you need more space attach a separate sheet.)

19. Do you authorize any physician, hospital, agency, employer or other organization (including the Social Security Administration) to disclose to the Department of Labor any medical records, or Information about your disability or any other information pertinent to your claim?

20. Do you authorize the Department of Labor to give information about the decision on your Black Lung Benefits claim to the Workers' Compensation, Unemployment Compensation, or Disability insurance agency of your State for use in connection with a claim you may have with that agency?

SIGNATURE OF MINER

I hereby certify that the information given by me on and in connection with this form is true and correct to the best of my knowledge and belief. I am also fully aware that any person who willfully makes any false or misleading statement or representation for the purpose of obtaining any benefit or payment under this title shall be guilty of a misdemeanor and on conviction thereof shall be punished by a fine of not more than $1,000, or by imprisonment for not more than one year or both.

21. Signature of Claimant (First, middle, last)	22. Date (Month, day, year)

23. Mailing Address (Number, street, Apt. No., P.O. Box or Rural Route)	24. City and State

25. Zip Code	26. County Where You Now Live	27. Telephone Number (Include area code)

Witnesses are required **ONLY** if this application has been signed by mark (X) above. if signed by mark (X), two witnesses to the signing who know the applicant must sign below, giving their full address.

28. Signature of witness	29. Signature of witness

30. Address (Number, street, city, state & zip code)	31. Address (Number, street, city, state & zip code)

Note: Persons are not required to respond to this collection of information unless it displays a currently valid OMB control number.

PRIVACY ACT NOTICE

APPENDIX 25:
DIRECTORY OF BLACK LUNG DISTRICT
OFFICES AND JURISDICTIONS SERVED

DISTRICT OFFICE ADDRESS	TELEPHONE	JURISDICTIONS SERVED
U.S. Department of Labor 105 N. Main Street Suite 100 Wilkes Barre, PA 18701	800-347-3755	Eastern Pennsylvania, the northeastern states and the District of Columbia
U.S. Department of Labo 1160 Dublin Road Suite 300 Columbus, OH 43215	800-347-3771	Illinois, Indiana, Michigan, Minnesota, Ohio, and Wisconsin
U.S. Department of Labor 319 Washington Street 2nd Floor Johnstown, PA 15901	800-347-3754	Central Pennsylvania and Virginia
U.S. Department of Labor 1999 Broadway Suite 690 Denver, CO 80201-6550	800-366-4612	all states west of the Mississippi River
U.S. Department of Labor 1225 S. Main Street Suite 405 Greensburg, PA 15601	800-347-3753	Western Pennsylvania and Maryland
U.S. Department of Labor, Charleston Federal Center, Suite 110, 500 Quarrier Street, Charleston, WV 25301	800-347-3749	Southeastern West Virginia
U.S. Department of Labor 425 Juliana Avenue Suite 3116 Parkersburg, WV 26101	800-347-3751	Remainder of West Virginia

APPENDIX 26:
CLAIMANT'S RIGHTS AND RESPONSIBILITIES

CLAIMANT RIGHTS AND RESPONSIBILITIES

RULES FOR FILING A CLAIM AND APPEAL RIGHTS

1. It is **your** responsibility to file this claim form promptly **after** you stop working due to your disability. Filing your claim before your last day of work will delay its processing. The law requires that claims must be filed within 30 days of the beginning of the disability. **Benefits may be denied or reduced if the claim is filed late.** If your claim is filed beyond the thirty day period, please attach a statement giving your reasons for the late filing.

2. If you disagree with a determination on your claim and wish to appeal, you must do so in writing within ten days from the date the decision was mailed. You do not need a lawyer at the appeal hearing.

CLAIMANT RESPONSIBILITIES:

1. Your signature certifies that you understand any misrepresentation of fact or failure to disclose a material fact may be punishable under the law. This includes any changes to the Medical Certificate or the Employer's Statement made by you without authorization by your physician or your employer.

2. If you receive a request for continued medical certification (Form P30), you must have your physician complete and sign the form. You should return it promptly.

3. When you recover or return to work, you should report this date immediately to the Division of Temporary Disability Insurance.

4. If you are requesting voluntary Federal Income Tax (F.I.T.) deductions to be withheld from your disability benefits, attach Form W-4S (Request for Federal Income Tax Withholding From Sick Pay) to your claim. Forms should be obtained from your employer or the Internal Revenue Service.

5. If your mailing address changes, you must notify the Division of Temporary Disability Insurance, PO Box 387, Trenton, NJ 08625-0387 immediately in writing. Notification must include your Social Security Number and signature. Disability checks cannot be forwarded by the Post Office.

Note: The NJ Temporary Disability Benefits Program is not a "covered entity" under the Federal Health Information Portability & Accountability Act (HIPAA). All medical records of the Division, except to the extent necessary for the proper administration of the Temporary Disability Benefits Law are confidential & are not open to public inspection. The Division protects all records that may reveal the identity of the claimant, or the nature or cause of the disability & the records may only be used in proceedings arising under the Law.

CLAIM ASSISTANCE:
If you require any assistance with your claim, call:
- **Customer Service Section (609) 292-7060.**
- **Telecommunication Device for the Deaf (TDD) (609) 292-8319**
- **New Jersey Relay Service: TT user 1-800-852-7899**
  Voice User: 1-800-852-7897

Division of Temporary Disability Insurance FAX number: (609) 984-4138
NOTE: If your disability is expected to last for one year or longer, you may be eligible for Federal Social Security Disability Benefits.
Toll Free number for Social Security: 1-800-772-1213.

READ THE FOLLOWING INSTRUCTIONS BEFORE COMPLETING THE
CLAIM FOR DISABILITY BENEFITS – DS-1

1. Complete the first page of this form (Part A.) YOU ARE RESPONSIBLE for having Part B completed by your doctor and Part C by your last employer. If you have worked for more than one employer during the past year, you may print Part C for completion by the other employer(s) to avoid processing delays. ANY MISSING OR INCORRECT ENTRIES ON THIS FORM WILL DELAY PROCESSING OF YOUR CLAIM. If you cannot have Parts B and/or C completed timely, complete Part A and return the application as soon as possible.
REMEMBER SENDING IN SEPARATE PARTS OF THE APPLICATION WILL DELAY YOUR CLAIM. MAIL OR FAX PART A, PART B AND PART C TOGETHER TO:

> **Division of Temporary Disability Insurance**
> **PO Box 387**
> **Trenton, NJ 08625-0387**
> **FAX No: (609) 984-4138**

2. Read all questions carefully! Print or write clearly since this information is used to determine your right to benefits. IF YOU NEED ANY ASSISTANCE IN COMPLETING THIS FORM, PLEASE CALL THE CUSTOMER SERVICE SECTION IN TRENTON AT (609) 292-7060 AND HOLD FOR AN AGENT.

3. BE SURE TO WRITE YOUR SOCIAL SECURITY NUMBER AND NAME ON EACH PORTION OF YOUR CLAIM.

Instructions For Part A – Claimant's Statement – Please complete all questions

Items 1, 4 & 7	Include your full name and complete address (this information is required). If your mailing address is different than your home address, be sure to complete Item 7.
Item 3	Please print or type your Social Security Number **CLEARLY**. An incorrect or illegible number will cause a delay in processing your claim.
Item 9	You must complete this item. If your answer to this question is "No," you must complete Items 10 and 11 and give your country of origin.
Items 12 –15	Please give exact dates. Remember to include the dates of any Emergency Room care you may have received for this disability. If available, provide proof of emergency room care.
Items 18	List the name and address of the physician who treated you for this disability. You must be under the care of a legally licensed physician, dentist, optometrist, podiatrist, practicing psychologist or chiropractor. If you have been treated by more than one physician, attach a separate piece of paper with their names and addresses.
Item 19	Starting with your most recent employer, list all employers, including those for whom you worked part-time, for the last **18 months**. If you had more than three employers, list the others with the dates you worked on a separate piece of paper and attach it to the claim form. Give business names and addresses as they appear on your pay envelopes, pay checks, employers' stationery or as listed in the telephone book.
Item 22	In the event that you are unable to telephone our agency, you may designate a representative in this space to obtain information on your behalf. **If there is no one listed, only YOU will be able to obtain information on your claim from this agency.**
Item 23	**Sign and date the claim form. Include your telephone number.**

Important: Keep a copy of the completed claim form and this instruction sheet for your records.

PART A	INFORMATION TO BE COMPLETED BY THE CLAIMANT – Print or Type	WDS1(07-04)
	N.J. DEPARTMENT OF LABOR & WORKFORCE DEVELOPMENT–DIVISION OF TEMPORARY DISABILITY INSURANCE	

1. Name: (Last, First, Middle)   **2. Birth Date**   **3.Social Security Number**

4. Home Address – required (Street, Apt #, City, State, Zip Code)   **5. County**   **6.** Male ☐ Female ☐

7. Mailing Address – if different (Street, Apt #, City State, Zip Code)   **8. Occupation**

9. Are you a citizen of the United States? Yes ☐ No ☐
If **NO**, answer #10 & 11 and give country of origin: _____   **10.** Alien Reg. No.   **11.** Work Authorization From ___ To ___

	Month	Day	Year

12a. Reason for separation: ☐ Illness/Accident/Maternity ☐ Terminated ☐ Quit
12b. What was the last day that you actually worked before your disability began? ➡

13. The **first day** you were unable to work due to present disability:
(Include Saturday, Sunday, or Holiday) Do not list future dates ➡

14. Date you recovered or returned to work:
(Do not use dates in the future) ➡

15. Date(s) of emergency room care: _____ or hospitalization: From _____ To _____
    Month/Day/Year   Month/Day/Year   Month/Day/Year

16. Describe your disability (How, when, where it happened) _____

17. Was this injury/illness caused by your job? Yes ☐ or No ☐ (This question must be answered.)
If Yes, date of work related injury/illness: _____
Was your employer notified that your injury was caused by your job? Yes ☐ or No ☐

18. Identify the physician or hospital treating you for this disability: Name: _____
Address: _____ Telephone: _____

Employment Information – Beginning with your last employer, list all employment (both full and part-time) in the past 18 months. If you had more than 3 employers, list the remaining employers on a separate sheet of paper and attach to this form.

19a. Name and address of your most recent employer: _____
Period of employment: From _____ To _____
Telephone: _____ Work Location _____
(Street) (City) (State) (Zip)   City   State
Occupation: _____ Full time ☐ Part time ☐ Union _____ Division _____

19b. Name and address: _____
Period of employment: From _____ To _____
Telephone: _____ Work Location _____
(Street) (City) (State) (Zip)   City   State
Occupation: _____ Full time ☐ Part time ☐ Union _____ Division _____

19c. Name and address: _____
Period of employment: From _____ To _____
Telephone: _____ Work Location _____
(Street) (City) (State) (Zip)   City   State
Occupation: _____ Full time ☐ Part time ☐ Union _____ Division _____

20. Other Benefits – You Must Answer Each Question Listed Below For the Period of Disability Covered By This Claim:
a. Have you worked after your disability began? (Including self-employment) Yes ☐ No ☐
b. Have you been receiving remuneration i.e , wages, salary or vacation pay? Yes ☐ No ☐
c. Have you been involved in a labor dispute? Yes ☐ No ☐

21. Since your last day of work have you received, claimed or applied for: c. Any other disability benefits provided by your
a. Federal Social Security **Disability** Benefits? Yes ☐ No ☐   employer or union? Yes ☐ No ☐
b. Pension benefits from your most recent employer? Yes ☐ No ☐   d. Unemployment Insurance Benefits? Yes ☐ No ☐

22. Please designate a representative to obtain claim information for you if you cannot call this Agency yourself. The Law only permits claim information to be given to you or your representative.   Birth Date: _____
Representative Name: _____ Phone ( )

23. Certification and Signature I was unable to work during the period for which benefits are claimed and hereby certify that I have read and understand my benefit rights and responsibilities. I am aware that if any of the foregoing statements made by me are known to be false, or I knowingly fail to disclose a material fact, I may be subject to penalties, which may include criminal prosecution. You are hereby authorized to: Verify my Social Security Account Number, and obtain any medical, employment and Social Security benefit entitlement information that is necessary to determine my eligibility for benefits.

Sign Here _____ Date _____
Witness signature if claimant writes an "X" _____ Phone No. ( )

Claimant's Name: _____ WDS-1(07-04)	**Social Security Number**
Claimant's Telephone No: _____	| |

MEDICAL CERTIFICATE
PART B (TO BE COMPLETED BY YOUR DOCTOR AFTER YOU BECOME DISABLED)

1a. Patient has been under my care for this period of disability: **FROM** _____ **TO** _____
(Month/Day/Year)   (Month/Day/Year)

b. Frequency of treatment: _____

c. Patient was last treated by me on: ⟶
| Month | Day | Year |

2. Enter the date the patient was unable to perform his/her regular work due to this disability: _____
| Month | Day | Year |

3. Estimated Recovery: (Give the approximate date patient will be able to return to work.) _____
| Month | Day | Year |

4. If now recovered, on what date was the patient first able to work? ⟶
| Month | Day | Year |

5. Diagnosis: (nature and cause of this disability which prevents patient from working) _____

_____ **ICD Code:** _____

Clinical data and tests to support diagnosis: _____

6a. If pregnancy, provide estimated date of delivery: ⟶
| Month | Day | Year |

b. Complications, if any _____

c. If pregnancy terminated, enter the date: ⟶
| Month | Day | Year |

And identify the reason: ☐ Birth ☐ C-Section ☐ Miscarriage ☐ Abortion

7a. Date(s) of emergency room care or hospitalization: FROM _____ TO _____

b. Name and address of any specialist treating patient: _____

8. Type of surgery: _____ Date of Surgery _____ Anticipated Surgery Date _____

Is surgery for cosmetic purposes only? ☐ Yes ☐ No

9. In your opinion, was this disability: ☐ Due to an accident at work? ☐ Not related to his/her work
☐ Due to a condition which developed because of the nature of the work.

10. I certify that the above statements, in my opinion, truly describe the patient's disability and the estimated duration thereof:

(Print Doctor's Name and Medical Degree)	(Original Signature of Doctor Required)	(Date Signed)
		If Resident, check ☐
(Address)	(Certificate License No. and State)	
(Address)	(Specialty of Treating Physician)	
(City) (State) (Zip Code)	( ) (Phone Number)	( ) (FAX Number)

I. CLAIMANT'S NAME:	SOCIAL SECURITY NUMBER
CLAIMANT'S TELEPHONE NO: WDS-1(07-04)	

PART C   **TO BE COMPLETED BY YOUR EMPLOYER OR COMPANY REPRESENTATIVE**

2. EMPLOYER STATUS
What is your Federal Employer Identification Number: _____

3. PRIVATE PLAN COVERAGE
a. Do you have a New Jersey approved Private Plan? ☐Yes ☐No
b. If "Yes", is claimant covered under this approved Private Plan? ☐Yes ☐No

4. LAST ACTUAL DAY WORKED before this disability
(do not use payroll week ending dates) ➡ ___|___|___
                                    (Month/Day/Year)

a. Exact reason for separation from work
(include labor dispute) _____
b. Is lack of work: ☐temporary? ☐ permanent?
c. Has claimant returned to work? ☐ Yes ☐ No
    If "Yes", give date: ___|___|___
                                (Month/Day/Year)
d. If the work was intermittent, list dates:

5. CONTINUED PAY (do not enter wages earned prior to disability)
a. Have you paid or expect to pay the claimant for any period after the last day
of work? ☐Yes ☐ No
b. If "yes" give dates: **FROM** ___|___|___ **TO** ___|___|___
                                (Month/Day/Year)   **(Month/Day/Year)**
c.   Amount per week $_____, if amount varies attach list of dates
and amounts.
d. Check the number that best describes the monies paid in item c.
    ☐ 1. Regular weekly wages and/or sick pay
    ☐ 2. Regular vacation (if designated for a specific time period)
    ☐ 3. Pension
    ☐ 4. Difference between regular weekly wage and disability benefits to be
       received
    ☐ 5. Full salary advanced to effect #4 above
    ☐ 6. Supplemental benefits or gratuities
    Note: Items 1, 2, and 3 may reduce benefits to the claimant

6. GOVERNMENT EMPLOYEES (Complete this section)
a. Payroll number (For N.J. State Employees) _____
b. Number of earned sick leave days as of the last day worked. _____
c. Has the claimant filed for or received Employment Disability Leave
(SLI)? ☐ Yes ☐ No
d. If claimant has applied for or received donated leave, attach dates and
amounts on a separate sheet of paper.

7. WORKERS' COMPENSATION LIABILITY
a. Did the claimant's disability happen in connection with his/her work or
while on your premises, or was the disability due in any way to his/her
occupation? ☐ Yes ☐ No
b. If "Yes", have you filed or do you intend to file a Workers' Compensation
claim on behalf of this claimant? ☐ Yes ☐ No
c. If "Yes," list Workers' Compensation insurance carrier below:
Name_____ Telephone ( ) _____
Address_____
Policy #_____ Claim #_____

**8. BASE WEEKS AND BASE YEAR GROSS
WAGES** A BASE WEEK is a calendar week in
which the claimant had New Jersey earnings of $103
or more during the Base Year. The BASE YEAR is
the 52 calendar weeks preceding the week in which
the disability occurred.

a. Total Number of **Base Weeks** _____

b. Total **Gross Wages in Base Year** _____
    Include all wages earned by the claimant
_____

9. REGULAR WEEKLY WAGE $_____

10. Weekly wages
Indicate below: dates and claimant's GROSS
earnings in N.J. employment during the listed
calendar weeks.

Description of Calendar Week	Calendar Week Ending Date	Gross Wages
Week Disability Began		$
Week Before Disability		$
2nd Week Before Disability		$
3rd Week Before Disability		$
4th Week Before Disability		$
5th Week Before Disability		$
6th Week Before Disability		$
7th Week Before Disability		$
8th Week Before Disability		$
9th Week Before Disability		$
10th Week Before Disability		$
TOTAL GROSS WAGES FOR ABOVE WEEKS ➡		$

Are you exempt from FICA tax? ☐Yes ☐No

Firm Name _____   **I CERTIFY THE INFORMATION GIVEN ABOVE IS CORRECT**

Address _____   Signed_____ Date_____

City, State, Zip _____   Print or Type Name _____

Mailing Address, If Different _____   Official Title_____

FAX No. ( ) _____   Telephone ( ) _____

GLOSSARY

Accrue—To occur or come into existence.

Action at Law—A judicial proceeding whereby one party prosecutes another for a wrong done.

Actionable—Giving rise to a cause of action.

Actionable Negligence—The breach or nonperformance of a legal duty through neglect or carelessness, resulting in damage or injury to another.

Activities of Daily Living—Impairments are generally defined as conditions which interfere with a person's "activities of daily living," including: (1) self-care and personal hygiene; (2) communication; (3) physical activity; (4) sensory function; (5) hand functions; (6) travel; (7) sexual function; (8) sleep; (9) social and recreational activities.

Actual Damages—Actual damages are those damages directly referable to the breach or tortious act, and which can be readily proven to have been sustained, and for which the injured party should be compensated as a matter of right.

ADA—The Americans With Disabilities Act (42 USC 12101 et seq.).

Ad Damnum Clause—The clause in a complaint which sets forth the amount of damages demanded.

Adjudication—The determination of a controversy and pronouncement of judgment.

Admissible Evidence—Evidence which may be received by a trial court to assist the trier of fact, either the judge or jury, in deciding a dispute.

Adversary—Opponent or litigant in a legal controversy or litigation.

Affirmative Defense—In a pleading, a matter constituting a defense.

Agency—The relationship between a principal and an agent who is employed by the principal, to perform certain acts dealing with third parties.

Agent—One who represents another known as the principal.

Aggravation—A worsening of a preexisting medical condition caused by a work-related injury or illness.

Air Quality Criteria—The levels of pollution and lengths of exposure above which adverse health and welfare effects may occur.

Allegation—Statement of the issue that the contributing party is prepared to prove.

Ancillary Care—Care such as physical or occupational therapy provided by a medical service provider other than the attending physician.

Answer—In a civil proceeding, the principal pleading on the part of the defendant in response to the plaintiff's complaint.

Appeal Rights—The right of the parties to a decision to seek review at a higher level.

Appearance—To come into court, personally or through an attorney, after being summoned.

Argument—A discourse set forth for the purpose of establishing one's position in a controversy.

Assumption of Risk—The legal doctrine that a plaintiff may not recover for an injury to which he assents.

Attending Physician—A physician primarily responsible for the treatment of an injured worker.

Attorney In Fact—An attorney-in-fact is an agent or representative of another given authority to act in that person's name and place pursuant to a document called a "power of attorney."

Beneficiary—The spouse, child, or dependent of an injured worker entitled to receive payments under workers' compensation law.

Benefits—An award of compensation paid under a claim, such as lost wages, medical and rehabilitation expenses, etc.

Bona Fide Dispute—A disagreement between the worker and the insurer about the compensability of a claim, which may be resolved by a disputed claim settlement rather than a hearing.

Breach of Duty—In a general sense, any violation or omission of a legal or moral duty.

Bureau of Labor Statistics—A division of the U.S. Department of Labor that compiles statistics related to employment.

Causation—A factor that contributed to the occurrence of an injury or illness.

Cause of Action—The factual basis for bringing a lawsuit.

Claim—An application for workers' compensation benefits brought by an employee alleging that he or she suffered a work-related injury or illness. A claim may also be brought by a deceased employee's surviving dependents.

Claimant—A person who files a claim for occupational disease or injury benefits under workers' compensation law.

Claim Closure—The process of closing a claim when an injured worker is found to be medically stationary.

Claims Examiner—Insurer representative who processes a claim filed by an injured worker.

Circumstantial Evidence—Indirect evidence by which a principal fact may be inferred.

Clinical Evaluation—The assessment of the health status of an individual and implementation of a course of treatment undertaken by a health care provider.

Closing Evaluation—A medical examination to measure impairment, which occurs when the worker is medically stationary.

Combined Condition—A preexisting condition that, combined with a compensable condition, causes disability or prolongs treatment.

Compensable Injury—An accidental injury arising out of and in the course of employment that requires medical services or results in disability or death.

Compensation—Refers to the benefits payable to claimants under a workers' compensation claim, such as lost wages, medical expenses, etc.

Compensatory Damages—Compensatory damages are those damages directly referable to a breach or tortious act, and which can be readily proven to have been sustained, and for which the injured party should be compensated as a matter of right.

Complaint—In a civil proceeding, the first pleading of the plaintiff setting out the facts on which the claim for relief is based.

Compromise and Settlement—An arrangement arrived at, either in court or out of court, for settling a dispute upon what appears to the parties to be equitable terms.

Conclusion of Fact—A conclusion reached by natural inference and based solely on the facts presented.

Conclusion of Law—A conclusion reached through the application of rules of law.

Conclusive Evidence—Evidence which is incontrovertible.

Consequential Condition—A condition arising after a compensable injury of which the major contributing cause is the injury or treatment rendered that increases either disability or need for treatment.

Contingency Fee—The fee charged by an attorney, which is dependent upon a successful outcome in the case, and is often agreed to be a percentage of the party's recovery.

Contributory Negligence—The act or omission amounting to want of ordinary care on the part of the complaining party which, concurring with the defendant's negligence, is the proximate cause of his or her injury.

Costs—A sum payable by the losing party to the successful party for his or her expenses in prosecuting or defending a case.

Counterclaims—Counterdemands made by a respondent in his or her favor against a claimant. They are not mere answers or denials of the claimant's allegation.

Cross-claim—Claim litigated by co-defendants or co-plaintiffs, against each other, and not against a party on the opposing side of the litigation.

Court—The branch of government responsible for the resolution of disputes arising under the laws of the government.

Cross-Examination—The questioning of a witness by someone other than the one who called the witness to the stand concerning matters about which the witness testified during direct examination.

Damages—In general, damages refers to monetary compensation which the law awards to one who has been injured by the actions of another, such as in the case of tortious conduct or breach of contractual obligations.

Death Benefit—The amount of money paid to the surviving spouse of a deceased Social Security beneficiary under certain circumstances.

Death Claim—A claim brought by a deceased employee's surviving dependents due to a work-related injury or illness resulting in the employee's death.

Decedent—A deceased person.

Decontamination—Removal of harmful substances such as noxious chemicals, harmful bacteria or other organisms, or radioactive material from exposed individuals, rooms and furnishings in buildings, or the exterior environment.

De Facto Denial—Failure of an insurer to accept or deny within the statutory time frame.

Degree—A unit of measure for permanent partial disability benefits that is used to convert disability percentages to dollar amounts

Dependent—Those individuals who, because of their financial dependency on the employee, are statutorily entitled to compensation on a death claim, such as surviving spouses and dependent children, etc.

Defendant—In a civil proceeding, the party responding to the complaint.

Defense—Opposition to the truth or validity of the plaintiff's claims.

Denied Claim—Written refusal by an insurer to accept compensability or responsibility for a worker's claim of injury.

De Novo Review – A second review of all the evidence.

Deposition—A method of pretrial discovery which consists of a statement of a witness under oath, taken in question and answer form as it would be in court, with opportunity given to the adversary to be present and cross-examine.

Disability—A medical impairment or disability that results in an individual's inability to carry on their usual activities, requires medical treatment, or adversely affects the individual's ability to earn a living.

Disability Payment—Payment for disability resulting from an accident or disease from which a worker is not expected to recover.

Disabling Compensable Injury—An on-the-job injury that entitles the worker to temporary or permanent, partial or total disability compensation or death benefits.

Discovery—Modern pretrial procedure by which one party gains information held by another party.

Disfigurement—An undesirable alteration of a body part usually due to an injury.

Disputed Claim Settlement—Settlement of a claim when there is disagreement about compensability.

Duty—The obligation, to which the law will give recognition and effect, to conform to a particular standard of conduct toward another.

Employability—The ability of an employee to meet the demands of a job and the conditions of employment.

Expert Witness—A witness who has special knowledge about a certain subject, upon which he or she will testify, which knowledge is not normally possessed by the average person.

Eyewitness—A person who can testify about a matter because of his or her own presence at the time of the event.

Fact Finder—In a judicial or administrative proceeding, the person, or group of persons, that has the responsibility of determining the acts relevant to decide a controversy.

Fatality Claim—Claim for benefits made by beneficiaries of a worker whose death resulted from accidental injury or occupational disease.

Federal employer Identification Number (FEIN)—The number assigned to a business by the Internal Revenue Service. This number is the primary identifier for employers in electronic data interchange (EDI) reporting.

Fee schedule—Maximum charges established for medical services under a workers' compensation program.

Finding—Decisions made by the court on issues of fact or law.

FMLA—The Family and Medical Leave Act of 1993, Public Law 103-3 (February 5, 1993), 107 Stat. 6 (29 U.S.C. 2601 et seq.).

Foreseeability—A concept used to limit the liability of a party for the consequences of his acts to consequences that are within the scope of a foreseeable risk.

Frequency Rate—Number of disabling injuries per 1,000,000 hours of work.

General Damages—General damages are those damages directly referable to the breach or tortious act and which can be readily proven to have been sustained, and for which the injured party should be compensated as a matter of right.

HIPAA—A federal law that ensures the privacy and security of protected health information and patients' access to their health-care records.

Immunity—As it relates to workers' compensation law, refers to the protection afforded an employer who is in compliance with workers' compensation statutes from common-law tort actions by employees arising out of the work-related injuries or illness.

Impairment—The loss, or loss of use of, any body part, system, or function.

Impairment Findings—A measurement, by a physician, of loss of use or function of a body part or system.

Independent Contractor—An individual who contracts to perform services for others without qualifying legally as an employee.

Indoor Air Pollution—Chemical, physical, or biological contaminants in indoor air.

Injury—Physical or mental harm or disability arising out of a work-related accident.

Insured employer—An employer who has a workers' compensation insurance policy in place to cover employees.

Insurer—An insurance company, self-insured employer, or self insured employer group that provides workers' compensation coverage to employers and benefits to injured workers.

Insurer Medical Examination (IME)—A medical examination of an injured worker by a physician other than the worker's attending physician at the request of the insurer.

Interim Compensation—Payment of time-loss benefits during the period between filing a claim and acceptance or denial.

Jones Act—The federal statute permitting a seaman, or a representative, the right to sue for personal injuries suffered in the course of the seaman's employment.

Judgment—A judgment is a final determination by a court of law concerning the rights of the parties to a lawsuit.

Jurisdiction—The power to hear and determine a case.

Jury—A group of individuals summoned to decide the facts in issue in a lawsuit.

Jury Trial—A trial during which the evidence is presented to a jury so that they can determine the issues of fact, and render a verdict based upon the law as it applies to their findings of fact.

Loss of Earning Capacity—The impairment of ability to earn a living attributable to a work-related injury or illness.

Lump Sum—Payment of all or any part of permanent partial disability award in one payment.

Major contributing cause (MCC)—A cause deemed to have contributed at least 51 percent to an injured worker's disability or need for treatment.

Managed care organization (MCO)—An organization that may contract with an insurer to provide medical services to injured workers.

Maximum Medical Improvement—The point at which an employee has reached maximum recovery after every method of treatment has been employed and a reasonable period of time has elapsed.

Mediation—The act of a third person in intermediating between two contending parties with a view to persuading them to adjust or settle their dispute but without the authority to make a binding decision.

Medical Arbiter—A physician selected by the director to perform an impartial examination for impairment findings.

Medical Only—A workers' compensation claim for an injury or illness that doesn't involve time loss or permanent disability but that requires medical treatment.

Medical Provider—A hospital, medical clinic, or other vendor of medical services.

Medical Service Provider—A person duly licensed to practice one or more of the healing arts.

Medically Stationary—The point at which the attending physician states no further significant improvement can reasonably be expected from medical treatment or the passage of time

Negligence—The failure to exercise the degree of care which a reasonable person would exercise given the same circumstances.

Negligence Per Se—Conduct, whether of action or omission, which may be declared and treated as negligence without any argument or proof as to the particular surrounding circumstances, because it is contrary to the law.

Noncomplying Employer—An employer who fails to provide workers' compensation coverage for its employees.

Non-disabling Claim—A workers' compensation claim for an injury or illness that doesn't involve time loss or permanent disability but that requires medical treatment.

Non-disabling Injury—Any injury that requires medical services only and does not result in an inability to work or permanent disability.

Notice of Closure—A document sent by the insurer to the injured worker that closes the claim, ends time-loss benefits, and states the extent of disability.

Notice of Compliance—A notice from DCBS required to be posted in an employer's place of business notifying employees that the employer has workers' compensation insurance coverage.

Objection—The process by which it is asserted that a particular question, or piece of evidence, is improper, and it is requested that the court rule upon the objectionable matter.

Objective Findings—Indications of an injury or disease that are measurable, observable, or reproducible; used to establish compensability and determine permanent impairment.

Occupational Disease—A disease or infection arising out of and occurring in the course and scope of employment, that is caused by substances or activities to which an employee is not ordinarily subjected or exposed other than during employment, and requires medical services or results in disability or death.

Occupational Safety and Health Administration (OSHA)—The federal agency that oversees workplace safety and health in federal offices and in states without state OSHA programs.

Opinion and Order—A formal decision issued by an administrative law judge at the Workers' Compensation Board to resolve a dispute.

Pain and Suffering—Refers to damages recoverable against a wrongdoer which include physical or mental suffering.

Palliative care—Medical services rendered to reduce or temporarily moderate the intensity of an otherwise stable condition to enable the worker to continue employment or training.

Parens Patriae—Latin for "parent of his country." Refers to the role of the state as guardian of legally disabled individuals.

Parties—The disputants.

Penalties—Monetary sanctions that can be assessed against employers, insurers, or medical providers for violations of workers' compensation laws or rules; workers may be penalized by means of suspended benefits.

Permanent impairment—The loss of use or function of a body part due to a compensable injury.

Permanent Partial Disability—A medical impairment, usually statutorily defined as a scheduled loss award which, although it is of indefinite duration, does not prevent the employee from returning to gainful employment.

Permanent Total Disability—A medical impairment that is unlikely to change in spite of further medical or surgical therapy, and which renders the employee unable to return to gainful employment.

Physical Capacity Evaluation—Measurement of a worker's ability to perform a variety of physical tasks.

Plaintiff—In a civil proceeding, the one who initially brings the lawsuit.

Pleadings—Refers to plaintiff's complaint which sets forth the facts of the cause of action, and defendant's answer which sets forth the responses and defenses to the allegations contained in the complaint.

Power of Attorney—A legal document authorizing another to act on one's behalf.

Preexisting condition—A condition that existed before the compensable injury or disease. Premium The amount an employer pays an insurance company for a workers' compensation policy.

Pro se—A party that participates in a formal or informal dispute process without an attorney.

Prima Facie Case—A case which is sufficient on its face, being supported by at least the requisite minimum of evidence, and being free from palpable defects.

Proximate Cause—That which, in a natural and continuous sequence, unbroken by any efficient intervening cause, produces injury, and without which the result would not have occurred.

Punitive Damages—Compensation in excess of compensatory damages which serves as a form of punishment to the wrongdoer who has exhibited malicious and willful misconduct.

Question of Fact—The fact in dispute which is the province of the trier of fact, i.e. the judge or jury, to decide.

Question of Law—The question of law which is the province of the judge to decide.

Reciprocity agreement—An agreement between states regarding jurisdiction in workers' compensation claims.

Release—A document signed by one party, releasing claims he or she may have against another party, usually as part of a settlement agreement.

Relief—The remedies afforded a complainant by the court.

Res Ipsa Loquitur—Literally, "the thing speaks for itself." Refers to an evidentiary rule which provides that negligence may be inferred from the fact that an accident occurred when such an occurrence would not ordinarily have happened in the absence of negligence, the cause of the occurrence was within the exclusive control of the defendant, and the plaintiff was in no way at fault.

Retainer Agreement—A contract between an attorney and the client stating the nature of the services to be rendered and the cost of the litigation.

Sanctions—Monetary sanctions that can be assessed against employers, insurers, or medical providers for violations of workers' compensation laws or rules; workers may be penalized by means of suspended benefits.

Scheduled disability—The permanent complete or partial loss of use or function of an arm, hand, leg, foot, or other extremity of the body, or the loss of visual or hearing ability.

Scheduled Loss Award—Compensation for the loss of, or loss of use of, certain body parts or functions, as defined by a statutory schedule, e.g. loss of vision, loss of a finger, etc.

Scope of Employment—Those activities performed while carrying out the business of one's employer.

Self-Insured Employer—An employer that has been authorized by the appropriate agency to administer and pay directly on employee compensation claims.

Service of Process—The delivery of legal court documents, such as a complaint, to the defendant.

Settlement—An agreement by the parties to a dispute on a resolution of the claims, usually requiring some mutual action, such as payment of money in consideration of a release of claims.

State—Any State of the United States or the District of Columbia or any Territory or possession of the United States.

State Insurance Fund—An insurance fund administered by the state instead of, or in addition to, private insurance.

Stipulation—A negotiated agreement between parties to a claim.

Summons—A mandate requiring the appearance of the defendant in an action under penalty of having judgment entered against him for failure to do so.

Supplemental disability—Payment of wage-replacement benefits to workers who held more than one job at the time of injury.

Supplemental Security Income (SSI)—The government program awarding cash benefits to the needy, aged, blind or otherwise qualifying disabled.

Survival Statute—A statute that preserves for a decedent's estate a cause of action for infliction of pain and suffering and related damages suffered up to the moment of death.

Suspension of benefits—An interruption of payment of benefits to an injured worker.

Temporary Partial Disability—A medical impairment that is expected to be of limited duration and which does not prevent the employee from returning to gainful employment.

Temporary Partial Disability Benefits—Payment for wages lost based on a worker's ability to perform temporary modified or part-time work due to a compensable injury.

Temporary Total Disability—A medical impairment that is expected to be of limited duration, but which prevents the employee from returning to gainful employment.

Temporary Total Disability Benefits—Payment for wages lost based on a worker's temporary inability to work due to a compensable injury.

Testimony—The sworn statement make by a witness in a judicial proceeding.

Third-party administrator—A company contracted by self-insured employer or insurer to administer its workers' compensation claims.

Time-loss payments—Compensation paid to an injured worker who loses time or wages as a result of compensable injury.

Tort—A private or civil wrong or injury, other than breach of contract, for which the court will provide a remedy in the form of an action for damages.

Tortfeasor—A wrongdoer.

Tortious Conduct—Wrongful conduct, whether of act or omission, of such a character as to subject the actor to liability under the law of torts.

Trial—The judicial procedure whereby disputes are determined based on the presentation of issues of law and fact. The trier of fact, either the judge or jury, decides issues of fact and the judge decides issues of law.

Trial Court—The court of original jurisdiction over a particular matter.

Unscheduled disability—The permanent loss of earning capacity as a result of physical limitations; modified by factors of age, education, and ability to return to work at injury.

Venue—The proper place for trial of a lawsuit.

Verdict—The definitive answer given by the jury to the court concerning the matters of fact committed to the jury for their deliberation and determination.

Verification—The confirmation of the authenticity of a document, such as an affidavit.

Vicarious Liability—In tort law, refers to the liability assessed against one party due to the actions of another party.

Vocational assistance—Services, goods, and allowances used to help injured workers return to work as soon as possible and as nearly as possible to a condition of self-support and maintenance.

Waiting Period—Statutory period of time, e.g. three days, from the date of work-related injury or illness, during which the employee is ineligible for workers' compensation payments, unless disability continues for a specified duration, e.g. two weeks.

Waiver—An intentional and voluntary surrender of a right.

Whistleblower—An employee who reports on violations of the law which occur in the workplace.

Worker—Any person who receives payment for work or services under the direction and control of an employer.

Workers' Compensation—Refers to the benefits payable to claimants under a workers' compensation claim, such as lost wages, medical expenses, etc.

Work-related Injury or Illness—An injury or illness which is causally related to one's employment.

Wrongful Death Statute—A statute that creates a cause of action for any wrongful act, neglect, or default that causes death.

Zone of Employment—The physical area in which injuries to an employee are covered by worker compensation laws.

BIBLIOGRAPHY AND ADDITIONAL RESOURCES

Black's Law Dictionary, Fifth Edition. St. Paul, MN: West Publishing Company, 1979.

Insurance Information Institute. (Date Visited: October 2005) <http://www.iii.org/>.

The National Institute for Occupational Safety and Health (Date Visited: October 2005) http://www.cdc.gov/niosh/>.

The Office of Workers Compensation (Date Visited: October 2005) http://owcp.gov/>.

United States Department of Health and Human Services Office of Disability, Aging and Long-Term Care (Date Visited: October 2005) <http://aspe.os.dhhs.gov/daltcp/home>.

The United States Department of Labor (Date Visited: October 2005) <http://www.dol.gov/>.

The United States Department of Labor, Bureau of Labor Statistics (Date Visited: October 2005) http://www.bls.gov/>.

The U.S. Department of Labor, Occupational Safety & Health Administration (Date Visited: October 2005) http://www.osha.gov/>.

The United States Environmental Protection Agency (Date Visited: October 2005) <http://www/epa.gov/>.

The United States Equal Employment Opportunity Commission (Date Visited: October 2005) <http://www.eeoc.gov/>.

The United States Office of Personnel Management (Date Visited: October 2005) <http://www.opm.gov/>.

The United States Social Security Administration (Date Visited: October 2005) <http://www.socialsecurity.gov/>.

The United States Department of Veterans Affairs (Date Visited: October 2005) <http://www.va.gov/>.